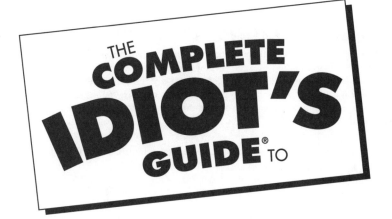

THE COMPLETE **IDIOT'S** GUIDE® TO

The FBI

by John Simeone and David Jacobs

Copyright © 2003 by John Simeone and David Jacobs

All rights reserved. No part of this book shall be reproduced, stored in a retrieval system, or transmitted by any means, electronic, mechanical, photocopying, recording, or otherwise, without written permission from the publisher. No patent liability is assumed with respect to the use of the information contained herein. Although every precaution has been taken in the preparation of this book, the publisher and authors assume no responsibility for errors or omissions. Neither is any liability assumed for damages resulting from the use of information contained herein. For information, address Alpha Books, 201 West 103rd Street, Indianapolis, IN 46290.

THE COMPLETE IDIOT'S GUIDE TO and Design are registered trademarks of Pearson Education, Inc.

International Standard Book Number: 0-02-864400-X
Library of Congress Catalog Card Number: 2002115293

04   03   02   8   7   6   5   4   3   2   1

Interpretation of the printing code: The rightmost number of the first series of numbers is the year of the book's printing; the rightmost number of the second series of numbers is the number of the book's printing. For example, a printing code of 02-1 shows that the first printing occurred in 2002.

Printed in the United States of America

Note: This publication contains the opinions and ideas of its authors. It is intended to provide helpful and informative material on the subject matter covered. It is sold with the understanding that the authors and publisher are not engaged in rendering professional services in the book. If the reader requires personal assistance or advice, a competent professional should be consulted.

The authors and publisher specifically disclaim any responsibility for any liability, loss, or risk, personal or otherwise, which is incurred as a consequence, directly or indirectly, of the use and application of any of the contents of this book.

For marketing and publicity, please call: 317-581-3722

The publisher offers discounts on this book when ordered in quantity for bulk purchases and special sales.

For sales within the United States, please contact: Corporate and Government Sales, 1-800-382-3419 or corpsales@pearsontechgroup.com

Outside the United States, please contact: International Sales, 317-581-3793 or international@ pearsontechgroup.com

Publisher: *Marie Butler-Knight*
Product Manager: *Phil Kitchel*
Managing Editor: *Jennifer Chisholm*
Acquisitions Editor: *Gary Goldstein*
Development Editor: *Suzanne LeVert*
Production Editor: *Billy Fields*
Copy Editor: *Michael Dietsch*
Illustrator: *Chris Eliopoulos*
Cover/Book Designer: *Trina Wurst*
Indexer: *Brad Herriman*
Layout/Proofreading: *Mary Hunt, Ayanna Lacey*

Contents at a Glance

Appendixes

Contents

Appendixes

Foreword

Many writers have tried to tell the complete story of the FBI, but few have been as successful as John Simeone and David Jacobs. They have done a masterful job of capturing the FBI's history beginning in 1908 and leading us right up to the present with stories as fresh as today's headlines. Today, FBI Agents are deployed all over the world bringing the war against terrorism home to the terrorists themselves. Working with their intelligence and law enforcement counterparts throughout the Middle East they conduct investigations and help to apprehend some of the most dangerous terrorists on the earth. With worldwide jurisdiction and an international reputation for tracking down the most elusive and dangerous criminals on the planet, they have evolved light years from the Bureau's humble beginnings.

Originally the entity that would become the FBI was an investigative unit within the Department of Justice known as the Bureau of Investigation. Unfortunately it was staffed with political appointees who had little training, discipline and fewer successes. It was not until J. Edgar Hoover was appointed as its new director that a corps of professional investigators became the backbone of the institution that would be renamed, Federal Bureau of Investigation. Lawyers and accountants made up the vast majority of the special agents that would staff this revitalized organization. As the Bureau became more and more successful, the United States Congress began to give the FBI more and more responsibility by way of increased jurisdiction. Initially FBI agents did not have the authority to carry firearms and had to rely upon local police to make arrests for them when faced with armed and dangerous criminals. Recognizing the need for armed agents, congress authorized FBI agents to carry firearms and today the FBI's reputation for marksmanship is legendary. Millions of Americans have witnessed the FBI's Fire Arms Demonstrations as they tour FBI Headquarters in Washington, D.C.

Co-authors Simeone and Jacobs have given us invaluable insights into the history and development of today's FBI. Their work not only chronicles the story of the FBI, but the very history of our country as well. David Jacobs has conducted his research with accuracy and thoroughness, and writes with a sense of humor that makes this a great read. Any credible story about the FBI has to include the involvement of a competent insider. John Simeone is not only a veteran FBI agent, but also is one of the most respected agents ever to carry the FBI badge. Mr. Simeone started his career as a highly decorated St. Louis, MO, police officer and later joined the FBI. Ultimately he became the Chief Firearms Instructor for the FBI and was one of the founders of the FBI's Hostage Rescue Team. John is an expert on terrorism matters and consults with nations all over the world in our War on Terrorism. It is his perspective on the agency that he served that helps to bring the stories to life.

This book has vast appeal. Journalists who cover the FBI will find it an invaluable resource tool. It should be required reading for any student involved in criminal justice studies, and it is a must for any young man or woman who has ever dreamed of being an FBI agent. And for those who love cops and robbers tales, you won't do better than *The Complete Idiot's Guide to the FBI.*

—Danny O. Coulson

Founder of the FBI Hostage Rescue Team and co-author of *No Heroes: Inside the FBI's Secret Counter-Terror Force* (Pocket Books, 2001)

Introduction

Eighty or so years ago, having just successfully concluded the First World War, the United States was alarmed by the rise of the international communist conspiracy and assaulted by a wave of anarchist terror bombings. War, revolution, and anarchy helped transform the Bureau of Investigation, a modest-sized investigative arm of the Justice Department, into the forerunner of the Federal Bureau of Investigation, one of the world's great law enforcement agencies.

An elite investigative body of dedicated law enforcement professionals, the FBI has served as a bulwark against a host of foreign and domestic foes threatening the United States. Throughout its existence, America's enemies have been the FBI's enemies.

The Bureau first came to national prominence as the scourge of Depression-era public enemies, such as Machine Gun Kelly and John Dillinger. Guarding against subversion in the 1930s, the FBI monitored and moved against fascist and communist groups pledged to the violent overthrow of the government. During World War II, the FBI neutralized Axis spies, saboteurs, and subversives operating in the hemisphere, from Alaska to Argentina. In the latter half of the twentieth century, the FBI's struggle against Soviet spies and double agents was counterpointed by its opposition to such homegrown threats as organized crime, the Ku Klux Klan, and violent anti-government extremist groups and militias.

One of the FBI's great strengths has been its ability to change, to adapt to changing times and new challenges by constantly reinventing itself, yet never losing sight of its guiding principles of professional, scientific law enforcement.

Today, after the terror strikes of 9/11 have inflicted the most damaging assault ever suffered on U.S. soil, the FBI must reinvent itself again, redefining its primary mission as the prevention of future terrorist attacks. In this time of national emergency and alert, it's vitally important for concerned citizens to know their FBI—what it is, where it's been, and where it's going.

How This Book Is Organized

Part 1, "The Director," describes the rise of the modern FBI. Created in 1907 as the Justice Department's investigative arm, the Bureau of Investigation dramatically expanded in response to the national security demands created by World War I. Appointed in the mid-1920s, Director J. Edgar Hoover reorganized the Bureau into the modern FBI. The bank robbers and gangsters of the 1930s gave way to the threat of Axis spies and saboteurs during World War II.

Part 2, "National Security State," details the FBI's vital role in protecting the nation's internal security during the Cold War. In the late 1940s, the FBI uncovered extensive Soviet spy networks penetrating the U.S. government. The USSR's detonation of an atomic bomb triggered an intensive spy hunt, culminating in the execution of the Rosenbergs for treason. The 1960s social dislocations and antiwar ferment prompted controversial FBI COINTELPRO operations. After successfully staving off Nixon White House efforts to politicize the Bureau, J. Edgar Hoover died in 1972.

Part 3, "Cold War Climax," tells how two new Directors, Clarence M. Kelley and Judge William Webster, retooled the FBI for the post-Watergate era, restoring Bureau morale and public confidence in the organization. A new, vigorous approach to combating organized crime resulted in the decimation of the Mafia. As the U.S./USSR superpower rivalry reached its peak, the FBI pursued a new breed of traitor, greedy double agents who betray their country for hard cash.

Part 4, "New World Order," examines the FBI's role in the post-Cold War era. The fall of the Soviet Empire resulted in new threats coming to the fore. At home, neo-Nazi and extremist hate groups struck, culminating in the horrific 1995 Oklahoma City bombing. Abroad, the shape of a dangerous future was demonstrated by Red China's massive espionage campaign to acquire U.S. atomic weapons secrets. The terror strikes of 9/11 caused the FBI to redefine its primary mission as one of counterterrorism.

Extras

Throughout the book are a number of informative and entertaining boxes and sidebars designed to increase your understanding of the subject:

Justice Jargon

Defining the FBI, these notes showcase the specialized vocabulary of the legal, intelligence, and national security sectors.

Official and Confidential

The case files open to alert you to fun facts, quotes, and anecdotes about the FBI and its times, its friends, and its foes.

Bu Stats

In these sidebars, you'll learn the FBI by the numbers, in plain figures.

Cops and Robbers

Here's a Who's Who of leading notables in the worlds of law and order, crime and punishment.

Acknowledgments

Persons without whom this book would not have been possible: John Talbot, Gary Goldstein, Krista McGruder, and Suzanne LeVert. Thanks!

Special thanks to Patrick O'Donnell and the gang at Devil Bat Media.

Special Thanks to the Technical Reviewer

The Complete Idiot's Guide to the FBI was reviewed by an expert who double-checked the accuracy of what you'll learn here, to help us ensure that this book gives you everything you need to know about the FBI. Special thanks are extended to Daniel Coulson.

Trademarks

All terms mentioned in this book that are known to be or are suspected of being trademarks or service marks have been appropriately capitalized. Alpha Books and Pearson Education, Inc., cannot attest to the accuracy of this information. Use of a term in this book should not be regarded as affecting the validity of any trademark or service mark.

Part 1

The Director

As the federal government grew, so did the Federal Bureau of Investigation. For almost 50 years, the FBI was headed by one of the most remarkable and controversial figures of the American twentieth century: J. Edgar Hoover. Reorganizing the Bureau along modern lines, stressing the goal of professional, scientific law enforcement, Hoover and his "G-men" gained national prominence in the 1930s, combating gangsters and kidnappers, fascists, and communists.

When war broke out in 1941, the FBI quickly rolled up pro-Axis groups it had been surveilling during peacetime years. During the war, the FBI protected vital U.S. national security interests in North, Central, and South America.

Chapter 1

Today's FBI

In This Chapter

- ◆ The FBI's mission and mandate
- ◆ An organizational overview
- ◆ The FBI's national and global reach
- ◆ Crime and investigations
- ◆ Counterterrorism and counterintelligence

One of the world's great law enforcement agencies, the Federal Bureau of Investigation is authorized to detect and apprehend those who violate federal laws. Founded in 1908, the FBI is the investigative component of the U.S. Department of Justice and is under the authority of the Attorney General. Its personnel are divided into special-agent investigators and technical and support staff. Working in close cooperation with local, state, federal, and international law enforcement agencies, the FBI is our national bulwark against crime, espionage, and terrorist activities. In order to maintain its independence, the director of the FBI must be nominated by the president of the United States then confirmed by the Senate before he can serve his ten-year term.

Meet Your FBI

To most people, the FBI occupies the same mental space as such safety devices as seat belts, electrical fuses, or smoke detectors. You take it for granted, not really thinking about it until it's needed—until, suddenly, in a split second, it may spell the difference between life and death. When a child is kidnapped or a bank robbed, when government top secrets are stolen or terrorists strike, most Americans assume that the FBI will take action.

For almost a century, the FBI has been the federal government's frontline force protecting the public against crime and maintaining national security against spies, saboteurs, and terrorists.

It's a two-way street, too, because the FBI looks to the American public as its partner in the ceaseless struggle to keep our nation safe from crime, espionage, and terrorism. Many major cases broken by the FBI began when an ordinary citizen contacted the Bureau with a tip about a suspected violation of federal law.

Cops and Robbers

On September 4, 2001, Robert S. Mueller III became director of the FBI. A week later, on September 11, 2001, terror strikes were launched against New York City's World Trade Center and the Pentagon in Washington, D.C. These brutal surprise attacks were a watershed event, presenting the FBI with possibly its greatest challenge, one that has already led to a redefinition of its mission and a restructuring of the organization.

Since the events of September 11 (a.k.a. 9/11), the FBI has been gratified to receive a record number of applications by citizens eager to work at the Bureau and help fight terrorism. The Bureau received more than 15,000 applications between September 2001 and March 2002, the most applications ever submitted within a six-month period. (Some of you reading this may become inspired to join the FBI. If so, we'll tell you how to do so later in the book.)

The FBI's work on behalf of the American public is being carried out by some of the most dedicated and talented people found anywhere in law enforcement today. All are committed to combating criminal activity through the Bureau's investigations, programs, and law enforcement services. They serve in accordance with the highest traditions of the Bureau's motto: Fidelity, Bravery, and Integrity.

What Is the FBI?

The federal government—and the world—has changed drastically since the FBI was founded in 1908, and the Bureau has changed to meet it, steadily evolving and adapting to meet changing patterns and dynamics of crime, espionage, and political terrorism. Like the law, crime is fluid, ever-shifting and mutating to exploit new technologies and demographics.

A branch of the U.S. Department of Justice, the FBI is responsible to the attorney general, who's nominated by the president and approved by the Senate. The Bureau is also charged with reporting its findings to federal U.S. attorneys across the country. It has the authority to provide other state and local law enforcement agencies with cooperative services, such as fingerprint identification, laboratory examinations, and police training.

More than 32 separate federal agencies are responsible for performing law enforcement tasks, but the FBI is the primary such vehicle for the U.S. government and thus is in charge of enforcing more than 200 federal laws. Not a national police force, the FBI is primarily an investigative body, although its preeminent position of leadership as one of the world's great law enforcement agencies has put it at the center of an anticrime network of local and state police forces, other federal agencies, and international police organizations.

From the beginning, the FBI has maintained that cooperation is the backbone of effective law enforcement and vital to combat domestic and international crime. Now, more than ever, the globalization of crime demands that cooperation. The FBI has been spearheading initiatives to prepare for both domestic and foreign lawlessness in the twenty-first century. A key part of this effort is the continuance of the Bureau's longtime advocacy of the instituting of standardized training of domestic and international police in investigative processes, ethics, leadership, and professionalism.

Due to limited federal law enforcement resources and increasingly complex criminal organizations, effective and efficient use of resources is essential. The FBI routinely cooperates and works closely with all federal law enforcement agencies on joint investigations and through formal task forces that address broad crime problem areas. On December 4, 2001, the Office for Law Enforcement Coordination was created, responsible for improving FBI coordination and information sharing with state and local law enforcement and public safety agencies.

FBI special agents work with state, local, or other law enforcement officers on task forces to investigate violations of many of the criminal laws which the FBI is charged to enforce. Task forces have proven to be a very effective way for

Justice Jargon

In law enforcement, **concurrent jurisdiction** exists when a crime may be a local, state, and federal violation all at the same time. High-profile crimes sharing such concurrent jurisdiction are often tackled by multi-agency task forces, teaming local or state police with the FBI.

the FBI and state and local law enforcement to join together to address specific crime problems that share *concurrent jurisdiction*. Task forces concentrate on organized crime, bank robbery, kidnapping, terrorism, drugs, violent gangs, and motor vehicle theft.

Police Academy

The FBI National Academy, founded in 1935, was established to provide college-level training to mid-level state, local, and foreign police officers. The FBI National Academy is located in the same facility as the FBI Academy, where the Bureau trains its own employees, at Quantico, Virginia. The FBI's Field Police Training Program provides qualified FBI police instructors to give training assistance at local, county, and state law enforcement agencies to improve the investigative and technical skills of local officers. This training program strengthens the cooperative effort between the FBI and local agencies in protecting the public.

Authority and Oversight

The mission of the FBI is to uphold the law through the investigation of federal criminal law; to protect the United States from foreign intelligence and terrorist activities; to provide leadership and law enforcement assistance to federal, state, local, and international agencies; and to perform these responsibilities in a manner that is responsive to the needs of the public and is faithful to the Constitution of the United States.

The FBI's authority derives from congressional statutes and executive orders issued by the president of the United States. The FBI's mandate is the broadest of all federal investigative agencies, authorizing it to investigate all federal criminal violations that have not been specifically assigned by Congress to another federal agency. The FBI's investigative functions fall into the categories of applicant matters, civil rights, counterterrorism, foreign counterintelligence, organized crime, drugs, violent crimes and major offenders, and financial crime.

Official and Confidential

In accordance with current law and Justice Department and FBI policy, information generated by FBI investigations is protected from public disclosure. This protection is designed to preserve the integrity of the investigation as well as the privacy and the rights of individuals involved in the investigation prior to the leveling of any public charge.

Although the agency is responsible for investigating possible violations of federal law, it is the office of the United States attorneys that ultimately decides who will be prosecuted and prosecutes the case. Information and evidence gathered in the course of an investigation are presented to the appropriate U.S. attorney or Department of Justice (DOJ) official who will determine whether prosecution or further action is warranted. Depending on the outcome of the investigation, evidence is either returned or retained for court.

There is no typical expenditure of time, personnel, or money in an FBI investigation. Some investigations are fairly uncomplicated and quickly resolved; others are long-term, complex, and involve multiple jurisdictions, subjects, and violations.

The FBI's activities are closely and regularly scrutinized by a variety of entities. Congress, through several oversight committees in the Senate and House of Representatives, reviews the FBI's budget appropriations, programs, and selected investigations. Also, the results of FBI investigations are often reviewed by the arms of the judiciary system during court proceedings.

File Facts

The FBI's central records system contains information regarding applicants, personnel, administrative actions, criminal, and security and intelligence matters.

The FBI shares information in its files with domestic or foreign investigative agencies and other governmental agencies. The National Name Check Program disseminates limited information from the FBI's central record system to other entities lawfully authorized to receive it, such as federal agencies in the executive branch, congressional committees, the federal judiciary, some foreign police and intelligence agencies, and state and local agencies within the criminal justice system. The FBI also provides fingerprint card checks for certain licensing and employment purposes. Latent fingerprint examinations are conducted for duly constituted law enforcement agencies.

Another area of traditional Bureau leadership is the compilation and dissemination of vital statistics on the patterns and demographics of crime, criminals, and victims. The FBI's Uniform Crime Reporting (UCR) Program receives crime data from nearly 17,000 law enforcement agencies, overseeing 94 percent of the U.S. population. The UCR Program collects information on serious crimes reported to law enforcement agencies, issuing annual Uniform Crime Reports which supply invaluable hard data to police, legislators, and concerned citizens.

Begun in 1929, the UCR Program's categories of serious crime are homicide, forcible rape, robbery, aggravated assault, burglary, larceny, theft, motor vehicle theft, and arson. Information is also collected on hate crimes and on 22 other less serious crime categories.

Field Offices

The FBI is a field-oriented organization. FBI Headquarters (FBIHQ) in Washington, D.C., provides program direction and support services to 56 field offices, approximately 400 satellite offices known as resident agencies, four specialized field installations, and more than 40 foreign liaison posts. The foreign liaison offices, each of which is headed by a legal attaché or legal liaison officer, work abroad with American and local authorities on criminal matters within FBI jurisdiction.

FBI field offices are located in major cities throughout the 50 states and Puerto Rico. In addition, resident agencies are maintained in smaller cities and towns across the country. The locations were selected according to crime trends, the need for regional geographic centralization, and the need to efficiently manage resources.

Each FBI field office is overseen by a special agent in charge (SAC), except for those located in Los Angeles, New York City, and Washington, D.C. Due to their large sizes, those offices each are managed by an assistant director in charge (ADIC).

Official and Confidential

All field offices may be contacted 24 hours a day, every day. The FBI encourages the public to report any suspected violations of U.S. federal law. You can do so by calling your local FBI office, legal attaché office, or by submitting a tip via the FBI Tips and Public Leads form.

Warning: should you suspect some type of criminal activity or violation of federal law, don't try to verify your suspicions before reporting them to the FBI. Playing detective is a good way to get yourself killed. The Bureau advises that citizens should never place themselves in harm's way or conduct their own investigations. Instead, any suspicious activity about matters under FBI jurisdiction should be reported to the FBI promptly.

Legat Chat

The FBI's jurisdiction extends far beyond national shores, reaching into 52 countries outside our borders, to protect U.S. citizens and businesses abroad. The Legal Attaché (Legat) program was created to help foster good will and gain greater cooperation with international police partners in support of the FBI's domestic mission.

The goal is to link law enforcement resources and other officials outside the United States with law enforcement in this country to better ensure the safety of the American public here and abroad.

Presently, there are 44 Legal Attaché (Legat) offices and four Legat sub-offices. The FBI believes it is essential to station highly skilled special agents in other countries to help prevent terrorism and crime from reaching across borders and harming Americans in their homes and workplaces.

Legats help international police agencies with training activities, as well as facilitate resolution of FBI's domestic investigations that have international leads. The Legat program focuses on deterring crime that threatens America such as drug trafficking, international terrorism, and economic espionage.

The program is overseen by the International Operations Branch (IOB) of the FBI at FBIHQ. The IOB keeps in close contact with other federal agencies, Interpol, foreign police and security officers in Washington, D.C., and national law enforcement associations.

Personnel Profile

Total FBI personnel numbers slightly less than 30,000, with about one-third of that being special agents and the rest members of support divisions. The special agent, or SA, is an active investigator who may be regarded as the Bureau's equivalent of police department detectives. SAs wear no uniforms but instead wear plainclothes on the job, generally neat business suits corresponding to those worn by civilian corporate executives. On undercover assignments, agents may be required to wear a variety of garb to promote and maintain their assumed identities.

Support staffers occupy a wide range of positions, including clerical workers, managers, analysts, financial experts, computer operators and programmers, crime scene technicians, and forensics lab personnel, to name only a few.

Fewer than 30,000 FBI employees must daily confront and overcome the threat of countless legions of criminals, spies, and terrorists. Yet it is the malefactors who fear the FBI, not the other way around, a testimony to the Bureau's legendary reputation for fearless crime-busting

Bu Stats

The FBI has approximately 11,400 special agents and over 16,400 other employees who perform support functions: professional, administrative, technical, clerical, craft, trade, or maintenance operations. About 9,800 employees are assigned to FBIHQ; nearly 18,000 are assigned to field installations.

efficiency. FBI members are united in their common desire to fight injustice and make a positive difference in the nation and world.

From the Director

The FBI is headquartered in Washington, D.C. The offices and divisions at FBI Headquarters provide program direction and support to 56 field offices, 400 resident agencies, four specialized field installations, and more than 40 foreign liaison posts known as legal attachés.

FBI headquarters in Washington, D.C., houses a number of divisions, each with a separate mission task, duties, and skills. At the summit is the Office of the Director.

The FBI is headed by a director who is appointed by the president of the United States and confirmed by the Senate for a term not to exceed ten years. The current director of the FBI is Robert S. Mueller III.

Official and Confidential

Currently listed as one of the FBI's Ten Major Investigations, the search for the person or persons responsible for the anthrax-letter attacks has been designated the Amerithrax Investigation. This is an open, ongoing investigation. Anyone having knowledge related to this matter is urged to contact the FBI.

Within a week of taking office, Director Mueller had to face the challenge of the attacks of 9/11. A month later, Washington and New York City were hit with a blizzard of anthrax-laden letters. The FBI quickly committed all resources at its disposal to investigate the terrorist attacks and anthrax-tainted letters and to prevent future incidents. Director Mueller announced a reorganization of FBI Headquarters, responding to the urgency of the Bureau's heightened responsibility in the field of counterterrorism and deterrence and detection of those who would use weapons of mass destruction against our nation.

Organization by Division

FBI divisions embody various components necessary to the efficient running of the organization and the successful completion of its mission. The largest division by far is the Criminal Investigations Division (CID). Other divisions have purely administrative functions relating to the organization itself, involving such in-house matters as personnel, financial, managerial, and the like.

Each of the divisions will be covered in greater detail later on, but for now, here's a quick survey of FBIHQ divisional components:

- **Office of Equal Employment Opportunity Affairs (Office of EEO Affairs).** Ensures equality of opportunity for all Bureau employees and applicants, in accordance with federal guidelines barring discrimination based on race, creed, color, disability, or national origin. The FBI is an equal opportunity employer. Qualified men and women of all backgrounds are always needed.

- **Office of the General Counsel (OGC).** The Bureau's legal staff, providing legal advice to the Director and other FBI officials. OGC's legal researchers and lawyers provide the legal framework and administrative background on matters of law enforcement and national security.

- **Office of the Professional Responsibility (OPR).** Investigates allegations of criminality or serious misconduct by FBI employees. Who polices the Bureau? They do, with oversight from the Department of Justice. Similar in function to a police department's Internal Affairs Division.

- **Office of Public and Congressional Affairs (OPCA).** The Bureau's public relations component, OPCA communicates information on FBI matters, investigations, policies, and directives to the public, Congress, and news media.

- **Administrative Services Division (ASD).** Responsible for FBI personnel management and recruitment, and for the management and security of all FBI facilities. Also responsible for FBI and non-FBI background checks.

- **Counterterrorism Division.** Consolidates all FBI counterterrorism initiatives. Assigned to this division are subunits the National Infrastructure Protection Center (NIPIC) and the National Domestic Preparedness Office (NDPO), the former dealing with infrastructure threats and the latter coordinating the response to *weapons of mass destruction* incidents.

- **Criminal Investigation Division (CID).** The FBI's single largest component, CID investigates a broad spectrum of federal criminal violations, including organized crime, white collar crime, election fraud, government corruption, kidnappings, bank robberies, serial murders, violent interstate fugitives, and many others.

Justice Jargon

Weapons of mass destruction (WMD) are conventional or unconventional delivery systems for the use of lethal nuclear, biological, or chemical (NBC) material. A missile or bomb is a conventional delivery system; anthrax-tainted letters are unconventional. Biological weapons use viruses or bacteria. Chemical weapons include nerve and poison gases and toxic agents. Because of their minimal cost and relative ease to produce, chemical and biological weapons have been called "the poor man's nukes."

- **Criminal Justice Information Services Division (CJIS).** Headquartered in Clarksburg, West Virginia, the CJIS is the central repository for criminal information services in the FBI, providing state-of-the-art identification and data to local, state, federal, and international criminal justice agencies.

- **Finance Division.** Handles budgetary and fiscal matters, payrolls, and property management. The assistant director is the FBI's chief financial officer and chairs the Contract Review Board.

- **Information Resources Division (IRD).** IRD creates the architecture for centralized information processing and handling and designing and implementing the hardware and software needed to maximize efficient data handling.

- **Inspection Division.** Reviews FBI investigations and programs and FBI personnel conduct to standards of a law officer and a gentleman (or gentlewoman). Unlike the OPR, which investigates major internal violations and criminality, the Inspection Division handles minor infractions and managerial streamlining.

- **Investigative Services Division (ISD).** ISD analysts mine the mountains of data from FBI case files and other sources, identifying future trends in crime and national security threats. ISD also oversees Bureau crisis management functions.

- **Laboratory Division.** The FBI crime lab is one of the largest and most comprehensive in the world. Dedicated to the scientific solution and prosecution of crimes, it's the nation's only full-service forensics laboratory. Activities include crime scene searches, DNA testing, fingerprint testing, and a plethora of scientific and technical services, all offered free of charge to all U.S. law enforcement agencies.

- **National Security Division.** Coordinating foreign counterintelligence operations, the NSD's mission includes the investigation of espionage, overseas homicide, and domestic security matters. The division's Security Countermeasures Program conducts background checks and probes physical security issues.

- **Training Division.** Located in Quantico, Virginia, the FBI Academy is one of the world's most respected law enforcement training centers. The FBI Academy trains FBI SAs and professional staff support, while the same-site FBI National Academy offers police training programs for local, state, federal, and international law enforcement personnel.

Investigation Nation

The FBI's war on crime is the area with which the average citizen is most familiar, thanks to the Bureau's Ten Most Wanted Fugitives list, wanted posters displayed in U.S. post offices, and FBI-themed movies and television shows. Investigation is at the heart of what the Bureau does, but not all investigations are focused on criminally related matters.

The FBI conducts background checks on individuals for a variety of reasons. For starters, all persons who apply for employment with the FBI are scrutinized to ascertain that they are who they say they are, and that there is nothing criminal, subversive, or discreditable in their past histories. It would be a coup indeed for organized crime or a foreign intelligence service to place one of their own, unsuspected, in the ranks of the FBI. Background checks are a forward-perimeter defense against penetration agents.

Additionally, the FBI conducts background investigations for certain other government entities, such as the White House, the Justice Department, the administrative office of the U.S. courts, and certain House and Senate committees. The results of background investigations are vital in assessing a person's suitability for employment or access to sensitive, classified, or top-secret materials.

> **Cops and Robbers**
>
> On June 7, 1999, the FBI placed Osama Bin Laden on the Ten Most Wanted List for his alleged involvement in the 1998 bombings of U.S. embassies in Kenya and Tanzania, Africa.

Crime in all its protean varieties is a major focus of investigation. A top priority of the FBI is the fight against organized crime, with more and more crime syndicates going international or even global. The FBI operates under an organized crime/drug strategy which focuses its investigations on major regional, national, and international groups which control large segments of the spectrum of illegal activities. Tactics such as the use of undercover operatives, informants, cooperating witnesses, and electronic surveillance and monitoring devices, are frequently used. Many of these investigations are conducted with foreign and domestic police agencies.

Drug trafficking is a primary source of organized crime revenues, generating byproducts such as mega-violence and pervasive corruption. The FBI uses the enterprise theory of investigation, targeting not single individuals but rather entire criminal enterprises. Through this process, all aspects of the criminal operation can be identified. A key component of the strategy is the seizure of the enterprise's assets and the disruption or dismantling of the entire criminal organization.

White collar crime is money crime, generally nonviolent in nature, such as check fraud, health care fraud, telemarketing fraud, Internet scams, money laundering, mortgage loan fraud, and fraud against the government. The FBI actively pursues a multiplicity of investigations of white collar crime.

Official and Confidential

When engaged in a potentially lethal confrontation with a violent felon, a special agent does not shoot to kill, he instead shoots to stop. The difference is more a matter of semantics than anything else, because the results are the same.

Graft and corruption of public officials falls under the investigatory purview of the FBI thanks to the Hobbs Act, which authorizes the investigation of those in local and state government and local police departments who have illicitly sold their influence for bribes, pay-offs, or other items of value. The categories of public corruption include legislative, judicial, regulatory, contractual, and law enforcement.

The FBI investigates all violations of federal civil rights statutes, including those prohibiting racial or religious discrimination, use of excessive force or police misconduct, involuntary servitude and slavery, and violations of the voting rights and civil rights laws.

Common civil rights complaints involve racial violence such as physical assaults and homicides, verbal or written threats, or desecration of property. The most common civil rights complaint, however, is the alleged use of excessive force by law enforcement personnel that causes injuries or death. About 40 to 50 law enforcement personnel are convicted of this offense each year nationwide.

Counterterrorism Command

In response to the terror strikes of September 11, 2001, the FBI's counterterrorism program has taken on a new urgency and priority. The FBI's role is to reduce the threat of terrorism in the United States and against U.S. persons and interests throughout the world through professional investigation and coordinated efforts with local, state, federal, and foreign agencies and governments.

Countering terrorism effectively requires the exchange of information and close, daily coordination among U.S. law enforcement, intelligence, and service entities, as well as international law enforcement agencies. To further that goal, on December 4, 2001, the Office for Law Enforcement Coordination was created to take responsibility for improving FBI coordination and information sharing with state and local law enforcement and public safety agencies.

The United States is both empowered and imperiled by its complex technological infrastructure. In his classic work of political philosophy, *Leviathan*, Thomas Hobbes famously compared the state to a single human being. So, too, may the modern infrastructure be compared to a living body, the body of technology. The computer system is the brain. The power grid is the nervous system. Power plants, electric or nuclear, supply the energy to make it all go. The transportation web is the circulatory system, with complex trunk lines and branches, highways and road grids, passenger and freight air lines, trucking, railroads, and shipping. Oil is the lifeblood.

Those who would destroy us may strike at any of these areas, singly or in combination. And our enemies are legion: terrorists foreign or domestic, fanatic fundamentalist religious groups, political extremist and hate groups—anyone who's got a grudge against Uncle Sam.

The Amerithrax anthrax attacks show the extensive financial and emotional devastation even a relatively mild bio-weapon with a haphazard, scattershot delivery system can unleash, inflicting casualties, causing scores of millions of dollars in damages, and paralyzing whole sectors of the federal government.

In 1998, to combat cybercrime, the FBI's National Infrastructure Protection Center (NIPC) was established. Located in FBIHQ in Washington, D.C. NIPC brings together representatives from U.S. government agencies, state and local government, and private enterprises to protect the nation's critical infrastructures.

Like NIPIC, a part of the Bureau's Counterterrorism Division, the National Domestic Preparedness Office (NDPO) coordinates all federal efforts to work in partnership with local and state governments to respond to a weapons of mass destruction incident.

Official and Confidential

Post-9/11, the FBI identified several vital skills that are currently in demand for countering the threat of international terrorism. They are computer science, engineering, foreign counterintelligence, military intelligence, physical sciences, and foreign language skills in Arabic, Farsi (Iran), Pashtu (areas of Afghanistan and Pakistan), Urdu (Muslim India), Chinese, Japanese, Korean, Russian, Spanish, and Vietnamese.

Working in partnership with foreign governments, leaders, and law enforcement officials, the FBI has focused on ways to strengthen security measures against possible theft of nuclear weapons and nuclear materials from Russia and other former republics of the Soviet Union. FBI initiatives have sharpened multi-nation task forces and joint efforts against organized crime, drug trafficking, and terrorism.

The FBI investigates domestic hate groups, potential terrorist groups in the United States, and foreign groups linked to terrorism abroad with members here in the United States. When conducting investigations, the FBI collects information that not only serves as the basis for prosecution, but also builds an intelligence base to help prevent terrorist acts.

Counterintelligence Capers

The era of Cold War superpower rivalry between the United States and the Soviet Union may arguably be called the Golden Age of Espionage. Those naïve enough to think that the end of the Cold War (and the Union of Soviet Socialist Republics) would put an end to the intricate game of spy/counterspy were soon disabused of that notion. The post–Cold War era has become the Silver Age of Intrigue, with political and economic espionage roaring along at full blast.

Electronic intelligence (nicknamed *elint*) gathering, spy satellite surveillance, and related uses of high technology have not done away with the need for human intelligence (also known as *humint*). High technology gives the intelligence officer anonymity, enhancing but not replacing the efforts of foreign spies. No clearer or more devastating example of the importance of humint may be seen than the ease with which Bin Laden's Al Qaeda terrorists were able to carry out their surprise attack on the United States.

Espionage and related matters cost the nation an estimated $100 billion per year. The FBI has defined economic espionage as intelligence activities, sponsored or coordinated by foreign powers, directed at the U.S. government or U.S. corporations, establishments, or persons designed to unlawfully or clandestinely influence sensitive economic policy decisions. This theft can provide foreign entities with a treasure trove of proprietary economic information at a fraction of the true cost of their research and development, causing significant economic loss.

Justice Jargon

Counterintelligence is activity designed to block the enemy's sources of information by concealment, codes, and other measures, and to deceive the enemy through deviousness, deception, and disinformation.

Intelligence is, simply, information. *Counterintelligence* is activity designed to keep the enemy from getting that intelligence. FBI counterintelligence efforts are run through the Bureau's National Security Division, which investigates espionage, overseas homicide, protection of foreign officials, domestic security, and nuclear extortion.

Most FBI responses to foreign intelligence activity results in neutralizing the threat, rather than by making arrests, and so the public knows nothing about them. You can help by raising your own security awareness, and by reporting any suspected espionage activity to the FBI. Apparent espionage activity may include unauthorized attempts to view records or plans, scavenging through trash, eavesdropping on live or telephone conversations, questioning from persons who have no need to know certain information to do their job, or persons loitering outside their normal work areas or at unusual hours. Security awareness is vital to the national interest.

Heraldry of the FBI Seal

The FBI's official seal is the hallmark of its ideals, the brand of the Bureau. Each symbol and color in the seal has special significance. The blue field and the scales on the shield represent justice. The circle of 13 stars denotes the original 13 states. The laurel leaf symbolizes academic honors, distinction, and fame. The 46 leaves in the laurel branches stand for the 46 states in the Union when the FBI was founded in 1908. Of the red and white stripes, red stands for courage, valor, and strength; whereas white conveys cleanliness, light, truth, and peace. As in the American flag, the red bars exceed the white by one.

The motto "Fidelity, Bravery, Integrity" describes the motivating force behind the men and women of the FBI. The peaked beveled edge which rings the seal symbolizes the severe challenges confronting the FBI and the ruggedness of the organization. The gold color in the seal conveys its overall value.

The Least You Need to Know

- Founded in 1908, the FBI is the investigative arm of the Justice Department and answers to the attorney general.

- A field-based organization, the FBI maintains 56 field offices, 400 satellite resident agencies, and 40 foreign liaison posts.

- FBI headquarters in Washington, D.C., (FBIHQ) operates 15 divisions to accomplish its mission, Criminal Investigative Division (CID) being the largest.

- The FBI believes that universal law enforcement cooperation is vital, and works closely with local, state, federal, and international agencies.

Chapter 2

Origins of the Bureau

In This Chapter

- Origin of the FBI
- World War I spies and spy-catchers
- Red Threat of the international communist conspiracy
- Enter J. Edgar Hoover
- Antiradical raids of 1919

At the start of the twentieth century, immigration, industrialization, and internationalism brought the United States into the modern era. Modern times demanded a different definition of the role of federal law enforcement. In 1908, the Justice Department established the Bureau of Investigation, a small permanent detective division with the responsibility of investigating violations of the law. World War I and the rise of the international communist conspiracy presented new challenges to the Bureau, which adapted to meet them. In the fight against anarchists, radicals, and subversives, the Bureau was greatly aided by the tireless efforts of a young Justice Department lawyer: J. Edgar Hoover.

Twilight of the Old-Time Badmen

On March 3, 1908, the last act of settling the American West took place in San Vincente, Bolivia, as government troops prepared to close in on a cornered gang of bandits. Among them were the celebrated Butch Cassidy and the Sundance Kid (Harry Longbaugh), once the mainstays of the Wyoming outlaw band known as the Wild Bunch.

The brand of violent frontier outlawry that the Bunch represented was ending. The frontier was closing and the onset of civilization was squeezing out the bandits. Telegraphs and trains narrowed the outlaws' margin of escape, allowing for a quick raising of alarms and posses at the sight of them. Hard-pressed local marshals and sheriffs were aided by nationwide detective agencies such as the Pinkertons, with their relentless bands of sleuths and manhunters.

Cops and Robbers

Sleuth Alan Pinkerton foiled an assassination plot aimed at President-elect Abraham Lincoln while he was en route to his 1861 inauguration in Washington, D.C. Pinkerton was made the head of Union Army intelligence, founding what later became the Secret Service. When he left government service, he founded the private detective agency which bears his name. In the first quarter of the twentieth century, the Pinkerton Agency was primarily used for antilabor activities and strikebreaking.

The dragnet caused Cassidy and Sundance to flee to South America, where their luck finally ran out. Trapped in a little mountain village by Bolivian troops, Sundance was killed and Cassidy committed suicide rather than be taken alive.

As the twentieth century continued to unfold, there would be other outbreaks of Wild West–type banditry, most notably that of the Depression-era bank robbers such as John Dillinger and Charles "Pretty Boy" Floyd. But the main trend of modern crime would be urban in nature, with organized crime mobs controlling lucrative vice rackets such as bootlegging, gambling, prostitution, and narcotics, ultimately creating a nationwide crime syndicate dominating a significant sector of the national economy.

Changing times demand new solutions. Just when the era of the Wild Bunch came to an end, the Bureau of Investigation, the embryonic organization that would eventually become the FBI, came into being.

Teddy Roosevelt's Bigger Stick

Starting in about 1880, the United States began experiencing a massive influx of European immigration, with most of the newcomers settling in the cities. Increased urbanization, industrialization, and new technologies such as the automobile, telephone, and electric light dramatically transformed the U.S. landscape, culture, and balance of power. Federal law enforcement needed to keep up with the changing times.

As New York City police commissioner Theodore Roosevelt had once told his men, "There's more law in the end of your nightsticks than in all the law books in the world." He also once famously observed, "Speak softly and carry a big stick." As president of the United States, he carried over this same vigorous, hard-driving approach to law enforcement. An activist trust-buster and conservationist, he demanded additional policing powers to protect the public.

Roosevelt's vehicle was the Department of Justice, which had been created in 1870 during the post–Civil War Reconstruction era. Heading the department was a presidentially-appointed attorney general. (The attorney general was one of the four original Cabinet posts established in 1789.)

Department of Justice duties included detecting and prosecuting violations of federal law, representing the federal government in civil suits, and assisting the president and other federal officials in fulfilling their lawful duties. Initially, the department had no staff of permanent investigators, borrowing them as needed from the Secret Service Division of the Treasury Department, or from private detective agencies, such as Pinkerton (a practice forbidden by Congress in 1892).

The Justice Department belongs to the government's executive branch, and Congress, jealous of its powers and prerogatives, was unwilling to cede additional authority to the president.

Bu Stats

By 1899, the number of immigrants arriving yearly at these shores numbered 300,000, rising to a peak in 1907 of one million immigrants per year. From 1908 to 1917, immigration rates remained at 650,000 per year.

Official and Confidential

In our constitutional system of checks and balances, the president proposes and Congress disposes. The legislative body has the power to authorize the funding of government agencies. Congressional Appropriations Committees control the amount of the federal budget allocated yearly to the FBI, giving them some measure of oversight regarding the Bureau.

This tug-of-war between presidential and congressional interests would prove to be a major factor not merely during the start-up of the Bureau, but throughout its history.

In 1908, Attorney General Charles J. Bonaparte (grandnephew of French emperor Napoleon I) requested congressional approval for the department to form its own investigative division. Not only was he turned down, but as payback for an earlier land fraud probe which had targeted legislators, he was forbidden by Congress to use Secret Service agents to carry out investigations.

Scheduled to go into effect on July 1, 1908, the prohibition was circumvented by Bonaparte, who used the discretionary funds at his disposal to hire a small staff of nine investigators and fourteen examiners and accountants. He put them on the Justice Department payroll before the expiration of the June 30 deadline.

The unnamed agency's first chief was Inspector Stanley W. Finch, who served from 1908 to 1912. On July 26, President Roosevelt officially authorized the new investigative division.

Bureau of Investigation

William Howard Taft won the 1908 presidential election. Appearing before the House Appropriations Committee in February 1909, outgoing Attorney General Bonaparte assured the members that he'd installed institutional safeguards on the new detective force. Congress agreed to fund the new division, while reserving the right to keep close tabs on it.

On March 16, 1909, new Attorney General George Wickersham named the agency the Bureau of Investigation. (In abbreviated form, BI.) Wickersham's 1910 report to Congress outlined the Bureau's area of operations: "enforce national banking laws, antitrust laws, peonage laws, the bucketshop law, laws relating to fraudulent bankruptcies, impersonation of government officials with intent to defraud, thefts and murders committed on government reservations, offenses committed against government property, and those committed by federal court officials and employees, Chinese smuggling, customs frauds, internal revenue frauds, post office frauds, violations of the neutrality act … land frauds and immigration and naturalization cases."

From its inception, the Bureau and politics would prove to be inseparable. Responding to national outrage over massive organized prostitution rackets, Congress passed the Mann Act, a.k.a. the White Slave Traffic Act, in 1910. Named for its sponsor, Illinois Republican Representative James Mann, the act made it a federal crime to transport a female across state lines for "immoral purposes." Congress voted to give the BI the responsibility of enforcing the Mann Act, thus extending its bailiwick to madams, prostitutes, and pimps.

Although the act was intended to check organized prostitution, loose wording in the statute had the perhaps unintended consequence of allowing for the prosecution of any man who took a female not his wife across state lines for a sexual encounter.

The Bureau's newly expanded powers also led to extensive contacts with "helpful" pimps and madams who gained favor by passing along potentially explosive information regarding payoffs to corrupt police, judges, and government officials, and the identities and sexual peccadilloes of highly placed customers. The arrangement was a prime potential source of ripe blackmail material.

Bu Stats

The inciting incident for the passage of the Mann Act was the revelation that a big-time pimp had procured more than 10,000 foreign-born women and girls to stock Chicago brothels, of which the Windy City had 192, according to Chicago Vice Commission statistics furnished to the police—a number which was undercounted by several hundreds.

War Clouds

The second decade of the twentieth century saw the United States beset by domestic and foreign woes. At home, decades of wholesale immigration from Italy, Eastern Europe, and the Balkans had enflamed the resentment of native-born citizens, pitting largely Protestant rural constituencies against predominantly Catholic urban dwellers. Many East Europeans and Mediterraneans were trade unionists, a trait hardly likely to endear them to militantly antilabor big business interests.

A leading indicator of domestic unrest was the movement to prohibit alcoholic beverages. Although Prohibition gained its momentum in rural America, consumption of alcohol was greatest in the cities. A more dramatic and dangerous bellwether was the 1915 revival of the white-supremacist secret society, the Ku Klux Klan, whose program now included a virulent anti-immigrant strain. Racial tensions prompted the steady migration of rural Southern blacks to Northern cities.

Internationally, the assassination of Archduke Ferdinand in August 1914 sparked a new Balkan war, the third since 1912. Unlike the others, this one flared up into a conflagration that put Europe's great powers at each other's throats, locked in a death spiral. Reelected in 1916 on the slogan, "He kept us out of war," President Woodrow Wilson on April 6, 1917, turned right around and brought the United States into war against Germany and the Austro-Hungarian Empire.

The Great War was nothing if not total, and total war demands total involvement. This involvement brought an increased U.S. public demand for federal surveillance of spies, saboteurs, and subversives. Wilson signed into law the 1917 Espionage Act, which included a clause criminalizing "*seditious* utterances during the course of the hostilities." Congress passed legislation restricting immigrants, excluding illiterates and those who advocated the use of force or violence to overthrow the U.S. government. This was followed by the 1918 Alien Act, also known as the Alien and Sedition Act, which banned alien anarchists from the United States.

Justice Jargon

Sedition is the incitement of discontent or resistance against legally constituted authorities or the government. Sedition may be expressed by the written or spoken word, visual displays such as posters or tableaux, symbolic acts, protest demonstrations, and the like.

Anarchists, radicals, and subversives were held to be equally dangerous to the war effort as German spies and saboteurs, most of whom had been rounded up when war was declared. (By war's end, the Justice Department had arrested 4,000 "enemy aliens.")

In September 1917, the BI moved hard against the country's most militant radical organization, the Industrial Workers of the World (IWW). Founded in 1905, the IWW, or "Wobblies," sought to bind the national workforce into one giant union. The group was strongly antiwar and not hesitant about saying so, thus putting itself in violation of wartime sedition acts.

Under the leadership of A. Bruce Bielaski (Bureau chief from 1912 to 1919), BI agents simultaneously raided 48 meeting halls and seized IWW membership lists, pamphlets, correspondence, and all documents great and small. This action was only the prelude for stronger action later that month, the mass arrest of 165 high-level IWW members for conspiracy against the draft and war effort and labor agitation.

In April, 1918 110 IWW defendants went on trial. The trial lasted five months, making it the lengthiest criminal trial held up to that time in the United States. IWW president William "Big Bill" Haywood and 14 others were sentenced to 20 years in prison, lesser terms were handed out to the underlings, and the organization was hit with a $2.5 million fine. The IWW was broken, never to recover.

Postwar Blues—and Reds

Across the globe, Lenin's Bolsheviks had stormed the Tsar's Winter Palace in St. Petersburg in November 1917, marking the beginning of the Russian Revolution. Even before the end of World War I, destabilized European governments began falling like dominoes. October 1918 saw revolt break out in Hungary, Austria, and Bulgaria. One month later, Germany's Kaiser was overthrown. Milan and other northern Italian cities seethed with unrest. Mutinies erupted in the French Army.

Cops and Robbers

In Russia, 1887, Alexander Ulyanov was one of five University of St. Petersburg students hanged for conspiring in a failed assassination attempt on Tsar Alexander III. Ulyanov's younger brother, Vladimir Ilyich, changed his name to Lenin and continued working for revolution, ultimately ordering the execution of Tsar Nicholas II and his family in 1918, ending the centuries-old Romanov dynasty.

Armistice was declared on November 11, 1918, a date which continues to be commemorated in the United States as Veteran's Day. Total U.S. dead in the Great War: 116,700. The political scene was further set boiling by a variety of leftist "isms" that even their own adherents sometimes found hard to tell apart:

♦ Socialism: social organization based on collective or government ownership and management of the means of production and distribution of goods.

♦ Marxism: socialism of Marx and Engels, which makes the class struggle the fundamental force in history.

♦ Anarchism: literally, "no government;" believers hold government is oppression and must be destroyed.

♦ Bolshevik: majority wing (*bolsheviki*) of Russian Social Democratic Party, which under Lenin's leadership stressed extremist revolutionary Marxism; in 1919 renamed Communist Party.

♦ Communism: (via Lenin and Bolsheviki) class warfare; all social, cultural, economic activities regulated by single authoritarian party representing the workers.

With the revolution triumphant in Russia, Lenin and his associate Leon Trotsky declared the Third Communist International, or Comintern on March 4, 1919. Their manifesto stated that henceforth the Russian Communist Party would become the vanguard of world revolution, spreading the doctrine of class warfare by means fair or foul, doing whatever it took to overthrow foreign governments and replace them with communist regimes. All would then be incorporated into a global union of soviet socialist "republics," headed by Lenin and the Party, of course.

Radical Terror

Delirious over Lenin's victory, American leftist radicals felt certain that the long-prophesied revolution was at hand. In January 1919, Seattle was hit by a general strike, which was crushed in four days.

On April 28, 1919, a bomb disguised in the form of a package was delivered to the house of Ole Hanson, the mayor who'd stopped the Seattle strike. The infernal device was disarmed before it could do any damage. The next day, a similar package bomb was delivered to the Atlanta home of former Senator Thomas Hardwick, blowing the hands off the hapless housemaid who unwrapped it.

Justice Jargon

An **agent provocateur** is one who commits the crime to incite, entrap, and punish a supposed criminal or discredit the cause for which he pretends to be working.

Thirty-four more bombs were delivered to prominent political and financial figures. The bombers' identities were never discovered. Predictably, members of the Left charged that the bombs were the work of *agents provocateurs*, working for the government to discredit their collectivist foes.

Cops and Robbers

A power in the Democratic Party and Wilson Administration, A. Mitchell Palmer (the "Fighting Quaker") headed the wartime Alien Property Bureau, where his public posture of moral rectitude did not deter him from redistributing confiscated German wealth to his political cronies. Succeeding Thomas Gregory as attorney general, Palmer was the frontrunner for the 1920 Democratic presidential nomination. He didn't get it.

A second wave of terror bombings followed. On the night of June 2, 1919, the Washington, D.C., home of Attorney General A. Mitchell Palmer ("the Fighting Quaker") was struck by a shattering blast. The front of the house was pulverized but no one inside was hurt. Strewn among the wreckage was what was left of the bomber, who'd apparently stumbled, prematurely triggering the blast. Among the debris were leaflets threatening the capitalist class, signed "the Anarchist Fighters."

The Palmer blast was only one of a number of bombings that took place at midnight in eight cities, including Boston, Cleveland, Pittsburgh, and New York City, where two people were killed by an explosion at a judge's house.

Young Mr. Hoover

Palmer struck back, first cleaning house at the Justice Department; he targeted BI Chief William A. Allen as a scapegoat and fired him. Successor to Bielaski, Allen's tenure had lasted only a short six months before the June 2 bombing prompted his replacement by former Secret Service head and celebrated detective William J. Flynn. Francis P. Garvan, former chief investigator at the wartime Alien Property Bureau, was put in as assistant attorney general with a mandate from Palmer "to deal with the radical threat."

Garvan was put in charge of the Radical Division, also known more accurately as the Anti-Radical Division (in 1920 its name would be changed to the General Intelligence

Division). As his assistant, Garvan chose a 24-year-old Justice Department lawyer named John Edgar Hoover.

During the war, Hoover had distinguished himself at the Justice Department's Alien Registration Bureau, where he'd worked with the Immigration Bureau to deport "undesirable" aliens. A tireless worker with an encyclopedic memory for details, Hoover was the BI's resident "alien expert."

On June 17, 1919, a high-level Justice Department war council decided on a mass roundup and deportation of "alien radicals." On July 1, 1919, Palmer chose Hoover to head the drive, appointing him assistant to the attorney general, reporting to Garvan.

Justice Jargon

In 1919, Bureau Director Flynn's yearly salary was $7,500. His second in command, Chief Burke, was paid $4,000. J. Edgar Hoover's promotion to assistant to the attorney general raised his salary from $1,800 to $3,000 a year. By 1920, Hoover's salary was $4,500, $500 more than Chief Burke. By comparison, a high-powered lawyer like A. Mitchell Palmer could earn $200,000 a year in private practice.

Like a dividing amoeba, Marxist-Leninist groups began fragmenting, and a particular split arose in the United States between foreign-born and native-born radicals. On August 31, 1919, foreign-speaking Left Wing radicals formed the Communist Party. September 3, English-speaking members met at Chicago's IWW hall to form the Communist Labor Party.

U.S. citizens could not be deported merely for holding and advocating radical beliefs. But the 1918 Alien and Sedition Act made it legal to deport noncitizens who believed in anarchism or the use of force or violence to overthrow the government.

The Comintern had put itself on the record in favor of overthrowing governments by whatever means necessary and replacing them with communist regimes. That "whatever means necessary" included the use of force and violence. Those organizations which had speedily endorsed the Comintern's manifesto had tacitly or explicitly associated themselves with its aims. That meant that anywhere from 40,000 to 70,000 radicals had advocated the violent overthrow of the U.S. government. Those who were also noncitizens had rendered themselves liable for deportation.

Now in charge of the Bureau's Radical Division, Hoover set it to work gathering *general intelligence.* Casting a wide net, the division

Justice Jargon

General intelligence is the gathering of background information on a particular subject, as opposed to information gathered during the course of an investigation to develop a criminal case for prosecution.

researchers studied the radical movement's books, pamphlets, newspapers, and other printed material. Translators labored over foreign language publications. Agents attended movement meetings and rallies, transcribing speeches and reporting on the proceedings. All-important membership lists were acquired, sometimes from paid informants.

Soviet Ark

The Justice Department first moved against the Union of Russian Workers, a New York City–based organization with between 4,000 and 7,000 members. The Labor Department ruled that membership in the UORW was grounds for deportation. On November 7, 1919, a date picked because it was the two-year anniversary of the Bolshevik revolution, teams of BI agents working with local police swept down on UORW branches in twelve cities. Several thousand people were arrested nationwide, 650 in New York City alone. The meeting halls were picked clean of all records, printed matter, and anything else that looked suspicious.

The total number of detainees was winnowed out to some 600 prisoners, who were sent across country and held at Ellis Island in New York harbor for imminent deportation.

> **Official and Confidential**
>
> Attorney Isaac Schorr of the National Civil Liberties Bureau (forerunner of the American Civil Liberties Union) inquired about beatings that some of the local police had inflicted on members of the UORW. Hoover said he didn't know about any beatings, advising Attorney General Palmer not to reply "lest the controversy be prolonged." For his temerity, Schorr was the first to make Hoover's enemies list; Hoover opened a file on him and urged his disbarment.

The Red-busting raid had its aspects of political theater and, like any other show, it needed some top headliners to ensure its success. Hoover selected three stellar radicals for the leads in this first production: Emma Goldman, Alexander Berkman, and Ludwig C.E.K. Martens.

Emma Goldman, "Queen of the Reds," born in Russia in 1869, had arrived in the United States in 1885, swiftly becoming a power in radical politics. An unabashed anarchist, feminist, and orator, she also advocated birth control and "free love." In 1890, she became lovers with Russian radical Alexander Berkman, who two years later tried but failed to assassinate Carnegie Steel Company's ruthless manager Henry Clay Frick. Frick survived and Berkman spent the next 14 years in prison. Martens was a German-born communist who was Lenin's unofficial trade representative in America—unofficial because the U.S. government had yet to diplomatically recognize the Soviet Union.

Goldman claimed U.S. citizenship through marriage, but Hoover used a technicality in her citizen status and her advocacy of the violent overthrow of the U.S. government to get a deportation order against her. No such legal maneuvers were needed to deport noncitizens Berkman and Martens.

Of the Ellis Island detainees, some 249 were ultimately selected for deportation, with Goldman, Berkman, and Martens making the final cut. A majority of the deportees were UORW members, a minority were anarchists, and the remaining handful made up a potpourri of assorted malcontents.

On December 22, 1919, they were loaded on to the troop ship USS *Buford*, which was manned with an armed guard of 200 soldiers who would also be making the voyage. Hoover and other Justice Department bigs were on hand at dockside to see the ship sail for Russia.

Bu Stats

In 1917, the American Socialist Party's Left Wing caucus had 80,379 members. Two years later, propelled in large part by enthusiasm for the Bolshevik revolution, its membership totaled 104,822. By summer of 1919, party leadership had expelled two-thirds of its membership for radicalism. The outcasts formed the Communist Party, whose 60,000 members were 90 percent foreign language-speaking aliens. Formed at about the same time, the rival Communist Labor Party had 10,000 members, mostly English-speakers, though many were foreign-born.

Red Raids

Nationwide raids took place on Friday, January 2, 1920, from 7:00 P.M. through 7:00 A.M. Hundreds of raids were launched in 33 cities in 23 states. As in November, BI agents worked in concert with local police augmented by anti-Red civilian auxiliaries. In the first mass sweep, 10,000 persons were arrested. Of these, 3,500 were held, and 556 were ordered deported.

Reporting the January antiradical raids, a *New York Times* front page headline bannered "Revolution Smashed!" Praising Attorney General Palmer, the *Times* editorialized,

"If any or some of us … have ever doubted the alacrity, resolute will, and fruitful intelligence of the Department of Justice in hunting down the enemies of the United States, the questioners and doubters now have cause to approve and applaud."

Then the negative reports and opinions began to come in. The first objections focused on the treatment of those arrested. Many had been badly beaten, with the civilian auxiliaries being the prime offenders in this regard. In various police station holding pens and cells, hundreds of the detainees were crammed together for days in conditions that were cramped, unhygienic, and inhumane.

The second wave of objections was more overtly political, with foes of the antiradical mass deportations launching a swift counterattack on the legal and propaganda fronts. Propagandists of the left shrewdly managed to shift the focus from the aliens' radical political views to the abuse they'd suffered as a result of the Palmer raids.

In April, ACLU founder Roger Baldwin appeared for the defense in a Boston deportation case. The trial against the Colyers, a British married couple who were part of a group of 18 radical defendants who'd been rounded up for deportation saw the surfacing of a memo written by BI Chief Frank Burke, the Bureau's Number Two man. Written before the January raids, the document indicated that the Bureau had a number of agents planted in the Communist Party and Communist Labor Party, agents so highly placed that they were able to schedule party meetings for the night of the raid to concentrate the targeted groups.

At Boston's Colyer Trial, Judge George Anderson rebuked the prosecution, opining, "What does appear, beyond a reasonable doubt, is that the government owns and operates some part of the Communist Party." J. Edgar Hoover fired back that the judge's statement was "an unjustifiable misconception of the facts … which the most perverted mind could not put on the evidence."

Reeling under the barrage of opposition, Attorney General Palmer warned that 1920's May Day demonstrations were sure to be the most violent yet, with thousands of radicals taking to the street to spread riot and anarchy. Across the nation, big city police forces mobilized for the big day, but when May 1 arrived, the prophesied violent crowds and revolutionary street action was nowhere to be seen. Palmer's credibility took a major hit, as did the credibility of the Red Scare.

The finish came on June 19, 1920, when Judge Anderson handed down his decision in the Colyer case, ruling that by itself, membership in the Communist Party or Communist Labor Party was not grounds for deportation. While the decision was later appealed and overturned, it effectively cut the legs off the antiradical drive. The question of whether or not Party membership was grounds for deportation remained to be settled, but it was clear that the federal government would no longer prosecute the issue.

"Return to Normalcy"

On September 16, 1920, a dynamite bomb was set off on Wall Street at the corner of a J. P. Morgan commercial building at lunchtime, killing thirty people and injuring hundreds more. Later, a New York postal clerk intercepted 16 bomb packages addressed to Morgan, Rockefeller, Holmes Jr., and so on. The identity of the bombers remains a mystery.

It was one of the worst terror bombings to that date, but still it failed to revive public apprehension about the Red Menace. The antiradical drive had run out of gas. In fact, despite revisionist attempts to portray them as a failure, the Red raids had been extremely effective. They destabilized, demoralized, and decimated communist, radical, and other leftist extremist groups. The numbers tell it: Within two years of the raids, Communist Party and Communist Labor Party membership shrank to a combined 5,000 members. The BI's hard-hitting tactics spooked the left, causing the communist parties to go underground and become conspiratorial organizations rather than vital political parties.

In late June 1920, the Democratic National Convention was held in San Francisco. At the start of the proceedings to nominate a presidential candidate, Attorney General A. Mitchell Palmer was regarded as the favorite. Billed as "the Great Red Hunter," Palmer had strong financial backing from industrialists who supported his anti-union activities, but was opposed by organized labor and Prohibitionists. After an exhausting 38 deadlocked ballots, Palmer dropped out of the race, which was won a few ballots later by Ohio Governor James M. Cox.

In Chicago, the GOP convention was similarly deadlocked until, in a classic smoke-filled-room episode that defined the genre, party bosses settled for everybody's second choice, Ohio Senator Warren G. Harding.

Heeding Harding's call for a "return to normalcy," the voters elected him president of the United States on November 2, 1920.

The Least You Need to Know

- The Justice Department's BI was founded in 1908 as a small permanent detective force to investigate violations of federal law.

- The entry of the United States into World War I put the Bureau in the business of catching spies, saboteurs, and subversives.

- Triumphant in the Russian revolution, Lenin's Comintern organization called for the violent overthrow of governments worldwide, to be replaced by communist regimes.

- ◆ J. Edgar Hoover transformed the Bureau's intelligence division into a high-powered, wide-ranging fact gathering operation, compiling voluminous files.

- ◆ The Justice Department's 1919 antiradical Palmer Raids hammered the American Communist Party, but political opposition soon halted the controversial drive.

Chapter 3

J. Edgar Hoover: America's Top Cop

In This Chapter

- ◆ Prohibition triggers gang violence and nationwide lawbreaking
- ◆ Political patronage and corruption nearly destroy the BI
- ◆ In 1924, J. Edgar Hoover is appointed BI director and cleans house
- ◆ The Bureau is reorganized along scientific principles of professional law enforcement

The 1920 election of Warren G. Harding as president showed that voters wanted a return to pre-war levels of governmental noninterference in the public sector. Working against this trend was national prohibition of alcohol, causing a rise in lawlessness. Political patronage and cronyism flooded the BI with incompetent and corrupt detectives and party hacks, until the Teapot Dome oil scandals caused a collapse of the Harding regime. Installed in 1924 as BI acting director, young J. Edgar Hoover cleaned up and reorganized the Bureau, within a year winning permanent appointment to the director's post.

"Best of the Second-Raters"

One of the political bosses at the 1920 Republican convention who'd helped pick Warren G. Harding said of the nominee, "He was nobody's first choice, but he was the best of the second-raters." Even by the freewheeling standards of a different era, the Harding presidency would prove to be one of the most corrupt administrations in U.S. history, resulting in the near-destruction of the BI.

Defeating Democrat candidate James M. Cox and his running mate Franklin Delano Roosevelt, Harding was inaugurated the twenty-ninth president of the United States on March 4, 1921. For attorney general, Harding picked his old crony, Ohio Republican Harry M. Daugherty, a lawyer, and political power broker. To the victor belongs the spoils, and Daugherty wasted no time sacking Democratic officeholders and replacing them with Republicans.

Official and Confidential

As a native Washingtonian, J. Edgar Hoover fell under the constitutional prohibition forbidding residents of the District of Columbia from voting because they were not citizens of an official state. He was not a registered member of either political party, although his pro-GOP sentiments were fairly well-known. Proud of never having voted, Hoover chose not to exercise the franchise when the right to vote in presidential elections was granted to D.C. citizens.

A holdover from the previous administration, Hoover was potentially expendable. However, a number of factors were working in his favor. Neither Democrat nor Republican, he belonged to no political party. He'd demonstrated loyalty to his superiors. Highly qualified, a bureaucrat supreme, he could maintain a continuity of experience in the Bureau. Not least, his willingness to share files on Harding's political foes with Daugherty didn't hurt his position, either.

The Old Sleuth

On August 18, 1921, Attorney General Daugherty fired William J. Flynn, celebrated detective and onetime head of the Secret Service, who'd been named BI head by Palmer. Daugherty installed his boyhood friend, William J. Burns, in the post of Bureau director.

Like Flynn, William J. "Billy" Burns was a famous sleuth and former Secret Service operative. Leaving the service, in 1909 Burns founded the William J. Burns Detective Agency. Advertising himself as "The Internationally Famous Sleuth," he soon lived up to his billing by solving the 1910 *Los Angeles Times* bombing case, which had killed twenty people and gutted the building.

Burns, 62, couldn't have been more opposite to the bureaucratic, buttoned-down J. Edgar Hoover, 26. The partnership of this law enforcement odd couple was cemented on August 22, 1921, when Daugherty named Hoover as BI assistant chief.

Back in 1920, the Radical Division's name had been changed to the General Intelligence Division or GID. Now that Hoover had been put in as assistant director, Attorney General Daugherty transferred the GID from the Justice Department directly to the BI, putting it under Hoover's control.

Publicly, the BI was out of the antiradical business, but in reality, throughout the 1920s, it continued its investigations more covertly, maintaining and adding to its files. During this period, a large part of the surveillance of Reds and radicals was undertaken by the U.S. Army's Military Intelligence Division (MID). During the war and the Palmer raids, Hoover had worked closely with MID head Major General Ralph H. Van Deman and his successor, Brigadier General Marlborough Churchill. In 1922, Van Deman gave Hoover a reserve officer's commission in the MID. By 1942, when Hoover resigned his commission, he had risen to the rank of lieutenant colonel.

How Dry I Am

Attorney General Daugherty and BI Director Burns turned the Bureau into a patronage mill, stocking it with politically connected hacks and Burns's often-shady old detective buddies. In the age of Prohibition, a Bureau post could be turned into a real money maker.

On July 15, 1920, at 12:01 A.M., the Eighteenth Amendment became law. The nation was officially *dry*. Instantly, alcohol became a prized commodity. Massive amounts of booze were smuggled in from other countries by land and sea. Entrepreneurs brewed up gin in their bathtubs. Long adept in the handling of contraband and other illegalities, organized crime moved into the booze business in a big way. Rival mobs warred with machine guns and bombs, big-time gangsters paid off police, judges, and politicians.

Justice Jargon

Drys were in favor of Prohibition, **Wets** against.

The Corruptors

Congressional appropriations limited the number of Bureau postings available. Daugherty and Burns got around that by appointing plenty of "dollar-a-year" men, who drew no salary but enjoyed the benefits of being BI agents, including payoffs on Prohibition cases of as much as $2,000 a month.

Meanwhile, J. Edgar Hoover was far from out of the antiradical game. His biggest raid while assistant director took place on the night of August 22, 1922 as Communist Party bigs, including William Z. Foster and Earl Browder, met at a house in the woods of Bridgman, Michigan, near Lake Michigan. It was a strategy meeting, held to decide whether the Party should retain its clandestine status or surface as a "legitimate" public organization. When the meeting broke up, its participants walked out and into a team of BI agents who arrested them.

Bu Stats

In 1921, the Bureau had 346 investigators. The number remained less than 400 a year until the mid-1930s.

Justice Jargon

Red Squads were local police investigative units specializing in collecting information and intelligence on prominent communists, socialists, and other extreme leftists within their jurisdiction. Most major cities had Red Squads, with those of Chicago, Los Angeles, and New York City being among the most formidable. The units were also long-lived, some of them remaining in operation well into the 1970s.

At congressional hearings, Hoover sat at Director Burns's elbow, feeding him statistics and facts, just as he'd done with Palmer. Coalition-building with like-minded outfits, Hoover continued to share information about communists, agitators, and dissidents with Army MID, local police *Red Squads*, and private detective agencies.

In September 1922, the BI involved itself in a national railroad strike, its investigation resulting in the arrests of 1,200 strikers and the breaking of the strike. That same month saw the opening of an investigation into KKK domination of the state of Louisiana that reached as far as the governor's office. The governor sent word via a go-between that the Klan was tapping phones and intercepting mail—his. President Harding, citing the constitutional provision authorizing the chief executive to suppress domestic violence, directed the Justice Department to investigate. Bureau agents unearthed the details of several Klan-inspired murders, but local grand juries refused to indict the Klansmen, from either intimidation or sympathy for the accused, or a mixture of both. Investigators turned up information resulting in the conviction of Imperial Kleagle Edward Y. Clark on a Mann Act violation.

On August 2, 1923, about two-and-a-half years into his administration, President Harding died under murky circumstances in a San Francisco Hotel; was it caused by fatigue from a recent Alaskan goodwill tour, ptomaine poisoning, or apoplexy? If nothing else, his demise showed good timing, sparing him the subsequent disgrace and downfall of his administration, which was set into motion by the revelation that members of his cabinet had illegally sold leases on the federally owned Teapot Dome oil reserves. Investigations into the matter revealed a pervasive pattern of corruption among Harding cabinet members, including the attorney general.

Teapot Dome Doings

Vice President Calvin Coolidge moved into the White House, while Teapot Dome set things boiling. Teapot Dome, Wyoming, was the site of one of the U.S. government's naval reserve oil fields. In 1922, Interior Department Secretary Albert M. Fall leased the fields to his chums in the oil industry for their private use, receiving in return $360,000 in bonds and cash from the oil company owners ("loans," they said).

In October 1923, the matter was first investigated by Montana senior Senator Thomas Walsh, who'd earlier had Palmer and Hoover on a congressional hot seat concerning the Palmer raids. He was soon joined in the questioning by the state's junior senator, Burton K. Wheeler.

Wheeler's star witness was ex-BI agent Gaston B. Means, whose account of dirty deals, graft money, and high living sank Daugherty and Burns, who retaliated by pressuring their accusers. Witnesses were paid off or scared off. Pro-administration newspapers avoided or buried the story. When Attorney General Daugherty made the mistake of defying a Senate request for departmental records, President Coolidge sacked him.

Cops and Robbers

Seeking better pay, Boston police joined the American Federation of Labor and went on strike in 1919, triggering days of lawlessness and mob rioting. Massachusetts Governor Calvin Coolidge sent a telegraph to AFL President Samuel Gompers, stating, "There is no right to strike against the public safety by anybody, anywhere, at any time." Coolidge called out the 6,000-strong state guard, which suppressed the violence after a ferocious six-hour battle against 15,000 rioters at Scollay Square. The man they called Silent Cal rode to Washington as Harding's vice president.

Acting Director

On April 8, 1924, Coolidge appointed Harlan Fiske Stone, former dean of Columbia Law School, to be attorney general. Stone was a big man, six-and-a-half feet tall, 250 lbs, with a gruff demeanor.

With Daugherty out, Coolidge then put Burns's head on the chopping block. Stone began looking around for a new Bureau director. Commerce Secretary Herbert Hoover's confidential secretary Lawrence Richey, a Masonic lodge brother of J. Edgar Hoover's, recommended Hoover for the job. So did Assistant Attorney General Mabel Willebrandt, who said that Hoover was "like an electric wire, with almost trigger response."

Bu Stats

In 1924, when Hoover became acting director of the BI, it had 657 staff members, of whom 441 were agents. In the peak year of 1920, the Bureau had a total personnel of 1,127, of whom 579 were agents.

Hoover convinced Stone, a notable Palmer Raid critic, that he'd merely been carrying out the policy of his superiors, Palmer and Flynn, during the Red raids. His lack of political affiliation took him off the hook in the patronage spoils system and subsequent housecleaning.

On May 9, 1924, Stone gave Burns the sack. Burns was never prosecuted for any offense. Interior Secretary Fall received a one-year jail term. Gaston B. Means served two years in prison.

On May 10, 1924, Stone named J. Edgar Hoover acting director of the Bureau. According to Hoover's version of the meeting, which Stone never contradicted, Hoover said that he'd take the job under certain conditions: the Bureau "must be divorced from politics and not a catch-all for political hacks. Appointments must be based on merit. Second, promotions will be made on proven ability and the Bureau will be responsible only to the attorney general."

Stone said, "I wouldn't give it to you under any other conditions. That's all. Good day."

The Hoover Dossier

John Edgar Hoover was born on January 1, 1895, in Washington, D.C., to Dickerson and Annie Hoover. His mother's granduncle had been the first Swiss consul-general to the United States. An uncle, William Hintz, was a federal judge. Father Dickerson Hoover headed the printing division of the U.S. Coast and Geodetic Survey. Edgar's grandfather had worked for it, too. The family house at 413 Seward Square was in a modest, middle-class district inhabited largely by mid-level bureaucrats and their families. It lay within sight of the Capitol Building.

The youngest of four children, Edgar's older brother and sister were Dickerson Jr. and Lillian. A third child, a daughter, died at an early age from diphtheria. Born two years after her death, Edgar was the "baby of the family." Dominant and doting, Annie made no secret of her confidence that Edgar would someday make his mark in the world.

At age 10, Edgar began keeping detailed journals, recording such things as the weather, neighborhood events, and his daily comings and goings. He was deeply involved in church activities and later taught Sunday school. For an after-school job, he worked for a local grocery store as a delivery boy, running from place to place and earning the nickname "Speed."

Official and Confidential

During one of Hoover's appearances at a judicial hearing, the court stenographer charged with transcribing Hoover's words, threw down his pad in protest, saying that while he could transcribe at a rate of 200 words per minute, Hoover was talking at twice that.

He went to the city's elite, all-white Central High School. Practicing for the debating team, he overcame a tendency to stutter by talking faster, developing his famous "machine gun"–style verbal delivery. He soon became a leader of the team.

He liked sports, at least as a spectator, but rarely participated in school athletics. In later years, he liked to claim that his famous "bulldog nose" profile resulted from boyhood days, when a thrown baseball flattened his nose. In truth, the shape of his nose was the result of an operation to remove a boil.

An area where he shone was in the school's precision drill team, the Central High School Cadet Regiment. He commanded one of the companies on March 4, 1913, leading them past the reviewing stand during President Woodrow Wilson's inaugural parade.

Voted class valedictorian, he was friendly but had few close friends, and was something of a loner. He liked practical jokes. He dated members of the opposite sex rarely, if at all. He considered joining the ministry, instead joining the bureaucracy, as his father before him.

Graduating high school in 1913, Edgar Hoover worked during the day, taking night courses at George Washington University. He earned his bachelor's degree in 1916, his master's in 1917, and later passed the D.C. Bar and thus was licensed to practice law. Going to work at the Library of Congress, Hoover swiftly mastered the Dewey Decimal System, a system of classification which would one day serve as template for the BI's filing system. A master of details with an impressive memory, he early on demonstrated remarkable archival and bureaucratic skills.

On April 5, 1917, one day before the United States entered the Great War, father Dickerson Hoover Sr. resigned his government post before becoming eligible for a pension, even after 42 years of government service. Money was always a concern with Edgar, especially now, with two aging parents and without his father's salary. Brother Dick Hoover had a wife and three children of his own, leaving most of the responsibility of financially taking care of their parents to Edgar.

Hoover Joins the Bureau

On July 26, 1917 (a date all agents, at one time, were expected to memorize), J. Edgar Hoover joined the U.S. Justice Department as a $990-a-year clerk, a post that automatically carried a draft exemption.

John Lord O'Brian, wartime special assistant to the attorney general, picked Hoover, 22, to head a unit in the Enemy Alien Registration Section. Hoover's duties involved the supervision of German aliens and involvement in antiradical activities. He became a strong proponent of dragnet raids, which were applied to potential spies and saboteurs, the IWW, and draft-dodging slackers.

Around this time, Hoover joined the *Masons*, beginning a lifelong commitment to the fraternal lodge that would ultimately see him awarded its highest grade and honors. He dressed well and was a bit of a dandy. In his youth he was thin, taut, a whippet. In later years, he filled out to a stockier physique, adding to his bulldog image.

Justice Jargon

Established in America in Colonial times, the **Masons** are a fraternal lodge whose members embrace the principles of fellowship and the doing of good works. Much fringe-element conspiracy theorizing has been generated about the organization; despite this, the Masons are not a secret society, but a fraternal order open to the public. Worth noting, though, is the fact that every U.S. president has been a Mason, with the exceptions of John F. Kennedy, George H. W. Bush, and George W. Bush.

In March, 1918, Hoover hired as secretary Helen Gandy, a 21-year-old file clerk originally from New Jersey. One of her qualifications for the job was that she said she wouldn't marry and leave government service. She was Hoover's secretary for the next 54 years.

In 1924, father Dickerson Hoover Sr. died. Edgar continued to reside at the family home with his mother Annie. He did not seem to seek out the companionship of young women his own age. One of the few friends he kept from his George Washington University days was T. Frank Baughman, a frequent guest at the Hoover home, whom he hired for the Bureau in 1919. A few years later, the close relationship cooled somewhat when Baughman married and another young man, Clyde Tolson, made his entrance onto the BI scene. Baughman became the Bureau's first ballistics expert and later, a firearms instructor at the Quantico, Virginia training academy, a position in which he served for many years.

Official and Confidential

How did John Edgar Hoover happen to become J. Edgar Hoover? One explanation is that the government employed another lawyer named John E. Hoover, and that Edgar adopted the name to distinguish between the two. Another version is that he was unable to get credit at a department store because of the record of a John Hoover who didn't pay his bills, causing him to make the switch.

The New Boss

Hoover's appointment by Attorney General Stone was provisional. He was acting director, but had not yet been permanently appointed to that post. Hoover was on trial and had to make good or make way for a successor.

In a sense, the Harding-era scandals had destroyed the old BI, and Stone intended to remake it the way he wanted. For starters, he announced that the Bureau was out of the political police business. There would be no more investigating citizens for whatever radical beliefs they might hold.

A third-generation Washington bureaucrat and master of organizational politics, Hoover set to work to remake the Bureau. Within three days, he returned to Stone with a plan: The first step was to get rid of crooked holdovers from the previous regime, especially the dollar-a-year men. Only those with a background in law or accounting would be hired. During the next seven months, 61 persons left the Bureau, half of them agents.

The apex of the BI's organizational pyramid would be the seat of government (*SOG*), the Bureau's headquarters in Washington, D.C., headed by the director and assistant director. Below that was "the field," the rest of the United States and its possessions (Guam, the Virgin Islands, and so on), divided into 53 unequal parts, each headed by an *SAC* (special agent in charge).

Justice Jargon

The **SOG**, or seat of government, is the Bureau's headquarters in Washington, D.C., headed by the director and assistant director. Each field office is headed by a **SAC**, or special agent in charge. A member of the investigatory force is an SA, or special agent.

The key to Hoover's reorganization was standardization: standardization of reports, files, property, procedures, and personnel. Hoover's directive of July 1, 1924, stated that each SAC was in charge of all the personnel assigned to him. To counter favoritism, agents would be graded according to efficiency, in a system of merits and demerits. Letters of commendation or of censure would be put in the individual files, and those would determine whether the individual's career path moved up, down, or out.

SACs tended to maintain their own fiefdoms. To counter that, Hoover put the SACs under his tight control. SACs would be responsible for the actions of their personnel. To ensure compliance, and as an enforcement mechanism, a special Inspection Division of the Bureau was set up in Washington, D.C. Inspectors from SOG would descend on various field offices, surveying caseloads, files, statistics, productivity, inventory of Bureau property, everything.

SACs were ordered to periodically return to SOG for retraining (later, so were all SAs). The SA would be a law enforcement officer and a gentleman, with a degree in accounting or law. Well-groomed, well-dressed, well-spoken. Use of intoxicants during Prohibition was cause for dismissal. The agent must be like Caesar's wife, avoiding even the appearance of impropriety.

In the Justice Department's chain of command, Hoover had to answer to the assistant attorney general in charge of the Criminal Justice Division, whose command included the BI and six other bureaus. In August 1924, Stone gave the post to William J. Donovan, a remarkable individual who for the next quarter-century would remain at the top of Hoover's enemies list.

Born January 1 (the same day as Hoover), 1883, in upstate New York, Donovan was a high-powered lawyer, politician, and World War I hero who'd won the Congressional Medal of Honor. The highest decorated U.S. serviceman of his era, he was also a founder of the American Legion, a patriotic veterans' organization. After the war, Donovan set a political course, making no secret to his intimates that his goal was to be elected as the first Catholic president of the United States.

The antipathy between Donovan and Hoover was mutual, with Donovan low-rating Hoover as a mere "detail man" and bureaucrat, while Hoover scorned Donovan's "lack of organization." Donovan opposed Hoover's being made permanent director. His candidate for the job was Internal Revenue Service agent Elmer Irey, who headed the government's effort to take down Chicago gang czar Al Capone for nonpayment of federal income tax.

Permanent Director

On December 10, 1924, Stone called Hoover into his office and told him that his appointment as acting director (at $7,500 per year) was going to be made permanent. On January 5, 1925, after serving less than a year as attorney general, Stone was nominated to the U.S. Supreme Court. Before Stone left his attorney general post, Hoover persuaded him that the best way to protect the newly reformed Bureau from having the good work of its reorganization undone, was to insulate it from politics. Stone wrote a letter stating that henceforth the Bureau director would answer only to the attorney general, which effectively freed Hoover from Assistant Attorney General Donovan's control. The director's secretary Helen Gandy put the letter in the Official/Confidential file for safekeeping.

 Official and Confidential

Hoover's Official/Confidential file contained items believed to be too important or sensitive to be kept in the Bureau's general files. Documents included key procedural and jurisdictional authorizations and potentially explosive data about highly placed politicians (including presidents) and private citizens, such as their drinking habits, sexual proclivities, arrest records, politically suspect beliefs and associations, and the like. The Official/Confidential file material was kept in Hoover's office.

At this time, BI agents were investigators only, forbidden by law to make arrests, which instead had to be carried out by the appropriate local or state law enforcement officers. They were not allowed to carry firearms, though some agents carried their own.

On October 11, 1925, unarmed SA Edwin Shanahan was shot dead by Chicago car thief Martin Durkin, making Shanahan the first special agent killed in the line of duty since the Bureau's founding in 1908.

After an intensive three-month BI effort, Durkin was located and apprehended on a train outside St. Louis. Bureau agents, unable to actually make the collar, stood nearby as local lawmen made the arrest. Hoover vowed to make Congress pass laws allowing agents to make arrests, carry and use firearms, and make the murder of a special agent a federal crime. It would take eight more years and the Kansas City Massacre to make those laws a reality.

Every leader needs a trusted lieutenant, and Hoover was no exception, finding his in the person of Clyde Tolson. Like Hoover a younger son, Tolson was born in 1900 in Cedar Rapids, Iowa. Clean-cut, good-looking, and athletic, Tolson became an aide to Secretary of War Newton Baker in 1920 and stayed on to serve two subsequent successors. Also like Hoover, Tolson studied law nights at George Washington University; he was admitted to the D.C. Bar in February, 1928. Hoover and Tolson were both Army MID reservists, and they were both Masons.

It is possible that Hoover and Tolson first met through their mutual Army Intelligence MID reservist connection. On April 2, 1928, Hoover hired Tolson as a Bureau agent. Assigned to the Washington field office, then to the Boston office, he was recalled within four months to SOG, within first year becoming an inspector.

Hoover decided this was whom he wanted as his second in command. Within three years, Tolson became assistant director. Hoover was quoted in Tolson's hometown newspaper: "I hardly recall any similar case where a man has risen solely on merit with such rapidity." Tolson became Hoover's lifelong companion. Tolson was Clyde or Junior, Hoover was Speed, Eddie, and the Boss. Like Hoover, Tolson never married. Both liked to say that they were "married to the Bureau."

Fingerprint File

In the 1920s, J. Edgar Hoover began presenting himself as an apostle of scientific law enforcement, a position he maintained long throughout his career as director. The creation of the BI's fingerprint files was a classic example of this approach. Previously, no centralized, standardized system of identifying fingerprints was in existence. In 1896, the International Association of Police Chiefs (IACP) began keeping its print collection in Washington. Beginning in 1909, the Justice Department's repository of federal criminal prints was kept at the Bureau of Criminal Identification at the federal prison in Leavenworth, Kansas, where clerical inmates handled the work of filing and retrieving.

Bu Stats

Following Attorney General Stone's (and the public's) mandate to pare down the Bureau, Hoover continued cutting employees from personnel and field offices. At the end of the 1920s, BI personnel numbered 581, 339 of whom were agents. Field offices were reduced to 30, declining by 1932 to a record low of 22.

In 1924, two months after Hoover was made acting director, the Bureau took control of the two fingerprint collections, consolidating and combining them. Hoover turned the Bureau of Identification (Fingerprint) Division into a national clearinghouse for fingerprints, a database that could be accessed by city or state law enforcement agencies.

A second major achievement promoting professional, scientific policing methods was the new director's reestablishment of a BI training school. Hoover was not the first to establish such a school; an earlier version had been founded in Washington by former Chief A. Bruce Bielaski. The training school had lapsed during the private detective reign of Flynn and Burns. A fledgling attempt at starting a school in New York City in 1925 failed to click, but Hoover revived it in November 1928, founding the BI training school at Quantico, Virginia. The school generated great publicity, projecting the image of the Bureau's agents as members of a scientifically trained, elite law enforcement agency.

Unhappy Warriors

Ending speculation about his prospects in the election year of 1928, President Coolidge declared, "I do not choose to run." The 1928 presidential election campaign of Republican Herbert Hoover and Democratic candidate, New York Governor Al "the Happy Warrior" Smith was one of the dirtiest in history, a poisonous collision marred by vicious anti-Catholic prejudice against Smith.

Herbert Hoover beat Smith by a landslide. When Hoover failed to offer campaign manager William J. Donovan the attorney generalship, which Donovan believed he'd been promised, Donovan resigned from the Justice Department and went into private practice. Washington had not seen the last of him—nor had that other Hoover, J. Edgar.

The Least You Need to Know

- The Eighteenth Amendment's prohibition of alcohol unleashed a wave of public lawbreaking and made the Twenties roar.

- Harding-era political patronage and corruption came close to destroying the Bureau.

- In 1924, President Coolidge's Attorney General, Harlan F. Stone, appointed J. Edgar Hoover acting director of the BI.

- Hoover reorganized the Bureau, firing corrupt or incompetent agents and standardizing procedures to promote professional, scientific law enforcement.

Chapter 4

Busting the Gangs

In This Chapter

- Prohibition profits fuel a nationwide expansion of organized crime
- The 1934 Kansas City Massacre outrages the public
- Congress votes broad new powers for the Bureau
- Public Enemy Number One John Dillinger
- G-men and the new FBI

The 1920s ended not with a roar but a whimper in a financial crash that quickly worsened into the Depression. Public outrage led to an increased federal role in combating organized crime. Elected in 1932 on a platform of a New Deal for "the forgotten man," President Franklin Roosevelt reappointed J. Edgar Hoover as BI Director, making the Bureau the high-profile law enforcement component of his administration. The machine-gunning of lawmen in the Kansas City Massacre led to legislation that broadly expanded BI powers. Battling a Midwestern crime wave, the G-man entered popular mythology, and the Bureau became the FBI.

Underworld, USA

The 1920s came by its nickname of the Roaring Twenties honestly, one of the few things that was honest about an era that also came to be known as the Lawless Decade. It was a wild time, but the BI was largely absent from the playing field, even as organized crime mobs were extending their reach from coast to coast.

This absence was not so much a matter of choice as ideology. Like his two GOP predecessors, President Herbert Hoover was determined to limit the expansion of the federal government into the private sector, and that included federal policing power. In effect, that meant taking the stance that organized crime and gangland violence were the problems of city and state police. This position eventually became insupportable as crime organized itself nationwide on a big business basis.

Cops and Robbers

Born in New York City, Alphonse "Al" Capone (also known as "Scarface") was the Roaring Twenties' King of Crime. At the height of his power in Chicago, he once knocked the mayor down the steps of City Hall, while police officers stood by doing nothing. He once famously noted, "Don't get me wrong, I'm not one of those goddam radicals knocking the American system."

Headlines trumpeted the crimes of colorful, murderous hoodlums and racketeers like Dutch Schultz, Vincent "Mad Dog" Coll, and Jack "Legs" Diamond, to name but a few. But the premier gang lord in the United States during the heyday of Prohibition was Chicago crime boss Al Capone.

It takes a tough man to keep a tough town like Chicago awash in bootleg booze, and Big Al was that man. Using strong-arm tactics, wholesale murder with bombs and machine guns, and pervasive corruption, Capone took over the Chicago rackets, starting with bootlegging and branching out to protection, extortion, prostitution, and dope peddling. He personally ordered the death of 500 men; in all, 1,000 were killed in Chicago's ceaseless gang wars.

The 1929 St. Valentine's Day Massacre, during which Capone's shooters machine-gunned seven members of rival George "Bugs" Moran's mob, spelled the beginning of the end for Big Al, prompting the feds to move against him. While Treasury Department agent Elliot Ness and the Untouchables bedeviled Capone, his real nemesis was IRS agent Elmer L. Irey, who helped convict the crime boss on tax evasion charges.

In October 1931, Capone was found guilty of owing a quarter-million dollars in taxes on more than one million dollars in revenue from 1924 to 1929, and sentenced to eleven years in prison (Atlanta then Alcatraz). He spent eight years behind bars, dying in 1947 at age 48 of syphilitic paresis, a degenerative brain disease causing insanity.

Wall Street Takes A Fall

An article of faith with President Hoover and his administration was that government should avoid interfering with business. Beginning in 1925, the country had experienced a rising tide of prosperity—Coolidge Prosperity, it was called. Millionaires were created overnight. The stock market was booming. Wall Street was the road to easy street. The market was going up, up, up!

October 24, 1929, a Thursday, saw a major sell-off swell into a panicked rout. On October 29, a Tuesday, forever to be known as Black Tuesday, came the Crash. The stock market imploded, stock prices rocketing to the basement. Thousands of fortunes were wiped out with each tick of the ticker-tape machine. With dizzying velocity, the national economy plunged into critical condition. So did the presidency of Herbert Hoover.

> **Official and Confidential**
>
> Financier and the youngest bank president in America Joseph P. Kennedy said that he knew it was time to get out of the market when he overheard a couple of shoeshine boys swapping stock tips. He got out in time to keep from losing his shirt. Most folks didn't.

Crime By the Numbers

Arrogant, big-spending, flamboyant gangsters and racketeers stood out in stark relief against the bleak economic landscape, the hoodlums being rendered steadily more obnoxious to the public as the depression deepened. The government might not be able to fix a broken economy, but it could still fix a bunch of crooks. For the first time in years, 1930 saw an increase in the number of BI staffers (rising to 655 total, with 400 agents) and a ten percent budget increase.

As far back as December 1925, J. Edgar Hoover had told the House Appropriations Committee that the nation needed a system for "assembling uniform crime statistics." In 1930, Congress finally gave permission for the BI to collect statistics; that same year saw the publication of the first issue of the Bureau's Uniform Crime Reports. This swiftly turned the BI into the nation's premier source of crime statistics. Crime was one of the Depression's few boom markets.

> **Bu Stats**
>
> In 1931, 4.5 million men were out of work; by 1932, the number was three times that, at 13.5 million. The national income had fallen to half what it was pre-October 1929.

Crime of the Century I

An already sullen and demoralized populace was first shocked and then outraged as vicious, gangster-style crime brutalized an American hero and his family.

On May 20, 1927, Charles A. Lindbergh, 25, aviator and mail plane pilot, had taken off from New York in his airplane, *Spirit of St. Louis*, becoming the first person to fly solo across the Atlantic. Lindbergh became an international celebrity, an authentic 1920s phenomenon of mass hero-worship. He married Anne Morrow, daughter of former New Jersey Governor Dwight Morrow.

On March 1, 1932, their 20-month-old son Charles A. Lindbergh Jr. disappeared from his nursery room at the family mansion in rural, isolated Hopewell, New Jersey. When news of the crime became public knowledge, it triggered a media frenzy and mass hysteria. Writer H. L. Mencken called it "the greatest story since the Resurrection."

At this time, kidnapping was not a federal offense, so the BI had no jurisdiction in the case, though J. Edgar Hoover kept on top of it from the start. Notified that a ransom note demanding $50,000 in small bills for the child's return had been found at the scene, Hoover set up a *special* Lindbergh squad to offer the Bureau's unofficial help.

Justice Jargon

A **special** is a case important enough to merit a number of agents assigned to it alone. Each special is headed by an agent on-scene, with the ability to call up as many agents and resources needed to follow up leads—a forerunner of the modern strike force.

Three days after the child vanished, Hoover went to Hopewell but didn't get in to see the family. He was referred to the law enforcement official in charge of the case, New Jersey State Police head Colonel H. Norman Schwarzkopf Sr. (father of the Gulf War general). New Jersey and New York lawmen working the case agreed to freeze out the federal "glory hounds." Unable to get hold of the ransom notes, BI sleuths had to settle for facsimiles.

Lindbergh didn't want the BI to get involved, didn't want a record to be made of the ransom money. Hoover's man on the scene reported his suspicions that Lindbergh was holding back vital information.

On the night of April 2, the ransom was to be paid at St. Raymond's Cemetery in the Bronx by Lindbergh and go-between Dr. John F. Condon, an eccentric schoolteacher. The Bureau knew of the arrangements but backed off to protect the child's safety. The ransom was passed to an obscure figure hiding in the shadows who gave Condon a piece of paper naming a ship at a location where the tot would be found.

No such boat existed, but on May 12, 1932, the child's body was discovered in a shallow grave in woods near the family home. An autopsy revealed that Charles A. Lindbergh Jr. had died on the night of the kidnapping. On June 23, 1932, Congress passed the Lindbergh Law, making kidnapping a federal offense and giving the BI jurisdiction if the victim was transported across a state line. The law was quickly amended to make kidnapping a capital crime.

A curious postscript to the Lindbergh tragedy was the resurfacing of ex-BI agent Gaston B. Means, key witness in the Senate probe of the Harding-era BI. Arrested for trying to swindle a well-meaning Washington socialite out of money he claimed would help deliver the missing child, Means was convicted of embezzlement (Hoover attended the trial) and sentenced to fifteen years in prison. Post-trial, claiming he'd reveal where the missing $100,000 was hidden, he led agents on a wild goose chase.

Confronting him, Hoover said, "Dammit, Gaston, you stop lying about it!" Means said, "This is the last straw, Edgar. You've lost faith in me!" Five years later, Means died in prison. The money was never found.

> **Official and Confidential**
>
> Apart from Means, Hoover admitted that he'd been conned twice in his life: once by a door-to-door salesman who claimed to be peddling fertilizer which turned out to be sawdust dyed black; and again by convict Robert Stroud, the famous Birdman of Alcatraz, who'd sold Hoover a canary that turned out to be a yellow-dyed sparrow.

New Deal

The 1932 presidential election saw a massive repudiation of Herbert Hoover and the election of Democrat Franklin D. Roosevelt, who'd campaigned on the platform of a New Deal for the "forgotten man." For J. Edgar Hoover, a bright spot in the election was the defeat of William J. Donovan's bid for New York Governor.

Hoover's prospects for continued BI Director tenure dropped precipitously with Roosevelt's announcement of the planned appointment of Montana Senator Thomas Walsh as attorney general. Along with Senator Burton K. Wheeler, Walsh had exposed Teapot Dome and Harding administration corruption. The old Billy Burns-headed Bureau of Investigation had tried to "get" Walsh, whose own sources of information had made him aware that Hoover had been involved in the effort, although he was unaware of the extent of that involvement. It was a sure bet that one of Walsh's first official acts as attorney general would be to give Hoover the sack.

That's when Hoover had a stroke of luck. That is, he had the luck and Walsh had the stroke. The 72-year-old senator had recently married a much younger woman and

Cops and Robbers

FDR's first appointee as attorney general was lawyer Homer S. Cummings, 63. From 1900 to 1925, Cummings represented the state of Connecticut on the Democratic National Committee. An early Roosevelt stalwart, Cummings called the New Deal "a political movement led by a government in action."

Bu Stats

According to a Roosevelt administration report, for each year of its 13-year existence, Prohibition had cost an estimated one billion dollars annually in lost tax revenue and federal spending to enforce the amendment. During that time, 512 local, state, and federal agents were killed trying to enforce the law; they killed 2,089 citizens.

was enjoying a honeymoon with her on a Washington, D.C.–bound train heading for Roosevelt's inauguration when he suddenly dropped dead of a massive heart attack, With Walsh gone, Roosevelt turned to lawyer Homer S. Cummings, an early and enthusiastic New Dealer.

Hoover convinced Attorney General Cummings to exempt the Bureau from civil service laws, arguing that ability not seniority was what was needed. He said he would resign rather than accept communists "and other undesirables." The ruling put Hoover in a position of extraordinary power, allowing him free rein to hire, promote, demote, or fire employees without having his actions subject to review.

On July 30, 1933, Cummings announced that he'd appointed Hoover, 38, to be the director of a new Division of Investigation, which combined the BI, the Bureau of Identification (fingerprint identification), and the Prohibition Bureau. The first two had already merged, the last was on the fast track out and soon ceased to exist, as did Prohibition. On December 5, 1933, the "Noble Experiment" was repealed by the passage of the Twenty-First Amendment to the Constitution.

Return of the Badmen

FDR's first hundred days in office (the Hundred Days) was a whirlwind of activity, as newly created government agencies (CCC, TVA, WPA, and so on) fought actively to lift the malaise of economic and cultural depression. Activist New Deal government could make a difference to "get the country moving again."

The BI was the law enforcement component for this ferment, and its vehicle was the outbreak of Midwest banditry from 1933 to 1934, what leading historian of the phenomenon Paul I. Wellmen described as the "atavistic genre" of old-time outlawry. This was far different from the big city organized crime syndicates with its gangsters and vice rackets. It was more rural in nature, a flare-up of the banditry of the Old West, the kind associated with Frank and Jesse James, the Daltons, and Butch Cassidy and the Sundance Kid.

There was a populist (and popular) component to the outbreak. Major outlaws such as Dillinger, Bonnie and Clyde, and Baby Face Nelson were highly aware of their celebrity status, reveling in it, often playing to the public whom they believed relied on them to provide thrills and excitement.

In a word, they were stars. Here was a challenge the government could not afford to ignore, and one much easier to counter than organized crime.

Kansas City Massacre

On June 17, 1933, captured bank robber and old-time desperado Frank "Jelly" Nash was being transported to Leavenworth Prison by four BI agents and three local policeman. At this time, special agents were still unauthorized to carry firearms and make arrests. Outside Kansas City's Union Station, three gunmen armed with pistols and machine guns confronted the lawmen as they were putting Nash into a car. Things happened quickly: The gunmen opened fire, cutting down the lawmen, killing four and wounding two. One of the dead was SA Raymond Caffery. The triggermen also killed Nash, the man they were supposedly trying to rescue. Nash lived long enough to shout, "For God's sake, don't kill *me*!" before being shot to pieces in the car.

The brutal daylight slayings were a national outrage. The shooters were identified as bad-men Charles Arthur "Pretty Boy" Floyd, Adam Richetti, and Verne Miller. Floyd hailed from Oklahoma's Cookson Hills, a district long associated with outlawry, hide-outs, and gunmen. Richetti was a racketeer, robber, and gunman. Verne Miller was a World War I hero and onetime sheriff turned bank robber, train robber, and killer.

 Official and Confidential

Was the Kansas City Massacre a failed attempt to free Frank Nash, or was it murder? And who really did it? To his dying breath, Floyd denied taking part. Richetti died in the electric chair, taking his secrets with him. One who was generally believed to have taken part in the shooting was Verne Miller, who was found in a ditch outside Detroit on November 29, 1934, tortured and murdered gangland-style, possibly for bringing so much heat down on the underworld. The slaying of Nash, whom the gunmen were ostensibly trying to deliver, indicates that they might have been hit men set in motion by top Kansas City mobsters wanting to rub out Nash before he could testify about the city's organized crime.

Attorney General Cummings chose to spin the brazen daylight killings as the underworld's declaration of war on the government, announcing he would respond in kind. Nudged by the slayings, Congress passed an important New Deal crime package:

- Robbery of a national bank or member bank of the Federal Reserve System was made a federal crime, giving the Bureau jurisdiction to investigate.

- Other crimes made federal offenses were the interstate transportation of stolen property, transmission of threats, interstate commerce racketeering, and flight across state lines to avoid prosecution or giving testimony.

- The Lindbergh Law was amended to make kidnapping a federal death penalty crime. Another amendment clause stated that if the victim in a kidnapping case had not been safely returned within seven days, it would be *presumed* that the victim had been transported interstate, an elastic clause that gave the BI jurisdiction to get involved.

- BI SAs were given the right to make arrests, execute warrants, and carry firearms.

- Killing or assaulting a government agent was made a federal crime.

These changes left the BI newly customized, super-charged, and ready to roar into action against violent crime. Soon, they would have a powerful gimmick for capturing the hearts and minds of the public—a catchy nickname, possibly supplied by a small-time crook with delusions of grandeur.

G-Men

George Kelly was a loudmouthed, backslapping braggart, a bootlegger who plied his trade throughout the Southwest. His ambitious wife Kathryn wanted him to make the grade as a big-time bank robber. His gimmick was a submachine gun. After some months of practice with the weapon, he could shoot a walnut off the top of a fence post, which was no mean feat.

Calling himself by his new handle of Machine Gun Kelly, he robbed a couple of small-town banks, and then hit the big money in the lucrative kidnapping racket sweeping the nation. On July 23, 1933, he and an accomplice kidnapped Oklahoma City oil millionaire Charles Urschel, holding him for $200,000 ransom. The money was paid, Urschel was released.

The BI got on the case, finally cornering Kelly on September 26, 1933, in a flea-bag hotel in Memphis, Tennessee. Instead of shooting it out with the feds in time-honored "come and get me!" style, Kelly meekly surrendered without firing a shot. Asked later why he hadn't opened fire, Kelly's sensible answer was, "Because I knew you'd kill me."

Bureau-connected popularizers circulated the story that when they moved on him, Kelly had frantically cried, "Don't shoot, G-men! Don't shoot!" The G stood for government. Government-men. *G-men*.

The local lawmen on the scene maintained that when apprehended, Kelly had simply said, "I've been waiting for you." Whatever the truth was, the G-man version made a better story, and that's the one that stuck. Kelly died in prison; his wife Kathryn was released from prison in 1958.

Hoover's good friend and Bureau booster, reporter Rex Collier, picked up the ball and ran with it, giving the G-man angle a heavy play in feature stories and articles. It was too good not to be used as part of the propaganda war, the battle for public opinion. The catchy G-man tag was tailor-made for the ongoing effort to mythologize the Bureau, its agents, and especially the director.

The G-man was the hero of the hour, the frontline trooper in the war on crime. It was a propaganda effort, coordinated with Bureau-friendly newspaper reporters, magazine writers, and Hollywood studio executives. There were G-men movies, radio programs, monthly pulp fiction magazines (*G-men* pulp magazine, begun in October 1935, ran for 18 years), and even comic strips.

Bu Stats

1930 saw the release of the film *Little Caesar*, the plot of which was loosely based on Chicago gangland doings. So began a lucrative cycle of gangster movies. In 1931, about 50 gangster movies were made. The Hollywood Production Code killed off such amoral entertainment. *G-Men*, made in 1935, set off an even more popular cycle of G-man type films, of which 65 were made that year.

The director promoted the premise that once the Bureau got involved in a case, the criminal was doomed for capture or killing. It didn't matter if the local law got the culprit, it was the Bureau's scientific law enforcement that counted. As Hoover noted in a speech, "Before science, all must fall."

Little Mel and Big Bad John

Agent Melvin Purvis, "Little Mel," was the scion of an aristocratic South Carolina plantation family. Five feet tall, and like Hoover a former captain of a high school cadet corps, Purvis joined the Bureau in 1927. By 1932, he had risen to become SAC of the Bureau's important Chicago field office.

This post put him on a collision course with *Public Enemy* (called "Public Rat" by J. Edgar Hoover) Number One, John Herbert Dillinger, who robbed more banks and stole more money in one year than Jesse James did throughout the length of his sixteen-year criminal career.

Justice Jargon

The term **Public Enemy** seems to have been originally coined by the Chicago Crime Commission, and was picked up shortly after by some of the New York City tabloid newspapers. The phrase was in common use by the time it was used as the title for the movie *Public Enemy*, which was made in 1931.

Born on June 22, 1903, in Indianapolis, Indiana, Dillinger was a farm boy with a wild streak. Paroled from prison for previous offenses in May 1933, Dillinger soon teamed up with a gang of crooks, unleashing a wild crime wave robbing banks throughout the Midwest. Key players in the gang were hardened professional criminals Homer Van Meter, Handsome Harry Pierpont, and Harry Mackley. The gang broke Dillinger out of the Lima, Ohio, jail, slaying Sheriff Jess Sarber.

Later arrested in Arizona, Dillinger was transferred to Indiana's Crown Point Jail, where he posed for newspaper pictures and was quoted that trying to keep him in jail was "an exercise in futility." On March 3, 1934, he escaped from jail, apparently bluffing his way out with a "gun" carved from soap and blackened with shoe polish (another version holds that a real gun had been smuggled into jail to him). Making his getaway, he stole the sheriff's car, driving it across the state line into Illinois.

Here Come the Feds

This federal violation allowed the BI to get on his case, triggering special operation JODIL, Bureau lingo for the hunt for John Dillinger. In mid-April, Purvis received a tip that the Dillinger gang was holed up at Little Bohemia, a remote Wisconsin summer resort. With him were some friends and associates, a super-gang that included Baby Face Nelson (Lester Gillis), Homer Van Meter, and Pretty Boy Floyd. As Purvis later ruefully noted, it was "probably the largest aggregation of modern desperadoes ever bottled up in one place."

Hoover sent squads from the nearest field offices (Chicago and St. Paul) to the scene. Surrounding the place at night, special agents opened fire on three men seen racing out of the house into a car, killing one and seriously wounding the others. They weren't part of the gang, though, but rather just some locals who'd stopped in at the lodge for a drink. The gang escaped through the back of the house, scattering. Making his break, Baby Face Nelson shot down three lawmen, killing SA Carter Baum.

John Dillinger was the bank-robber's bankrobber—seen by many as a Depression-era Robin Hood. He actually escaped from one prison by carving a gun out of a bar of soap and covering it with black shoe polish.

(Courtesy of Corbis)

The spectacular debacle handed the Bureau its worst black eye in years, causing Attorney General Cummings to publicly deny that J. Edgar Hoover would be removed from office. Purvis submitted his resignation, but it was not accepted. Hoover put SA Sam Cowley, a former Mormon missionary, in charge of the Dillinger Squad.

On June 22, 1934, Dillinger's birthday (age 31), Hoover declared the outlaw Public Enemy Number One. There was already a $10,000 Bureau reward on his head.

Chicago Melodrama

In July, in Chicago, Purvis was contacted by Anna Sage (Romanian-born Anna Cumpanas), a madam and landlady facing deportation hearings on a morals charge. Sage said that one of her female boarders was keeping company with Dillinger, and she offered to put him on the spot for the reward money and the dropping of the deportation charges. All this was taking place while Dillinger was the object of what was perhaps the most intensive manhunt in U.S. history. On July 22, 1934, Sage called Purvis, telling him that it was a go for that night. Dillinger, now calling himself "Jimmie Lawrence," his girlfriend, and Sage went to the Biograph theater, to see the movie *Manhattan Melodrama*. The Dillinger Squad staked out the movie theater. At 10:30, Dillinger exited, flanked by his girlfriend and Sage.

Official and Confidential

Top-billed at the Biograph Theater the night Dillinger was killed, *Manhattan Melodrama* was a 1934 MGM release starring William Powell and Clark Gable. The plot was the old one (even then) about two boyhood pals from the old neighborhood, one of whom grows up to be a gangster, while the other becomes the district attorney who must prosecute him.

The squad moved in, Purvis reportedly shouting for Dillinger to surrender. Dillinger pulled a gun, three agents opened fire. They were Herman Hollis, Clarence Hurt, and Charles Winstead. Hollis missed, the others didn't.

Dillinger was dead. A crowd gathered, becoming an excited, hysterical mob as the word spread as to the dead man's identity. Hoover made the announcement to the press that Dillinger was done. Years later, when asked by an interviewer what his greatest thrill had been, Hoover said, "The night we got John Dillinger."

At the Biograph that night, Anna Sage had worn an orange dress, but under the marquee lights it looked red. That inspired the legend of Dillinger's betrayal by a Lady in Red, as well as the popular tune of the same title. In popular mythology, The Lady in Red symbolizes a female Judas. Anna Sage received a $5,000 reward and was soon deported. Dillinger's white plaster death mask, straw hat, and gun were put in a glass display case at SOG at Bureau headquarters in Washington, D.C., near the director's office, remaining there until 1972, when L. Patrick Gray became director.

On October 22, 1934, Purvis was in on the killing of Pretty Boy Floyd, who was mortally wounded during a shootout with Bureau agents at an Ohio farm. Purvis questioned the dying Floyd about his involvement with the Kansas City Massacre, with Floyd denying to the end that he'd taken part. On November 27, 1934, Sam Cowley and Herman Hollis (both members of the Dillinger Squad) were shot dead by Baby Face Nelson, who died shortly after of wounds he'd sustained in the gun battle.

The Carpenter and the Airman

That eventful fall of 1934 saw the first big break in the hunt for the Lindbergh baby kidnapper. When the ransom money had originally been collected, ace IRS agent Elmer Irey (who'd convicted Capone on tax fraud) had included gold certificates and marked bills in the pay-off bundle. On September 15, 1934, a motorist paid for gas with a ten-dollar gold certificate. The alert attendant noted the license plate. Sleuths discovered that the car belonged to Bruno Richard Hauptmann of the Bronx, a German immigrant and unemployed carpenter. A BI search of Hauptmann's house and garage located $14,600 of the ransom money.

The Trial of the Century (and its attendant media circus) found Hauptmann guilty of the kidnapping and murder of the Lindbergh baby. On April 3, 1936, he was electrocuted in the Trenton, New Jersey, death house. Was he guilty? A Hoover secret memo noted, "I am skeptical as to some of the evidence."

Initially opposed to the use of marked money, after Hauptmann's capture Lindbergh publicly stated that he gave all the credit for the arrest to Irey and the Treasury Department. This endeared him not at all to Hoover, who one day soon would be taking a closer look at the celebrated aviator with a ripening over-fondness for Nazi Germany.

Carping Critics and Creepy Karpis

In 1934, Hoover demanded that the BI come up with a new name, a single, recognizable name, preferably with catchy initials, something on the order of Scotland Yard's CID (Criminal Investigation Division). SA Edward Tamm, third-highest Bureau official, came up with the name, Federal Bureau of Investigation, adding that the initials FBI also stood for Fidelity, Bravery, Integrity.

The BI duly became the FBI. Hoover publicly gave the credit for the name change to Attorney General Homer Cummings. Stung by Congressional foes who taunted him as a "briefcase cop" who'd never actually made an arrest, Hoover was presented with a chance to do just that when hardened criminal Alvin "Old Creepy" Karpis was spotted in New Orleans. Last surviving associate of the Ma Barker gang, Karpis was a notorious thief, jailbird, bank robber, and killer.

Hoover, Clyde Tolson, and Bureau publicity chief Lou Nichols flew to New Orleans. When Karpis got into his car, agents moved in with drawn guns. He surrendered without a fight. Hoover was present during the arrest, though it's unlikely that he took part in the actual apprehension. But officially Hoover had made his arrest, throwing it back in the teeth of his critics.

Official and Confidential

While being held in San Francisco's Terminal Island prison in the early 1960s, Alvin Karpis gave guitar lessons to a fellow inmate, a young West Virginia-born car thief, pimp, and penny-ante crook Charles Manson, whose sex-drug-cult Family would commit the horrific Tate–LoBianco slayings in Los Angeles in 1968.

G-Man's Fate

Continually harassed by Hoover, who resented the other's celebrity as Public Hero Number One, the Man Who Got Dillinger, Melvin Purvis left the FBI on July 10, 1935, telling reporters he wished to "pursue business opportunities." He authored *American Agent*, a best-selling book about his crime-busting experiences. Other job offers closed when the prospective employers learned that hiring Purvis would incur the displeasure of the FBI director. In 1936, Purvis became the announcer for the children's radio program, *Junior G-Men*. He later hosted *The Melvin Purvis Law and Order Patrol* show, sponsored by cereal Post Toasties.

During World War II he would join the OSS spy agency (forerunner of the CIA) and work for Hoover's nemesis William J. Donovan. In 1960, terminally afflicted with cancer, Melvin Purvis shot himself with a pistol given him at his FBI retirement party.

The Least You Need to Know

- Prohibition brought organized crime into the modern era, causing it to establish itself as a nationwide big business.

- As the economic Depression set in, the public began demanding more of a federal role in smashing the organized crime mobs.

- After the election of President Franklin D. Roosevelt, Attorney General Homer Cummings reappointed J. Edgar Hoover BI Director.

- The Kansas City Massacre led to the passage of laws expanding federal jurisdiction and allowing FBI agents to carry guns and make arrests.

- The 1933–1934 outbreak of Midwest bank robbery was suppressed by the FBI, establishing the modern-day mystique of the G-man.

Chapter 5

Nazis and Reds

In This Chapter

- Depression-era America is besieged by fascists and communists
- The FBI foils a millionaire fascist plot to overthrow the government
- Pro-Nazi paramilitary German-American Bund's ties to Hitler
- U.S. Communist Party's sneaky "front" organization tactics
- The FBI takes charge of all domestic intelligence operations.

In the aftermath of World War I, the Russian Communist Party and Germany's Nazi Party rose, each committed to overthrowing other countries' governments and installing their own types of regimes. Economic woes, joblessness, and despair made the United States a ripe breeding ground for extremists of the right and left. Charged by President Roosevelt to monitor subversive activities, the FBI foiled a plot by the pro-Nazi Liberty League to take over the country in 1934. Throughout the 1930s, the United States was plagued by the Hitler-controlled German-American Bund and the Moscow-directed CPUSA. With the threat of war looming, FDR put Director Hoover's FBI in charge of all domestic intelligence operations.

World Woes

The Great War had toppled kings and undone em-pires. The Austro-Hungarian Empire dissolved virtually overnight. In Russia, Lenin's Bolsheviks exterminated the ruling royal Romanov dynasty and established the first soviet state. In the 1920s, Italian *fascist* dictator Benito Mussolini, Il Duce (from the Latin *dux*, lord) had taken over the country. In Germany, the Kaiser had been forced to abdicate, replaced by a weak Weimar republic beset by famine, hyper-inflation, and ferocious near-civil war between communists and right-wing militarists. Under the charismatic, ruthless leadership of Adolf Hitler, Germany's National Socialists Workers Party—the Nazis—were poised at the end of the 1920s to make their move to take supreme power over a flailing government.

Justice Jargon

Fascism: In Imperial Rome, *fasces* were bundles of rods tied together, symbolizing the power and authority of the state. In the modern era, fascism is a program for setting up a centralized autocratic regime with an ultra-nationalist agenda; exercising regimentation of industry, commerce, finance; and imposing rigid censorship and the forcible suppression of opposition.

Justice Jargon

Coup d'état: French for a blow or strike against the state. A coup d'état is a sudden decisive use of force to subvert or overthrow an existing government.

Final Crisis?

The financial Crash of 1929 triggered a world crisis in capitalism and a trial of faith in the western democracies, not least in the United States. Economic chaos inevitably brings with it social chaos, which worsened as the slide continued. Millions of people out of work, with no way to pay the rent or feed their families, was potential dynamite.

Disaster for the masses spelled opportunity for the extremists. The global communist movement was energized in a way it hadn't been since those heady days of 1919, when it seemed the Red revolution was unstoppable. Equally encouraged were the fascists, the ultra right-wingers. To them, the Crash proved that the weak, decadent democracies with their moral depravity and lack of direction and purpose were doomed to fall, to be replaced by a New Order sanctifying force, power, and nationalistic empire-building.

Even before the Depression, communists and fascists alike had already been working to undermine the U.S. government. Now, they began to move into high gear. A particularly sinister coalition was already taking shape as Roosevelt took office. Behind it lay some of the biggest names in America, household names, members of some of the 50 most important ruling families in the nation. Their goal: a *coup d'état* to overthrow the democratically elected president and take over the United States. Standing between them and success was the FBI.

Liberty League

In 1933, Hitler came to power in Germany, inspiring and energizing like-minded sympathizers in the United States. During most of his first two terms, Roosevelt was more concerned about the threat of a fascist takeover of this country than of a similar communist attempt. He had cause for alarm.

U.S. fascists had sharp teeth and claws. Behind them lay the power of the ruling class, masters of capital, who intended to protect their interests from communist redistribution by any means necessary. "I'd spend half my fortune to save the other half," said a multi-millionaire conspirator in the crypto-fascist Liberty League.

What came to be known as the Smedley Butler incident would reveal the extent of the American proto-fascist movement and how far it was prepared to go. Countering its machinations, J. Edgar Hoover would ultimately become czar of all domestic intelligence operations.

Hero General

Major General Smedley Butler, ex-commandant of the U.S. Marine Corps, had twice earned his country's highest decoration for valor, the Congressional Medal of Honor. One of the most popular military men in America, Butler was forced to retire after refusing to apologize for an anti-Mussolini speech. He had little respect for Herbert Hoover or FDR, and was not shy about saying so, especially in public. He toured the country, making a number of anti–New Deal speeches.

In the spring of 1934, Butler was approached by attorney Gerald C. MacGuire and his associate William Doyle, a pair of front men representing what they described as an anti-Red coalition of concerned wealthy individuals. The duo had recently returned from a European tour on behalf of their well-heeled sponsors, where they'd been researching the role of veterans' groups in the rise of the Nazi party, the Italian *fascisti*, and the French Croix de Feu extremist group. The cabal wanted Butler to spearhead a coup d'état by leading a half-million veterans in a march on Washington to overthrow the government. After the takeover, they said, if Roosevelt was compliant, he would be allowed to stay on as a kind of figurehead, like the role of the King of Italy under Mussolini. If he wouldn't play ball, well, he would be "removed."

The go-betweens said that the plotters were prepared to spend millions to get the job done, and that a three-million-dollar fund was already in place. Playing along, Butler feigned guarded interest to draw out the conspirators.

Bu Stats

In 1933, the Liberty League maintained a lavish 31-office headquarters in New York City, branches in 26 colleges, and 15 subsidiary organizations that distributed 50 million copies of Nazi pamphlets. The League's wealthy backers controlled an astonishing $37 billion worth of corporate assets.

Two weeks after the meeting, the other shoe dropped, with the official announcement of the founding of the American Liberty League. Demanding the suppression of "radicals in government," the League charged that Roosevelt and other prominent New Dealers were communists. The League took a militant pro-Nazi, anti-Semitic, and antiblack line. Its primary sponsors were a clique of fascist industrialists, notably members of the du Pont family, General Motors interests, and Morgan Bank associates.

The Bureau Strikes Back

Butler disliked Roosevelt, but he hated fascism even more. Learning that the League was behind the plot to mobilize veterans groups for a coup attempt, Butler contacted J. Edgar Hoover, warning that it looked like a treasonous plot to overthrow the U.S. government. Putting teeth into the threat was the revelation that arms and ammunition for the takeover attempt would be made available through the du Ponts' control of the Remington Arms Company.

Hoover took the plot seriously. After all, as he liked to point out, the Russian revolution had been made by a hardcore cadre of 23 conspirators. Hoover and Butler conferred with Roosevelt. All were agreed that the cabal would require careful handling. During this delicate time early in the administration, with the economy collapsed, a too-strong move against the leaders of du Pont, General Motors, and the Morgan banking interests all at once might trigger the very instability that the plotters sought.

Hoover advised that the plot be deactivated by leaking it to the press, and by having Butler tell his story to a House committee that was specially formed to investigate the conspiracy.

On November 20, 1934, Butler testified before House probers, as did the national commander of the Veterans of Foreign Wars, who stated that he'd also been approached by the plotters. Butler further turned up the heat by holding a press conference to announce that General Douglas MacArthur was part of the plot.

The special House Committee's final report was so explosive that four years passed before it was released. It concluded that, "There is no question that these attempts were discussed, were planned, and might have been placed in execution when and if the financial backers deemed it expedient."

But the plot had already been neutralized in the fall of 1934, thanks to J. Edgar Hoover's subtle, canny maneuverings behind the scenes that led to press exposure of the conspiracy. Burned by the fire of bad publicity, which they publicly ridiculed as an absurd misreading of their intentions, the League's big backers nonetheless pulled their support for the coup attempt. Their immediate plans were abandoned by necessity, but their overall intentions remained the same. They would find and fund other vehicles to promote their fascist agenda.

Cops and Robbers

The three du Pont brothers, Irénée, Pierre, and Lammot, were bulwarks of the pro-Nazi, anti-Semitic, American fascist movement. The du Ponts funded the Liberty League to the tune of $500,000 a year. Irénée, the most militant, gave a speech in 1926 calling for the creation of chemically created supermen. A vehement Hitlerite, he was instrumental in the creation of the Black Legion, a Klan-like terrorist organization.

Despite the foiling of the coup, the Liberty League was far from out of business, remaining a growing concern with an impact that would be felt in the 1936 presidential elections. But motivated fascists found other, more militant organizations more to their liking, such as the paramilitary Sentinels of the Republic, William Dudley Pelley's paramilitary Silver Shirts (20,000 members), and Clark's Crusaders (1.25 million members in 1933).

Just as the Communist Party U.S.A. was controlled by the Comintern in Moscow, the American fascist movement took its inspiration and direction from Nazi Party bigs in Hitler's Berlin.

Strike Up the Bund

On May 8, 1934, Roosevelt called a White House conference to discuss the growing Nazi threat in the United States. Present were J. Edgar Hoover, Attorney General Cummings, Secretary of the Treasury Morgenthau, Secret Service Chief Moran, and Secretary of Labor Perkins.

Roosevelt authorized an FBI-led probe of the Nazi movement and its connections with German government members in the United States. Director Hoover set in motion a general intelligence operation, which meant that the information would be used for background and fact-finding purposes, not for prosecution, at least for the moment.

Another Flower of Evil was Father Coughlin (pronounced cog-lin), Detroit's Radio Priest, whose weekly nationwide broadcasts from his headquarters at the Shrine of the Little Flower had an audience of 10 million. Originally a New Deal supporter, Coughlin had turned violently against Roosevelt; he was anticommunist, pro-fascist, pro-Hitler, and rabidly anti-Semitic.

In August 1936, he tried to persuade General Butler (of all people!) to lead a military force against an anticlerical Mexican president who'd been confiscating church property. Again, Butler contacted J. Edgar Hoover, and the plot came to naught. Less hare-brained and more insidious were Coughlin's exhortations to his followers in the military to commit obstructionism, subversion, and outright sabotage. But that came later, as war neared—and when it did, the FBI would be there to confront the challenge.

A major stockholder in General Motors, Irénée du Pont financed the creation of the Black Legion, a Klan-like terrorist organization centered in Detroit, the main purpose of which was to thwart the unionization of the company workforce. At its height, the Black Legion had 75,000 members. Its action squads dispensed beatings, whippings, burnings, and shootings to labor organizers and others on its hate list, and were responsible for about 50 deaths.

A prime target of FBI investigations and intelligence-gathering was the pro-Nazi German-American Bund. Originally formed in July, 1933, as the Association of Friends of the New Germany, the Bund was a creature of Germany's Nazi Party. Just as Communist Parties around the world were guided and directed by the Kremlin-controlled Comintern, so, too, were the Bund-type organizations under the sway of the Nazi International, directed from Berlin.

The German-American Bund's goal was the subversion, destabilization, and collapse of the United States's constitutional democracy, and then its replacement with a homegrown Nazi overlordship subordinate to the Third Reich's Führer, Adolf Hitler. In 1938, when membership peaked, the Bund had 100,000 members.

The Bund divided the United States into three sections, each ruled by a sub-leader: one each in New York City, Chicago, and Los Angeles. The supreme leader was Fritz Kuhn, the American Führer. The fanatically pro-Nazi paramilitary organization was of course restricted to Aryans, and all prospective members had to be able to demonstrate their "pure-blooded" pedigree. The nationwide organization was made of up 55 cells. Members wore Nazi-style brown uniforms in the manner of Hitler's Brownshirts, the strong-arm cadre of toughs and enforcers who provided the muscle for Nazi Party demonstrations, street fights, and generalized thuggery.

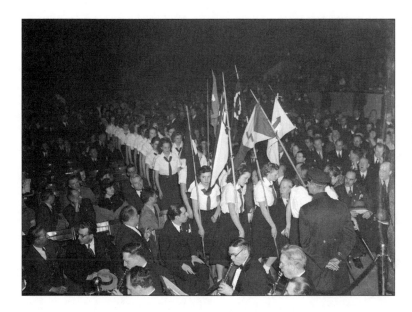

A German-American Bund rally in the late 1930s; the Bund, which operated openly, was an American pro-Nazi organization that was most active in the years immediately proceding America's entry into World War II. Their membership consisted of German-American citizens loyal to the Fatherland.

(Courtesy of Corbis)

Like their German counterparts, Bundists were big on mass marches, rallies, and torchlight parades, all awash in a sea of swastika flags and banners. From coast to coast, training camps were established where the members were instructed in the use of firearms and explosives in anticipation of the day when they would rise to overthrow the U.S. government. The Bund's Hitler Youth style organization operated a number of similar training camps for youngsters, the largest of which was on Long Island, New York.

FBI sleuths discovered direct links between the Bund and Berlin. The Bund was under the control of Hitler's hatemongering spinmeister, Dr. Joseph Goebbels, through the Ministry of Propaganda, of which Goebbels was the overseer. Through Goebbels, the Bund had direct links to the Führer himself, as well as to Third Reich Army and Naval Intelligence.

In the election year of 1936, the Bund threw its support to GOP presidential candidate Alf Landon, as did Father Coughlin and the Liberty League, which poured thousands of dollars in contributions to the campaign. To his credit, Landon repudiated the support of the League and its fascist cohorts.

Cops and Robbers

Fritz Kuhn, the self-styled American Führer, was born in Germany in 1896 and fought for that country in World War I as an infantry lieutenant. Emigrating to the U.S. after the war, he became an employee of the Ford Motor Company in Detroit. An ardent Nazi, Kuhn took over the German-American Bund in 1936 and went to jail in 1939.

Roosevelt was reelected in a landslide and the League soon withered and faded away. But the Bund grew stronger, even as the FBI steadily, stealthily enmeshed it in an invisible dragnet that would become manifest as the next world war neared.

Red Tide

To Roosevelt, the real danger lay on the right, from homegrown fascists and Nazis. For most of his first two terms, he turned a blind eye to the depredations in the form of the American Communist Party, the CPUSA. But Hoover's FBI wasn't going to be caught napping where the Red Menace was concerned.

During the 1920s, the prime target of Soviet spymasters had been Great Britain. As the succeeding decade demonstrated the importance of the United States as an emerging world power, Soviet espionage resources were allocated to meet the rising challenge. The 1919 Palmer raids had indeed dealt the Communist Party a crippling blow, while the wild, get-rich-quick mentality of the 1920s was heedless of the Reds' call for the downfall of capitalism. After the Crash, the communists redoubled their efforts.

Official and Confidential

In 1919, British and U.S. intelligence made a secret treaty to share counterintelligence information, cementing the special relationship between the two countries. Today that treaty is still in effect.

Cops and Robbers

Feliks Dzerzhinsky, the grandmaster of all Russian spymasters, was an aristocratic Polish revolutionary who'd spent a total of eleven years as the Tsar's political prisoner. Charged by Lenin to "Combat Counterrevolution, Speculation, and Sabotage," Dzerzhinsky formed the Soviet spy system, Sword and Shield of the Revolution, a ruthless secret police apparatus.

Stalin's ultimate goal was still world communist revolution, but he overhauled the Comintern's strategy and tactics. The USSR needed diplomatic relations with other countries, trade agreements, access, and influence. This material support would not be readily forthcoming if Russia was seen to be openly supporting the violent overthrow of the governments of the very countries which the Soviets were courting. What was needed was deniability.

Open, violent revolution, or even revolutionary rhetoric, was counterproductive. What was called for was deception, subterfuge, covert operations. Burrowing from within. Revolution would be achieved not by storming the Winter Palace, but by subverting the government and infrastructure of the capitalists. Once the targeted country had been sufficiently undermined, revolution might then be achieved. The vehicle for this secret war was a sophisticated multi-level operation that bore all the hallmarks of a product of a nation of chess-players.

Red Spies Rising

The attack was two-pronged. One head was directed by the Russia secret police spy system under a variety of names and acronyms: first the Cheka, morphing into the GPU, OGPU, NKVD, MVD, and, ultimately, the KGB. They may have had different labels, but also the same organizational continuity. Its primary mission was to prevent the subversion of the USSR from within.

The second head of the Soviet espionage effort was a creature of Russian Military Intelligence, the Red Army's GRU. Its principal target was industrial and scientific technical intelligence. GRU spymasters believed that the only valuable intelligence is secret intelligence, called *razvedka* or true intelligence, and they labored to get it.

Ultimately, Stalin, the supreme leader, directed both entities. One of his precepts to his spies was, "An intelligence hypothesis may become your hobbyhorse on which you will ride straight into a trap." Another: "Don't tell me what you think. Give me the facts and the source."

Resident Evil

During the 1920s, a principal Soviet penetration vehicle for overseas espionage was the use of trade missions as secret spy centers from which to direct operations against the host country. In 1927, British Intelligence investigators raided the Soviet's ARCOS Trade Mission in London, unearthing a massive spy nest.

In response, Moscow radically overhauled its overseas spy system. The result of the reorganization was the *resident* system. Spies operating out of their countries' embassies or trade missions usually pose as members of the diplomatic corps, conferring diplomatic immunity on them. If caught, they are deported. Spies without that diplomatic immunity ("*illegals*"), if caught by the host country, are subject to imprisonment and, in case of war, death.

The residence system used illegal spies to build its secret network. The illegals were furnished with false identities and papers to match. Avoiding contact with the local Soviet embassy, they would take up deep cover residence in the target country. Contact with Moscow headquarters was maintained by covert means.

Justice Jargon

In Russian spy jargon, **illegals** are spies without diplomatic immunity. They operate according to the residentura system, as **residents** hiding in deep cover in the host country, where they run an **apparat**, a secret network. They seek **razvedka**—true intelligence.

The resident director ran the operation with two or three assistants, each a trusted staff officer from Moscow. They were the hard core of the illegal network or *apparat*. Each would control anywhere from two to five group leaders, each of whom were running a number of sources (informants). Their purpose: to recruit government employees to aid the cause.

Up Front

After the initial enthusiasm and excitement engendered in Party circles by the Crash of 1929 and its immediate aftermath, the CPUSA realized that a revolution was not imminent and that they would have to prepare for the long pull and moderate their overt approach. The communists' principal vehicle in the U.S. during the 1930s was the front group. A front is an organization seemingly without any connection to the Communist Party, usually on behalf of some humanitarian or do-good cause.

The front was ideal for roping in those who wanted to change the world without openly signing on with Stalin. "Fellow travelers" were those sympathetic to the cause without being card-carrying Party members. But all the front groups were directed by the Comintern, and many people who unthinkingly signed some do-good petition or made a donation to some seemingly innocuous cause would have reason to regret it in the future.

Bu Stats

In the 1930s, fellow travelers in front groups outnumbered card-carrying Party members ten to one.

The years 1935 to 1939 marked the heyday of the CPUSA's Popular Front. Alarmed by the rise of Nazi Germany and its military might, the Kremlin changed its tune, stressing the antifascist angle.

FBI Counterattack

On August 24, 1936, FDR met J. Edgar Hoover for one of the regularly scheduled intelligence briefings that the director delivered to the president on a routine basis. There was nothing routine about this meeting, however. Hoover reported that communist-infiltrated and -dominated labor unions included the West Coast longshoremen, John L. Lewis's Mineworkers Union, and the Newspaper Guild. Should the subversives in the unions unite to act in common in a general strike, they could effectively paralyze the nation.

Roosevelt charged Hoover with intelligence gathering on fascist and communist movements to determine how they might affect the "economic and political life" of the nation. As with the 1919 Palmer raids, a legal framework had to be established to anchor the underpinnings of whatever action would be taken.

Legally, the FBI could not act without some violation of federal law having been committed, of which none were on the table. Ever the master of bureaucratic detail, Hoover pointed out that there was a loophole, however: a clause in the FBI appropriation allowing the Bureau to investigate any matters if requested by the State Department to do so.

On August 25, another meeting was held, at which Secretary of State Cordell Hull requested said investigations, allegedly saying, "Go ahead and investigate the hell out of the so-and-sos." Only he didn't use the phrase, "so-and-sos."

It was all the authorization Hoover needed to make it legal to investigate private citizens, not only for the moment, but for the future. Along with executive orders issued by the president of the United States and certain other statutes that Congress eventually passed, that verbal directive would serve as the basis of Hoover's legal authority to conduct domestic intelligence operations for the next 40 years.

Hoover formed the General Intelligence Section to process the information arising from the new domestic intelligence operation. In recent years, the Bureau had already compiled an index of 2,500 individuals involved in Communism, Nazism, and foreign espionage. Hoover recommended to the attorney general that no formal request for a new appropriation be made to Congress to fund the section, to avoid alerting the numerous communist and fascist sympathizers in that body.

Official and Confidential

A document outlining the preliminary strategy for domestic intelligence operations surveyed potential investigatory targets including "maritime, steel, coal, clothing, garment and fur industries; newspapers; government affairs; armed forces; educational institutions, communist and affiliated organizations, fascist and antifascist movements; and activities in organized labor organizations." Hoover's handwritten comment in the outline's margins: "A good beginning."

Rumors of War

Beginning in 1936, the Spanish Civil War pitted a leftist, democratically elected, government against Generalissimo Francisco Franco's Fascist Phalange movement. Supporters of the Republic were called Loyalists. Spain became the proving ground for World War II, with Moscow backing the Loyalists and Berlin backing the Phalange. The brutal civil war saw some of the first extensive bombing of civilian populations.

Several thousand communists and leftists, with a dash of thrill-seekers and adventurers, went to Spain to fight for the Loyalists. Many died on the battlefield. Adding to the gloom of Communist Party members was the 1937 Moscow purge trials, in which hundreds of top Party members, many of them veteran Bolsheviks who'd helped make the revolution, "confessed" to crimes against the state in kangaroo court-type show trials. Behind it lay Stalin, ruthlessly consolidating his power by eliminating any who might dare to challenge it or even offer mild criticism.

War Jitters

As international tensions mounted, on June 20, 1938, FBI investigations led to the indictments of 18 top American Nazis, a coup hailed by Bureau publicists as having cracked "the greatest peacetime spy ring in history." On October 1, 1938, Hoover posted domestic intelligence security specialists at each of the Bureau's 45 field offices, also establishing new field offices in Alaska, Hawaii, and Puerto Rico.

Cops and Robbers

In 1937, a young recent law school graduate from California applied to join the FBI but was rejected: Richard M. Nixon, a future president who would one day be Hoover's boss. The official Bureau line was that Nixon had been turned down for having been found "lacking in aggression." A recent theory suggests that he was rejected for withholding the fact that he'd been arrested (for a college prank), an omission duly noted by FBI background checkers.

March 1939, saw the final collapse of Spain's Republican government and the triumph of General Franco, who would remain in power for the next 40 years. On June 26, 1939, Roosevelt apportioned intelligence responsibilities between the Army, Navy, and FBI, giving Hoover responsibility for the Western hemisphere. August witnessed the signing of the Hitler-Stalin pact, the two tyrants pledging their countries to mutual nonaggression and potential future alliances. This exercise in realpolitik winnowed out a lot of CPUSA members, particularly those unable to adapt to the latest whirlwind changes in the party line. Now the new line was pacifism, disarmament, and isolationism. In other words, keep the United States out of war at all costs. The pact lasted from August 24, 1939, through June 22, 1941—the day Nazi Germany invaded Soviet Russia.

Bund Blunderer

German-American Bund leader Fritz Kuhn had come down a long way in the world since 1936, when he'd traveled to Germany on behalf of the Bund and was photographed shaking hands with Hitler at the Berlin Olympics.

In 1938, the Bund's peak year, the organization took in a million dollars a year in dues. Success went to Kuhn's head and he grew less inclined to follow orders from Berlin. Berlin then tried to force him from his post. His U.S. position slipping, Kuhn's last, desperate ploy was a monster rally at Madison Square Garden on February 22, 1939—George Washington's birthday. One of the damnedest spectacles ever enacted staged on the American scene, the Nuremberg-style rally massed 22,000 people on-site, requiring 2,000 police officers to keep order.

Some Bund funds stuck to Kuhn's fingers. Tried and convicted, in December, 1939 he went to New York's Sing Sing prison to begin serving a $2^{1}/_{2}$–5 year sentence for embezzlement.

Official and Confidential

In September 1939, the month that Germany invaded Poland, journalist Whittaker Chambers defected from the Communist Party. Confessing to FDR's security adviser Adolf Berle, Chambers fingered prominent New Dealer Alger Hiss, his wife Priscilla, and his brother as members of a clandestine communist cell. Reviling it as an attempt to discredit his administration, Roosevelt told Berle to tell Chambers to "go chase himself." Only he didn't say "chase." The Hiss case had not yet even begun.

The Least You Need to Know

- The worldwide economic Depression empowered extremist groups of the far right (fascists) and far left (communists), who plotted the overthrow of the U.S. government and republic.

- Alerted by General Butler, in 1934 the FBI forestalled the American Fascist Liberty League from an attempted coup against President Franklin Roosevelt.

- FBI monitoring of the German-American Bund, a paramilitary group with 100,000 members, discovered the group was directly controlled by Nazi Germany.

- During the 1930s, the Kremlin-controlled U.S. Communist Party (CPUSA) used "do-gooding" front organizations with no overt Party connections to promote their subversive agenda.

- As war neared, FDR authorized Director Hoover and the FBI to conduct extensive domestic intelligence operations against Communists, Nazis, and other national security threats.

Chapter 6

World War II: The Big One

In This Chapter

- ◆ Enemies stalk prewar America at home and abroad
- ◆ Pearl Harbor, December 7, 1941: Infamy
- ◆ The FBI's wartime internal security strategy
- ◆ Nazi saboteurs vs. America
- ◆ FBI Special Intelligence Service operations in South America

In the run-up to World War II, Nazis, fascists, and Soviet Communists all plotted against America, prompting President Roosevelt to authorize the FBI to intensify operations against the conspirators. Imperial Japan's devastating surprise attack on Pearl Harbor thrust the United States into war, as the FBI moved quickly to secure the nation against saboteurs and spies. The Bureau's Special Intelligence Service handled wartime security and counterespionage operations in Central and South America.

Fifth Column

On March 16, 1940, the White House Press Club dinner was the scene of some prime political theater, as President Franklin D. Roosevelt engaged

FBI Director J. Edgar Hoover in a seemingly casual exchange. For all its studied informality and jocular mutual "ribbing" between pols and press, the high-profile gathering was a snapshot of who's where on the Washington power pyramid.

With war—and a presidential election—imminent, political foes on the right and left, and in Congress, were trying to make moves on the director. His post was, after all, a political appointment, a prize one. Roosevelt was sending a message when he hailed Hoover in front of the press corps, calling out, "Edgar, what are they trying to do to you on the Hill?"

Hoover said, "I don't know, Mr. President."

Turning his hands in a thumbs-down gesture, Roosevelt said, "That's for them." Which also meant that he was giving the director a very public thumbs-up.

For most of Roosevelt's two terms, Hoover's FBI had been monitoring ultra-right extremists, communists, socialists, and subversives of all stripes. In the late 1930s, as Nazi aggression mounted overseas, Roosevelt authorized the FBI and military intelligence to use broader methods to keep tabs on potential enemies within the gates, to quell a homegrown *fifth column* of spies and saboteurs working against the national interests in the run-up to war.

Justice Jargon

A decisive Spanish Civil War battle was the siege of Loyalist Madrid by Phalangist General Mola, whose attacking forces were arrayed in four columns of troops. Materially aiding the victorious Mola were pro-Franco forces inside the city, what he called his "**fifth column.**" Fifth column has generally come to mean secret pro-enemy forces who are committing espionage, sabotage, and subversion behind defense lines.

In August, 1936, Roosevelt had used Secretary of State Cordell Hull's verbal authorization to officially put the FBI in the business of collecting general intelligence on fascists, communists, and other subversive elements. In reality, the Bureau had been doing that since early in Roosevelt's first term, but Hull's "request" made it official (and legal), though the arrangement was kept confidential for the next three years.

On June 26, 1939, Roosevelt issued a directive formally notifying the heads of other federal agencies that all espionage, counterespionage, and sabotage matters would henceforth be the province of Army Intelligence (formerly MID, now G-2), the Office of Naval Intelligence (ONI), and the FBI.

At this time, the Intelligence Coordinating Committee, consisting of representatives of those three divisions, was founded to investigate foreign espionage and sabotage in the United States. With their traditional reluctance for meddling in civilian affairs, the army and navy left the investigation of all nonmilitary personnel to the FBI, effectively giving the Bureau control for all domestic intelligence investigations.

Official and Confidential

On June 24, 1940, FDR issued a directive dividing the global areas of responsibility for espionage, counterespionage, and sabotage between the Big Three intelligence agencies. The navy's ONI was given jurisdiction in the Pacific. Army G-2's jurisdiction encompassed Europe, Africa, and the Panama Canal Zone. The FBI's field of operation was the Western Hemisphere, which included the continental United States and Central and South America. Hawaii was designated a joint army-navy area—mutual hot potato for both services following the Japanese attack on Pearl Harbor.

On the heels of Nazi Germany's September 1, 1939, invasion of Poland, Roosevelt issued an executive order of September 6, requesting that all local, state, and federal law enforcement agencies promptly pass along any information on possible spies and saboteurs—and subversive activities—to the FBI. On September 9, 1940, the president proclaimed a state of emergency.

Smear Campaign

Moving fast after Roosevelt's emergency proclamation, Hoover hired 150 new special agents (bringing the total number of SAs to 947), and opened ten new field offices. On November 30, 1939, Hoover went before the House Appropriations Subcommittee to request in addition to the Bureau's annual $9 million budget, an emergency supplemental allocation of $1.5 million. Which he got.

During that appearance, Hoover informed the committee members that he'd reformed the General Intelligence Division, which had already compiled lists of subversives. Twenty years after the Palmer Raids, the GID was still an object of abhorrence on the left, triggering a series of attacks on Hoover.

Undaunted, Hoover ordered a pair of raids that had critics on the right and the left boiling. On January 14, 1940, FBI agents rounded up 17 members of hatemongering Detroit "radio priest" Father Coughlin's Christian Front extremist group, charging them with conspiracy to commit terrorist acts. On February 6, G-men arrested 12 veterans of the Abraham Lincoln Brigade, who'd fought as Loyalist volunteers in the Spanish Civil War. They were charged with a 1937 violation of federal law prohibiting the recruitment on U.S. soil of persons to fight in foreign armies.

The two raids stirred up a hornet's nest, making unlikely allies of isolationist, anti–New Deal newspapers the *Washington Times-Herald*, *New York Daily News*, and *Chicago Tribune* with leftist ministers, labor unions, and the ACLU.

As the controversy heated up, Hoover was further destabilized by the departure of key ally Attorney General Frank Murphy. His replacement, liberal Robert Jackson, was destined to butt heads with Hoover a number of times over matters of policy and procedure. Most of the disputes would be resolved by Roosevelt in Hoover's favor.

Shortly after taking office, and much to Hoover's displeasure, Attorney General Jackson dropped the charges against the Spanish Civil War veterans. Hoover's counterattack was handled by Lou Nichols, head of the Bureau's Crime Records division, its public relations arm. The campaign included pro-Hoover articles from reliable supporters in the press. Friendly congressmen made speeches singing Hoover's praises. Hoover charged that the attacks on him were authored by "anti-American forces," that the communists were behind the "smear campaign."

Cops and Robbers

Lou Nichols joined the FBI in 1934, swiftly establishing himself as Hoover's publicity chief and all-around troubleshooter. Following the departure of Assistant to the Director Ed Tamm, Crime Records head and Bureau publicity chief Nichols became Hoover's Number Three man. The architect of much of the FBI's favorable media coverage, Nichols also invented the "not to be contacted list," naming unfriendly press elements who were to be denied FBI cooperation. Once, being upbraided by the director for not quashing a negative newspaper article, Nichols said, "If I'd known they were going to print that story, I would have gone over there and hurled myself bodily into the presses!" Hoover reportedly said of Nichols, "He may not be smart, but he's loyal." Nichols retired from the FBI in 1957.

Peace and War

In the presidential election year of 1940, public opinion polls showed that a large majority of Americans hated and feared Hitler and his regime. By almost the same margin, those polled also said that they wanted the United States to stay out of war. The last war's horrific mass slaughter had left its imprint on the national psyche.

Others whose motives were not so pure included German-American Bundists, Fascists, and other pro-Nazi sympathizers. They would have liked to have seen the United States get in the war but on Hitler's side. If not, they wanted the country to stay strictly neutral. To them, fascist dictatorships were the wave of the future and they'd have liked one in America.

For a while, the most vociferous voices calling for the United States to make war on fascism were those of the communists, until the Hitler-Stalin pact motivated the CPUSA to join the peace-at-any-price crowd. One of the terms of that pact was Stalin's agreement not to interfere if the Nazis took Poland. That was a term the Red tyrant found agreeable, as he, too, took a piece of Poland.

By the end of September, 1939, the Third Reich's conquest of Poland was complete. After that, further aggressive Nazi maneuvers were temporarily suspended, leading to the nerve-wracking period known as the Phony War. On November 9, 1939, J. Edgar Hoover set in motion the hush-hush compilation of a *Custodial Detention* list, naming persons to be rounded up and detained in the event of war.

Justice Jargon

The **Custodial Detention** list was an index of persons to be rounded up and held in preventative detention in times of national emergency. The list included U.S. citizens and resident aliens who were Nazis, Communists, subversives, and potential saboteurs. The list was kept confidential from Congress and the public.

This, then, was the situation going into the election year of 1940, as FDR decided to run for an unprecedented third term as president. His announcement threw anti-New Dealers into predictable paroxysms of outrage. Apart from the Republican opposition, Roosevelt had to guard against disaffection and hostility from within his own ranks.

Most potentially destabilizing on that score was Roosevelt's ambassador to Britain, financier, and power broker Joseph P. Kennedy. A prominent New Dealer, Kennedy had won his appointment partly as reward and partly as a way to keep him from stirring up trouble for the president and party at home. An apologist for fascism, Kennedy's tenure as ambassador began with appeasement and ended in defeatism. Yet Roosevelt feared that a Kennedy defection to the GOP could potentially peel off millions of Irish-Catholic votes from the Democratic ticket.

Enemy Within

In May 1940, the Phony War ended as the Nazis rolled across Holland. Around that time, at Roosevelt's request, Hoover ran background checks on 130 prominent critics and foes of the administration. Among them was leading isolationist and longtime Hoover foe, Montana Senator Burton K. Wheeler, who'd torpedoed the old Daugherty-Billy Burns Bureau of Investigation back in 1924. Before the presidential campaign season was done, the FBI would conduct a total of 200 such political investigations.

Technically, many of these investigations were in a legal gray area, since they probed into the private lives of Roosevelt's political foes. Their justification was that they also involved matters that might potentially impact U.S. national security. Still, it was a case that the administration would prefer not to have to argue in an open forum. Roosevelt knew he could rely on Hoover's keeping the matter confidential.

Official and Confidential

FDR was the first president to have a secret recording system installed in the White House. In 1940, he had the Oval Office wired, with a hidden microphone on his desk connected to a recording device. But the primitive state of such unwieldy, inaccurate equipment caused the abandonment of the system within a few months. When Roosevelt wanted a confidential transcript of a particularly sensitive conversation or meeting, he would have it taken down by a stenographer hidden behind the scenes.

Hoover's intelligence gathering was hampered by the obstructionism of Attorney General Robert Jackson, a doctrinaire liberal who confided to an intimate that he "hated" the FBI director. Jackson's fastidiousness about *wiretapping* led to his March 15, 1940, order prohibiting wiretapping by the FBI.

Justice Jargon

Wiretapping occurs when a third party listens to a private telephonic communication. In the dawn of such techniques, the phone conversations would be intercepted by physically "tapping" into the line, usually by splicing into it with a wire the other end of which would be connected to a pair of headphones worn by an agent secreted nearby in a closet or basement. The agent would take notes of the conversation. As the technology improved, the tap wire was connected to recording devices. Ultimately, evolving sophistication did away with the need for an actual spliced wiretap, with the monitoring being done via electronics.

Behind the scenes, Hoover labored to undo the ban, insisting that it hindered ongoing investigations of Nazi spies. Roosevelt instructed Jackson to authorize wiretaps in cases of "grave matters involving the defense of the nation," including the use of listening devices to monitor suspected spies and subversives. The attorney general unhappily complied with the presidential directive.

One of those Roosevelt wanted kept under close tabs was Ambassador Kennedy, whom he once described as "a very dangerous man." In this case, the surveillance was a matter of national security, since the ambassador was conducting his own foreign policy in Britain, one contrary to the administration's. In the language of Wall Street, where he'd made a fortune, Kennedy was bullish on fascism and bearish on democracy.

Publicly, Kennedy praised Roosevelt; privately, he mocked and derided him. As war in Europe neared, the ambassador made no secret of his belief that the British were "washed up," that Nazism and fascism would win out, and that democracy was probably washed up in America, too. Violating official diplomatic protocols, he conducted covert meetings with top Nazi leaders.

On May 3, 1940, Hoover reported to Roosevelt that his sources stated that Kennedy and his Wall Street crony, shady financier Ben Smith, had met in Vichy with Nazi Party big and Air Force (Luftwaffe) Minister Hermann Göring and donated a large sum of money to Nazi Germany.

Airman and the Appeasers

Officially opposing Roosevelt's bid for a third term was Republican presidential candidate Wendell Wilkie. Roosevelt had to walk a fine line where overseas intervention was concerned. In the summer and fall of 1940, most of the voters were alarmed by the war in Europe but still determined to stay out of it. Roosevelt campaigned on a platform of "keeping our boys out of foreign wars."

The antiwar opposition crystallized in September 1940, with the formation of the America First Committee, which steadfastly opposed any U.S. involvement in the European conflict. The Committee ultimately had five million members nationwide. Its leadership included pacifists and isolationists, as well as others with a more sinister hidden agenda, notably famous aviator Charles A. Lindbergh. In the years since Bruno Hauptmann's execution in 1936 for the kidnap/murder of the flyer's son, Lindbergh had traveled a twisted odyssey to become a dedicated pro-Nazi.

Warmly welcomed on his visits to Germany by top Nazi bigs, Lindbergh ominously warned the democracies that Hitler's Luftwaffe was the world's best air force and would be irresistible in any coming war. An appreciative Führer awarded Lindbergh the Service Cross of the Order of the German Eagle with the Star, the Nazis' highest civilian award. Postwar Nazi documents revealed Lindbergh's hyperbolic assessment of Luftwaffe capabilities was dead wrong.

Winning reelection, Roosevelt moved swiftly to put his administration on a war-ready basis. He'd already won enactment of a peacetime draft and the Alien Registration Act (Smith Act) to curb subversives. Now, he purged isolationists from the cabinet, adding Republicans for bipartisanship.

All these actions could arguably be considered part of homeland defense. But when it came to global strategy and tactics, Roosevelt was forced to move more circumspectly. He'd run and won on a policy of noninterventionism in foreign wars. Still, he was unabashedly pro-British and anti-Hitler. He was determined to aid Britain by every legal (and sometimes extra-legal) ploy available, while avoiding the violation of America's neutral status. He and his military planners believed that if Britain fell, the U.S. island continent would be pressed on the Atlantic side by Nazi Germany and by Imperial Japan in the Pacific. In December, 1940, he proposed his program of Lend-Lease, which would provide billions of dollars worth of wartime supplies to Britain.

Roosevelt's reelection allowed the America First Committee to focus its energies on noninterventionism. Charles Lindbergh became a leading opponent of Lend-Lease, traveling around the country making speeches to defeat it. He also went north to Canada, delivering a radio broadcast warning the Canadians that they, too, had no part in the European war.

Never one to forget or forgive an insult, and mindful of how Lindbergh had publicly given all credit for the capture of Bruno Hauptmann to Elmer Irey and the Treasury Department, J. Edgar Hoover ordered FBI agents to probe deeply into the shady affairs of Lindbergh and the America First Committee.

Official and Confidential

"If I were to die tomorrow, I want you to know this: I am convinced that Lindbergh is a Nazi." So declared FDR in private to Secretary of the Treasury Morgenthau. Publicly, on April 25, 1941, Roosevelt called Lindbergh a "copperhead," the term for pro-Confederate Yankees during the Civil War. In response, Lindbergh resigned his commission in the Army Air Corps Reserve. After December 7, 1941, he tried to regain it, but Roosevelt refused to reactivate it, causing Lindbergh to remain a civilian throughout the war.

In June 1941, the FBI reported that leading isolationist (and Hoover foe) Senator Burton K. Wheeler was using mailing lists supplied by the German-American Bund. In September 1941, a Bureau interrogation of a captured German spy elicited the information that America First was an arm of the Third Reich, used for the dissemination of propaganda and the creation of political destabilization. That same month, Lindbergh delivered a speech that was so virulently anti-Roosevelt, anti-British, and anti-Semitic that even the America First steering committee moved to disassociate itself from his remarks.

Hoover's secret report to Roosevelt in February 1942, summarized the results of the confidential investigation. Opining that America First was even more dangerous than the Bund, Hoover revealed that, had England fallen to Nazi Germany, America First would have spearheaded an effort to impeach Roosevelt and have him replaced by— who else?—Charles A. Lindbergh.

By the time Hoover delivered that confidential summation, America First had already been defanged in the aftermath of the Japanese attack on Pearl Harbor. Prominent members of the Committee were monitored for the duration of the war.

Infamy

December 7, 1941, an unseasonably warm Sunday, found J. Edgar Hoover weekending in New York City. At about 2:30 P.M., an emergency communications hookup established by FBIHQ in Washington put him in contact with Robert L. Shivers, special agent in charge of the Honolulu office. Also patched into the line at FBIHQ was Assistant to the Director Ed Tamm, the number three man at the Bureau.

Shivers described as it was happening the Japanese attack on the vital U.S. naval base at Pearl Harbor, linchpin of the Navy's entire Pacific Fleet strategy. In the background, Hoover and Tamm could hear the sound of bombs blasting. Shivers said, "It's war!"

In New York City, Hoover caught a flight to the capital. The Bureau was put on 24-hour alert, with all leaves canceled. The FBI blocked all travel and communication to Japan and put guards at all Japanese facilities.

Long-held FBI contingency plans for such an emergency now went into effect. Years of monitoring real and potential citizen and alien spies, saboteurs, and subversives, and putting them on the Custodial Detention list, were about to pay off. Within a few hours of the attack, FBI agents were ordered to put potentially dangerous listed individuals under tight surveillance. President Roosevelt proclaimed a state of emergency, allowing Francis A. Biddle, who'd replaced Robert Jackson to become wartime attorney general, to sign the warrants allowing the G-men to proceed with the arrests.

Within 72 hours of the bombing of Pearl Harbor, the FBI arrested 3,846 Japanese, German, and Italian alien enemy suspects. This was no dragnet-type roundup. A case had been made against each individual detainee, and Attorney General Biddle had personally approved every arrest.

Far from forgotten was the German-American Bund. Several of American Führer Fritz Kuhn's top lieutenants were FBI informants; the Bureau had many such sources in place throughout the organization. FBI agents had also managed, through the use of surreptitious break-ins at Bund headquarters and regional branches, to acquire copies of the all-important membership lists, which proved invaluable in identifying every member and neutralizing the Berlin-controlled organization.

Bu Stats

From 1938 to 1945, with the bulk of them falling within three months after Pearl Harbor, FBI arrests resulted in 91 convictions for spying. During World War II, the FBI arrested 16,062 suspected enemy aliens, of whom one-third were deemed dangerous enough to be interned or repatriated to their home countries.

From 1941 to 1944, the number of FBI special agents rose from 1,596 to 4,886. Their work being vital to the national security, personnel judged vital to the FBI were draft-exempt, which included all SAs and most lab and clerical staffers. Even so, the Bureau's numbers were too small to directly handle the massive domestic security apparatus needed.

Instead, the FBI followed its time-tested strategy of serving as the central coordinating nerve center of a network of local, state, federal, and law enforcement agencies and patriotic civilian organizations. Already in place (by presidential fiat) was the directive that all other parties refer suspected instances of espionage and sabotage to the FBI. A network of 20,718 FBI informants was quickly established in 4,000 defense plants reporting on sabotage or suspicious incidents. The Bureau's American Legion Contact Program recruited some 60,000 Legion members into a domestic security program.

One controversial policy that Hoover opposed was the rounding up of 120,000 American citizens of Japanese descent, who were transferred from their West Coast homes to internment camps in the Rocky Mountains for the duration of the war. By February 1942, intelligence experts agreed the FBI, ONI, and G-2 had effectively broken up the Japanese spy organization in the United States. But a condition of near-panic existed on the West Coast, uncertain whether Imperial Japan would attack in the aftermath of Pearl Harbor.

Official and Confidential

Among those who favored the internment of Japanese Americans at the start of WWII were reactionary anti-New Deal columnist Westbrook Pegler, progressive columnist Walter Lippman, and then-Governor of California Earl Warren, later to become an avowedly liberal Chief Justice of the Supreme Court. J. Edgar Hoover opposed the move, saying that the only fair and efficient way to process citizens for loyalty was on an individual, case by case basis.

Roosevelt let himself be persuaded by Secretary of War Stimson and Assistant Secretary McCloy, overruling Hoover and signing Executive Order 9066, authorizing the removal of 120,000 Japanese Americans to camps in the Rocky Mountain states. In the years since, the U.S. government has officially apologized and paid compensation to the internees.

They Came to Blow Up America

On December 8, 1941, Nazi Germany joined its ally Imperial Japan in declaring war on the United States. Mindful of America's formidable industrial might, the Third Reich set eight human time bombs on a collision course with the United States. In charge of the effort, which was labeled Operation Pastorius (Pastorius being an early German explorer of the New World), was the Abwehr, Nazi Germany's fearsome, deadly efficient foreign intelligence system. Eight operatives, fluent in English and familiar with American folkways, were instructed in the arts and sciences of destruction at the Abwehr's school for sabotage. Their potential targets in the United States (especially noteworthy in the light of current terrorist alerts) included the Alcoa aluminum processing plants, the massive hydro-electric generating complex at Niagara Falls, and the water supplies and reservoirs of New York City. Other niceties of their planned itinerary included setting off time-delayed bombs in movie theaters, department stores, and other public assemblies, to generate maximum panic and fear.

On the night of June 13, 1942, a German submarine U-boat surfaced off Long Island's Amagansett Bay, on a lonely section of coast, and landed four saboteurs. (Another four were delivered by U-boat to the Florida coast). Dressed in civilian clothes, the invaders buried crates of explosives and other supplies on the sandy beach. The date would prove to be an unlucky 13 for the Nazis, who soon discovered that the beach was not as lonely as they would have liked.

Along came Coast Guardsman John Cullen, on beach-watch patrol. Alone, he confronted the suspicious gang of four, whose spokesman, George Dasch, told Cullen that they were a group of fishermen who'd gotten lost, come aground, and were waiting for daylight to resume sailing.

The saboteurs had been instructed to kill any bystanders who might see them land. Although they were four and armed, and Cullen was alone and unarmed, for whatever reason they shrank from their duty, preferring instead to offer him a bribe of $260 to forget what he'd seen. Pretending to accept the bribe, Cullen got away from the group, returned to his post, and raised the alarm.

By the time pursuit was raised, the saboteurs had already boarded the Long Island Railroad, taking it to New York City and disappearing among the crowds. The pursuers dug up the saboteurs' beach caches, discovering explosives, fuses, detonators, and the like.

What followed next was one of the most intensive manhunts ever launched by the FBI. Rather than raise a general alert, warning its quarry and giving them a chance to escape, the Bureau operated quietly, throwing out a far-flung investigatory web.

A major break, as welcome as it was unlikely, was the decision of group leader George Dasch to turn himself in to the FBI, appearing on June 18 at FBIHQ in Washington with a suitcase full of Abwehr money. Identifying the other three members of his group, he told FBI interrogators of the landing by a U-boat in the Jacksonville, Florida, area of the other four saboteurs. He also said that these landings were only the first, and that additional such landings of sabotage groups was planned to occur every six weeks.

Within two days, the FBI had arrested the three saboteurs denounced by Dasch. In an extraordinary feat of sleuthing, by June 27, 1942, the Bureau had tracked down and arrested all four members of the Florida group, before they had committed a single act of sabotage.

Being taken in a time of war, behind enemy lines while dressed in civilian clothes with the intent of committing espionage and sabotage, the prisoners fell under the Articles of War decreeing that they were liable for the death penalty. Trial began on July 8, 1942 by a *military tribunal* held under heavy guard in the Department of Justice building, the eight were swiftly found guilty and sentenced to death.

A presidential commutation spared Dasch and one other, sentencing them respectively to 30 years hard labor and a life sentence. Within a month after the tribunal began, the other six saboteurs were executed at dawn by electrocution in the Washington, D.C. District jail. In 1948, President Harry S Truman ordered the two survivors released from prison and deported to Germany.

Justice Jargon

A **tribunal** is a military trial proceeding, though not a court martial, which allows for looser rules of evidence and greater secrecy, excluding the public and the press. It has been used, but rarely in America: during the Revolutionary War against Britain; against the Lincoln assassination conspirators; and in the 1942 proceedings against the eight Nazi saboteurs. In the latter, the defendants were tried before a commission of seven generals, with the attorney general serving as prosecutor.

Intelligence Matters

In May 1940, Hoover proposed to Roosevelt that the FBI establish a Special Intelligence Service (SIS) which would allow Bureau agents to operate outside the United States. A month or so later, when FDR issued his directive apportioning intelligence duties between G-2, ONI, and the FBI, the Bureau's newly designated Western Hemisphere territory became the field of operations for the SIS. Agents were assigned to Central and South America, some working undercover, others as legal attachés to U.S. embassies, others working in conjunction with indigenous police forces.

The region seethed with Axis (Germany, Japan, and Italy) spies, saboteurs, and propagandists. During World War I, Imperial Germany's plans to use Mexico as a staging ground to foment sabotage and terrorism against the U.S. had been revealed in the Zimmerman telegram, a leading cause of America's entry into the war. Now, with its many foreign embassies and cadres of spies, Mexico City was a cockpit of intrigue. Large and influential German enclaves existed in Brazil, Chile, and Argentina; Japanese colonies were especially strong in Peru and Brazil. An Axis spy and communication network overspread the South American continent.

The Axis's grand South American strategy consisted of denying vital raw materials to the Allies, and using the continent as a springboard for espionage, sabotage, and propaganda efforts against the United States. To further these goals

Bu Stats

There were about 360 FBI SIS agents operating in South America during the war. They arranged the arrests of 389 Axis agents, of whom 105 were convicted. Two hundred eighty-one propaganda agents were identified, 60 arrested. Just over 7,000 enemy aliens were relocated, 2,172 interned, and 5,893 deported. Twenty-four enemy radio stations were shut down. Four SIS agents were killed in action.

required overthrowing neutral or hostile governments and replacing them with friendly, pro-fascist regimes.

Countering them, SIS worked in concert with South American police and secret police forces. South American security officials were brought to Quantico, Virginia, for training in state-of-the-art investigatory and counterespionage techniques at the FBI's National Police Academy.

A notable SIS triumph was the thwarting of a planned Axis coup d'état in Bolivia, a primary supplier of tungsten, a metal vital to the U.S. war effort. In Argentina, agents documented links between Vice President Juan Peron (whose rise was masterminded by his ambitious wife, Evita) and Hitler. In Brazil, a single roundup of Axis agents netted 500 arrests. In Brazil, Argentina, and Chile, top Nazi agents were apprehended by SIS agents and held in U.S. military detention in the Panama Canal Zone. Smugglers of vital war materials were apprehended, and clandestine sources of Nazi funds for destabilization purposes were intercepted.

In later years, Hoover called the FBI's wartime Western Hemisphere activities the Bureau's "greatest untold story."

The Least You Need to Know

♦ President Roosevelt's division of foreign intelligence duties made Army G-2 responsible for Europe, Naval ONI responsible for the Pacific, and the FBI responsible for Central and South America.

♦ The FBI's extensive prewar monitoring of subversive groups and individuals allowed it to move swiftly after Pearl Harbor, rounding up potential enemy spies and saboteurs.

♦ The Bureau served as the wartime nerve center of a nationwide internal security program organizing local, state, federal, and civilian agencies against domestic foes.

♦ Eight Nazi saboteurs were captured by the FBI, tried by a military tribunal, and executed.

♦ FBI Special Intelligence Service agents thwarted Axis espionage and sabotage efforts in Central and South America.

Part 2

National Security State

For a short time after World War II, the American people basked in the sunny certainty of a peace guaranteed by their sole possession of the ultimate weapon, the atomic bomb. In 1949, the idyll was shattered by the Soviets' detonation of a nuclear device. They had the A-bomb, too. In fact, they had stolen U.S. atomic secrets years earlier, thanks to the help of spies and double agents.

So began the Cold War. In the late 1940s and early 1950s, FBI investigations decimated the top ranks of the Communist Party USA. By 1960, for all intents and purposes, the Party was washed up.

Sixties-era social unrest and antiwar activism were countered by the FBI's controversial COINTELPRO operations. An aging Hoover feuded with Bobby Kennedy and Martin Luther King, Jr. In his final years, the erstwhile Top Cop resisted Nixon White House efforts to politicize the Bureau.

Chapter 7

FBI, CIA, and Moscow Center

In This Chapter

- ◆ FBI wartime rivalry with the Office of Strategic Services
- ◆ Exit FDR, enter President Harry S Truman
- ◆ The postwar Communist Party turns hardcore Stalinist
- ◆ Government security risks, FBI spy hunters, and highly placed Soviet agents

The historic intelligence failure leading to the attack on Pearl Harbor highlighted the need for an agency that would coordinate information and operations of military intelligence agencies and the FBI. As we'll see in this chapter, this realization led to the creation of the wartime Office of Strategic Services, headed by Hoover's nemesis William J. Donovan. Roosevelt's successor, President Harry S Truman, disbelieved FBI reports about suspected secret Communist agents in high-level positions in his administration.

But some key defections put the FBI on the trail of a massive wartime Red spy system which had been operating against Britain, Canada, and the United States, leading to a massive national security showdown between Hoover and Truman.

Central Intelligence

When the United States entered World War II, the FBI controlled all civilian domestic intelligence operations and the Western Hemisphere Special Intelligence Service (SIS) foreign intelligence operations in Central and South American. The Bureau had made a good start toward realizing J. Edgar Hoover's not-so-secret ambition for the FBI to be in charge of *all* intelligence gathering worldwide.

But President Roosevelt liked getting his intelligence from more than one source. The competition between the Army's G-2 division, the Office of Naval Intelligence (ONI), and the FBI kept all three agencies on their toes, combating the complacency that comes from monopoly. It allowed for diversity, for the surfacing of a multiplicity of facts and opinions. Each bit of data was a piece of the informational mosaic, which when assembled and properly analyzed revealed the true intelligence picture. Also (and not to be underestimated), as a matter of practical politics and for reasons of balance, Roosevelt felt it was best not to let any one agency get too much more powerful than its rivals.

Justice Jargon

A **central intelligence agency** coordinates all government intelligence efforts and analyzes all intelligence information. Such coordination is especially needful in orchestrating covert intelligence operations of various military and federal branches. In the United States, it is a civilian service that is part of the executive branch. It is designed to serve the President directly and allows for a wide flexibility and freedom of movement.

This power-sharing arrangement was wrecked on the shoals of Pearl Harbor, as a consensus developed that one of the main causes of the debacle was the lack of central intelligence and a *central intelligence agency* that would have coordinated and analyzed the information and operations of the fragmented American intelligence agencies.

After Pearl Harbor, G-2, ONI, and the FBI agreed that the United States needed a centralized, coordinated intelligence, but not on whom should run it. On whom should *not* run it, however, they were all agreed: The universally unacceptable choice was war hero and East Coast political powerhouse William J. Donovan.

Some people opposed Donovan on principle. The military felt that a civilian central intelligence service would address civilian intelligence needs. Some of the opposition was personal. Brash, hard-driving, blunt-spoken Donovan had made many enemies, not least of whom was J. Edgar Hoover. As assistant attorney general in 1924, Donovan had fought Hoover's appointment as permanent director of the FBI.

But Donovan was a man of proven courage, a decorated war hero, a pillar of the East Coast establishment, and an internationalist with countless high-level contacts and connections throughout Europe. Most important, Roosevelt liked him and recognized his worth, believing that Donovan might someday well become president.

Oddly, America's ambassador to Great Britain, Joseph P. Kennedy, was responsible for Donovan's ultimately landing the coveted central intelligence post. Defeatist where Britain and democracy were concerned, Kennedy's official dispatches from London during the Luftwaffe's bombing raids (the Blitz) extolled Nazi military prowess and denigrated Britain's ability to resist the foe.

Would the British fight? Could they fight? Wanting a fresh appraisal from an independent observer, and in a display of bipartisanship, Roosevelt in July 1940, sent GOP stalwart Donovan to Britain on an inspection and fact-finding tour. Here Donovan successfully liaised with King George VI, Prime Minister Winston Churchill, and Colonel Stewart Menzies, head of the British Secret Intelligence Service. Returning home in August, Donovan reported to Roosevelt. His conclusion was the opposite of Kennedy's: British morale was high, the British *would* fight, but they were in desperate need of military armaments and supplies. Donovan's trip was a key component in the launching of Roosevelt's Lend-Lease plan to furnish Britain with those needed supplies.

In May 1940, the British Secret Intelligence Service appointed Sir William Stephenson as liaison with U.S. intelligence services. Heading the U.S.-based British Security Coordination (BSC), with offices in New York City's Rockefeller Center, Stephenson worked closely with Donovan on intelligence matters starting in the fall of 1940. He helped Donovan with the planning for an American central intelligence service and helped pave the way in December for Donovan's second, lengthier trip to Britain and the Mediterranean, North African, and Balkan war zones.

> **Cops and Robbers**
>
> Canadian-born Sir William Stephenson was a man of many parts: boxing champion, World War I flying ace, and millionaire businessman. As head of British Security Coordination, he was spymaster for all British Intelligence operations in the United States during World War II. His code name was Intrepid; his biography, *A Man Called Intrepid* (authored by a William Stevenson), was an international bestseller.

COI/OSS and the FBI

On June 18, 1941, FDR appointed Donovan coordinator of information (COI), heading the Office of the COI, a civilian organization answering directly to the president in his role as commander in chief and advised by the heads of other intelligence agencies, to coordinate the analysis and collection of information. An elastic clause in the agency's charter allowed it to carry out "such supplementary activities as may facilitate the securing of information important for national security." Without spelling it out, this authorized Donovan to create a division to specialize in what he called "unorthodox warfare": propaganda, psychological operations, and paramilitary and guerrilla operations.

To soothe military qualms, the Office of COI was prohibited from "interfering or impairing" military operations and duties. Protecting his turf, Hoover got Roosevelt's approval to keep Central and South America under FBI SIS's jurisdiction, free of COI operations. Hoover also continued to maintain his own, separate arrangement with Stephenson's BSC.

That arrangement had begun in spring of 1940, when Roosevelt had issued a directive ordering close cooperation between British Intelligence and the FBI. Hoover was opposed to even a friendly or allied nation running intelligence operations on U.S. soil, but orders were orders, and for a time the arrangement was mutually beneficial. Stephenson communicated with London on an FBI-supplied transmitter; FBI agents helped prevent sabotage of British ships; and the two agencies exchanged information and documents. Posing as a trade commission, the British Security Coordination (which was named by Hoover) operated about 1,000 agents in the United States. and 2,000 in Canada and Latin America. Within a year, the BSC had furnished the FBI with over 100,000 reports.

Official and Confidential

In May 1941, British Director of Naval Intelligence Rear Admiral Godfrey and Commander Ian Fleming met with Hoover at FBIHQ to propose intelligence integration between Hoover and Donovan. The future creator of James Bond described Hoover as "a chunky, enigmatic man with slow eyes and a trap of a mouth who received us graciously ... and expressed himself firmly but politely as being uninterested in our mission. Hoover's negative response was soft as a cat's paw."

This period of cooperation ended in June 1941, when the COI was formed and Donovan was installed at its head. Stephenson's advocacy of Donovan for the post caused Hoover to sour on him and the BSC. It was petty and vindictive yet, in an odd twist of events, it would turn out to be ultimately beneficial to the United States once the full extent of Soviet penetration of British Intelligence became clear. But that would come later.

In point of fact, Hoover was temperamentally unsuited to the post of central intelligence czar. He lacked global vision. Far from being an internationalist, Hoover traveled outside the United States only once in his entire life, when he vacationed in the Caribbean during the 1930s. William Sullivan, a key lieutenant of later years, said that Hoover "didn't like the British, didn't care for the French, hated the Dutch, and couldn't stand the Australians." And that was just the Allies.

Hoover's lack of cooperation with the BSC curdled to active harassment of the COI. Learning that COI agents were operating in Mexico, he protested vehemently until the operations ceased. Whenever the COI made a mistake, Hoover pounced and highlighted it. COI agents were kept under FBI surveillance.

But COI's strength lay in its analysis of information. The FBI approach was to transmit massive amounts of raw information, leaving the analysis and interpretation to its ultimate consumers, the president and his advisors. By contrast, COI's focus was on interpretive analysis, on finding the pertinent patterns and viewpoints that turned information into user-friendly intelligence.

The search for the maximally effective wartime use of COI led to Roosevelt's reforming it on June 1942, into the *Office of Strategic Services* (*OSS*), maintaining its civilian status while putting it under the control of the military's Joint Chiefs of Staff. Donovan was appointed Director of OSS. The Chiefs identified OSS's mission as espionage, counterespionage, sabotage, propaganda, psychological warfare, and covert action. By war's end, it had some 24,000 operatives.

Hoover's most outrageous harassment came in October 1942, when a team of OSS agents broke into the Washington, D.C., embassy of officially neutral but objectively pro-fascist Spain. The operation was a repeat of similar successful sorties earlier in July, August, and September, when agents had managed to photograph the embassy's cipher room codebooks, keeping abreast of the latest changes in the maritime codes.

On that October night, however, three OSS men were inside the building when two FBI cars pulled up with lights flashing and sirens wailing, causing the intruders to flee. Donovan complained, "The Abwehr gets better treatment from the FBI than we do!"

Justice Jargon

The **Office of Strategic Services (OSS)** attracted many Ivy League grads and Establishment upper-crusters, generating the popular joke that the organization's initials stood for "Oh So Social." According to Hoover, whose FBI had the responsibility of running security checks on COI/OSS recruits, the fact that OSS's enrolled a number of socialists and even communists in its membership despite the Bureau's negative referrals meant that the spy agency's initials stood for "Oh So Socialist."

But there was more to the Hoover-Donovan feud than mere personal enmity, petty empire-building, and turf protection (although there was plenty of all three). OSS's hiring of socialists and communists ensured that Bureau cooperation, if any, would be minimal. Donovan himself was an idea man, with plenty of hits and misses. While OSS scored some notable successes in Europe, it also came up with some bad blunders. One of the worst surfaced early in 1943, when Donovan proposed an OSS alliance with the Soviet secret police NKVD, one which would allow the two agencies to run operations in each other's countries. Learning of the proposal, Hoover pointed out that that public knowledge of arrangement allowing Red spies to freely operate in the United States would be political suicide for the administration. Roosevelt killed the proposal.

The limiting factor on OSS was that it had been created as a wartime entity. In November 1944, looking toward war's end, Donovan offered Roosevelt a plan for transforming OSS into a peacetime spy agency that would report directly to the president, laying the groundwork for what would eventually become the Central Intelligence Agency. It doesn't take an intelligence analyst to guess that Donovan's candidate for agency director was Donovan.

The plan was quashed when it was prematurely leaked to the virulently anti–New Deal *Chicago Tribune*, which in February 1945 bannered headlines that warned of a Roosevelt plot to create an American "Gestapo-style" secret police. The resultant uproar killed Donovan's chances to head such an agency, but not the idea of the agency itself.

Harry Gives 'em Hell

In 1940, FDR's vice presidential running mate was ultra-liberal Midwesterner Henry A. Wallace. Post-election, Wallace displayed political associations that were unwise if not dangerous. The FBI began scrutinizing such associations during an investigation that could not have been undertaken without the express authorization of the president himself.

Investigators learned that Wallace had lent the support of his name and office to Communist front organizations on numerous occasions. A charitable interpretation of his acts was that his extreme political naïveté made him the unwitting pawn of the Communist Party USA (CPUSA). But Hoover believed that Wallace was consciously aiding the Communists, though he was able to find no hard evidence to support that contention. Bureau wiretaps of top CPUSA leaders showed that they felt Wallace was a "useful idiot" who was easily manipulated by the party.

In the 1944 election, Roosevelt dropped Wallace from the ticket and replaced him with Missouri Senator Harry S Truman (note: it's Harry S Truman; the S is no abbreviation, Truman having no middle name). On Thursday, April 12, 1945, while vacationing in Warm Springs, Georgia, Roosevelt suffered a stroke, dying with his longtime love Lucy Mercer at his bedside. Harry Truman was now the president of the United States.

During an appropriation hearing at the start of the decade, then-Senator Truman had defended Hoover from the attacks of Tennessee Senator McKellar. Since then, the positions of the two senators had changed, with McKellar becoming a supporter of Hoover and Truman a critic. During hearings into the intelligence failure leading up to Pearl Harbor, Truman had criticized the FBI for not doing enough.

Now, Truman was Hoover's boss. Trying to court favor with him, Hoover sent a young agent from Truman's home state of Missouri to express Hoover's good will and readiness to be of service. Truman bluntly told the go-between to tell Hoover that if he needed anything from the FBI, he'd go through his attorney general. That really put Truman in solid with J. Edgar.

Truman's attorney general was Texan Tom Clark, genial and undistinguished, who at first got along pretty well with Hoover. Truman soon learned what other presidents had known, namely that the FBI was an important instrument for carrying out actions both official and confidential, including the surveilling of one's political foes and friends. Hoover was charged by the White House with monitoring political fixer Tommy "the Cork" Corcoran and other shady, high-level politicians.

In September 1945, one month after the war ended, Truman fired William Donovan and abolished the OSS. Hoover moved fast, resurfacing his proposal to extend the FBI's Western Hemisphere intelligence operations throughout the world. Not only did Truman thumbs-down the proposal, he also cut $6 million from the FBI's planned 1946 budget. On January 22, 1946, Truman established the Central Intelligence Group, forerunner of the CIA.

Official and Confidential

In early 1946, Hoover made a personal visit to the White House to try to convince President Truman to put the Central Intelligence Group under FBI authority. Truman, who'd already confided to an aide that no one man should be in charge of both agencies, lest he "get too big for his britches," listened to Hoover's pitch before turning it down. When Hoover pressed the point, Truman told him, "You're getting out of bounds."

Unpopular Front

Truman had little love for the FBI, more than once expressing his determination to prevent the empowering of an "American Gestapo." He had less love for Hoover, yet made no move to replace him. While this choice no doubt reflected political considerations that the sacking of the United States's Top Cop would lose plenty of votes in the upcoming Congressional election, it may also have reflected the reality that the director was in a position to know plenty about "Boss" Tom Pendergast's political machine, which had been the vehicle for Truman's advancement in Missouri politics and beyond.

Bu Stats

The CPUSA reached its greatest growth during the World War II era, when its enrollment totaled some 80,000 members. This, from a low point of some 5,000 members after the 1920 Palmer Raids. FBI estimates reckoned that for every open, card-carrying party member, there were at least ten undeclared sympathizers and fellow travelers.

Early in his administration, Truman had something of a blind spot where communism was concerned. This attitude was characteristic of New Dealers, who'd identified fascism as the major national security threat but tolerated leftists, socialists, and communists whose alliance helped facilitate the administration's plans. This way of thinking had persisted during World War II, when Soviet Russia was an ally against the Axis powers.

Even before the war was over, the USSR began emerging as the next challenger and threat to the United States. In the new postwar shape of things, the sun was setting on the British Empire. Where Britain had once been the top target of Soviet penetration agents, now America had become Priority Number One.

Things changed quickly after the war, as the USSR moved to extend its control throughout Eastern Europe. The changed geopolitical realities extended to the CPUSA. CPUSA got its orders from Moscow Center, the secret police's Kremlin headquarters, which now decreed a dramatic shift in strategy and tactics.

The era of the Popular Front, of the party wrapping itself in a mantle of phony Americanism and seeming to be openly cooperative with the government, was done. Judged by Moscow as having been too accommodationist, CPUSA head Earl Browder was expelled from post and party, replaced by hardcore Stalinist William Z. Foster. Among party circles, "Browderite" became the ultimate term of opprobrium, what "Trotskyist" had once been. Trotsky himself was long-gone, having been assassinated in 1940 in Mexico City by one of Stalin's agents.

The party's hand had already been tipped by the *Amerasia* incident in February 1945. Reading an article in an issue of the foreign affairs journal *Amerasia*, an OSS analyst was startled to discover almost verbatim excerpts from a confidential report he'd written some months earlier. That the document had been stolen was the only conclusion. Heading the investigation, in March OSS chief investigator Frank Brooks Bielaski led a squad of agents on a surreptitious entry of *Amerasia* offices in New York City. The searchers found literally thousands of secret government documents (including those from the State Department, ONI, OSS, and British Intelligence) that could only have been acquired by a major espionage ring.

The case was turned over to the FBI, which launched a major investigation, on June 6, 1945, arresting for espionage six *Amerasia* editors and writers. The arrests generated a strong negative media reaction, that painted the raid as an attempt to intimidate the press. Defense lawyers learned of several warrantless FBI entries of the editorial offices. The Truman administration refused to vigorously prosecute the case, leading to bad blood between Attorney General Tom Clark and Hoover. *Amerasia* editor Phillip Jaffe was found guilty on a lesser charge of theft of government property and fined.

> **Cops and Robbers**
>
> OSS Chief Investigator Frank Brooks Bielaski, a onetime Bureau of Investigation (BI) agent who'd taken part in the Palmer Raids, was the brother of A. Bruce Bielaski, who from 1912 through 1919 headed the old BI. A sister, Ruth Bielaski Shipley, was in charge of the U.S. Passport Office during the early 1950s, and was a strong Hoover ally.

But the wall of Red secrecy had been breached, leading to the first intimations of the extent of Communist infiltration of the Roosevelt administration. A few years down the road, Truman's refusal to prosecute the espionage cases with full vigor would be used against him by the GOP.

In short order, more cracks opened in the wall. In August 1945, Elizabeth Bentley walked into FBI offices in New Haven, Connecticut, confessing that for the past eleven years, she'd been a Communist and courier for a Red espionage ring operating in Washington, D.C.

> **Cops and Robbers**
>
> Born in New England in 1908, future "Red Spy Queen" Elizabeth Bentley was a Vassar graduate who claimed that her post-graduate sojourn in Italy made her a confirmed anti-Fascist, resulting in her joining the CPUSA. Going underground in 1938, code-named "Helen," she'd become the lover of high-ranking Soviet spy Jacob Golos, acting as his go-between to various Communist spy rings operating in the government in Washington, D.C. Golos's death from heart trouble in 1943 and her dislike of his successor led to her subsequent disenchantment and break from the party in 1945.

Case of the Dangerous Defector

Close on the heels of Bentley's walk-in came the September 1945 defection of Igor Gouzenko, a cipher clerk in the office of the Russian embassy in Ottawa, Canada. Gouzenko's duties had centered around encoding the dispatches to Moscow of the ambassador and of military attaché Colonel Zabotkin, head of GRU (Soviet Military Intelligence) operations in Canada. Fleeing with his pregnant wife, young son, and over a hundred top-secret Soviet cables and documents, including pages from Zabotkin's handwritten diary, Gouzenko became a political hot potato, being bounced from one Canadian government ministry to another by bureaucrats and politicians who feared offending the mighty USSR. As NKVD manhunters closed in on the defector, an eleventh-hour intervention by the Royal Canadian Mounted Police (RCMP) rescued Gouzenko and his family.

Gouzenko provided investigators with a roadmap to wartime Soviet penetration operations against the Canadian, British, and U.S. governments. RCMP interrogators were soon joined by FBI special agents. Most alarming was information provided by Gouzenko about Soviet espionage efforts to uncover the secrets of the atomic bomb. His tips led to the arrest of British nuclear physicist Allan Nunn May, who confessed to having passed top-secret technical details about the bomb's construction, and samples of enriched uranium 235 and 233, to his Soviet controls. Ultimately, Nunn May would lead FBI sleuths to an American atomic spy ring.

The Gouzenko revelations led to an intensified FBI investigation of Elizabeth Bentley's claims. Bentley ultimately identified, as part of the Soviet's Washington espionage network, over a hundred individuals from six different government agencies. Among them were six OSS officers, including the organization's chief counsel; three Pentagon officers; seven State Department officials; and eight Treasury Department officials.

According to Bentley, the leader of the ring was Gregory Silvermaster, a New Deal economist whose agents in all the important government agencies supplied him with information and thousands of documents, which he photographed in his darkroom and turned over to Bentley for delivery to her control, Golos. Another she named as a Soviet spy was Harry Dexter White, the chief lieutenant of Secretary of the Treasury Henry Morgenthau since the 1930s.

Armed with this information, the FBI now turned fresh attention on Whittaker Chambers, who in 1939 had contacted Assistant Secretary of State Adolf Berle, claiming that the State Department was penetrated by secret Communists, among them brothers Alger and Donald Hiss. At the time, FDR had met the accusations with contemptuous hostility, and the charges were filed and forgotten.

> ### Cops and Robbers
>
> An Eastern establishment mandarin, Alger Hiss was a Harvard Law School graduate, where he'd been a protégé of then-Professor and later Supreme Court Justice Felix Frankfurter. A New York lawyer, Hiss joined the New Deal administration as a legal staffer for an agricultural committee, joining the State Department in 1936, where he became one of its leading lights. Playing a major role in FDR's Yalta conference with Stalin and Churchill, Hiss served as temporary secretary general of the newly formed United Nations after the war. His strong Soviet support had him on the inside track to become permanent secretary general, until questions about his Communist affiliations surfaced.

In light of the Bentley revelations, the charges took on new life. Gouzenko's clues about a high-level Communist spy in the wartime State Department also seemed to point to Alger Hiss. Also generating renewed interest was a 1941 meeting between British Ambassador to the United States Lord Halifax and FDR, a meeting called by a worried Halifax to denounce Harry Dexter White as a "highly-placed Russian agent." Again, there had been no real follow-up on the charges.

Now, in late 1945, Hoover warned Truman about Hiss and Harry Dexter White. Disliking Hoover and feeling that the charges were alarmist and without merit, Truman in early 1946 nominated White as the first American director of the International Monetary Fund.

With 1946 also being a Congressional election year, the stage was set for an explosive national security confrontation between Hoover and Truman. When it ultimately came, one of its unexpected byproducts would be the making of freshman Representative and future President (and lifelong Hoover ally) Richard M. Nixon.

The Least You Need to Know

- Forerunner of the CIA, the wartime Office of Strategic Services was designed to centralize and coordinate the information collecting and operations of military intelligence and the FBI.

- Russia's Canadian embassy code clerk Igor Gouzenko defected, exposing the workings of a massive Red espionage network to FBI spy hunters.

- "Red Spy Queen" Elizabeth Bentley and ex-Communist Whittaker Chambers denounced high government officials Harry Dexter White and Alger Hiss as Communist agents.

- President Truman's blind spot about communist subversion and infiltration of the U.S. government set the stage for a national security showdown with J. Edgar Hoover.

Chapter 8

Atom Spies, Double Agents, and Subversives

In This Chapter

- Alger Hiss and the Pumpkin Papers
- The Battle of Foley Square
- The Rosenberg atomic spy case
- Venona: greatest U.S. intelligence secret of the Cold War
- British traitors and the mysterious Third Man

By 1947, rising Cold War tensions intensified the FBI's domestic spy hunt. In a pivotal early case of the period, ex-Communist Whittaker Chambers led FBI agents to a treasure trove of prewar documents and evidence buttressing his contention that New Deal State Department powerbroker Alger Hiss was a secret Communist agent. The 1949 prosecution of top CPUSA leaders revealed that the Bureau had highly placed informants throughout the party.

As discussed in this chapter, the Soviet Union's detonation of an atomic bomb triggered the FBI's hunt for the Red spies who'd passed bomb-making secrets to the Soviets. Ultra top-secret Venona-decoded messages helped the Bureau expose a spy operation reaching deep into the heart of British Intelligence.

Alger Hiss and the Pumpkin Papers

While J. Edgar Hoover worked behind the scenes trying to get Truman to dump Alger Hiss and Harry Dexter White, the FBI put a heavy surveillance program on Hiss, White, their families, and their associates. They and their homes were watched night and day, their comings and goings minutely noted. Their phones were tapped, their mail was scrutinized, their pasts examined with a fine tooth comb.

Where the goal was to actually catch them in possession of stolen government documents, meeting covertly with other communist cell members, communicating with a Soviet control—in other words, to actually catch them in the act of espionage—the results were nil. And why not? Igor Gouzenko's defection warned Soviet GRU controls to immediately shut down their spy operations, while the leaky sieve that was (and is) the Washington establishment would undoubtedly have alerted Hiss and White, and all the others known to Gouzenko or Elizabeth Bentley, to cease all covert activities.

Even so, during the three-month investigation of White, he'd been observed meeting with a number of individuals that Bentley had named as members of the D.C. spy ring, many of whom had already been under FBI suspicion of being secret Communists even before Bentley had started talking. A *"black bag"* break-in of suspected spy ring leader Nathan Gregory Silvermaster verified Bentley's claim that he had a darkroom, which she'd charged he used to photograph thousands of classified government documents.

Justice Jargon

A **black bag** job is a surreptitious break-in conducted to retrieve information about a person by illegal means.

This was still a long way off from developing evidence that could be used in court to convict the suspects. In Silvermaster's case, nothing from the warrantless break-in could be entered into the court record. Harry Dexter White's nomination went forward, and in May 1946, he was confirmed as one of three executive directors of the International Monetary Fund.

Playing the anti-Communist card, Republicans won big gains in the November 1946 Congressional elections. This turn of events strengthened Hoover's national security hand, since the Truman administration, already burned, was becoming leery of leaving itself open to charges of being soft on communism. In March 1947, President

Truman signed an executive order dividing responsibility between the FBI and the Civil Service Commission for the investigation of federal employees accused of disloyal or subversive backgrounds. Unwilling to settle for half a security loaf, Hoover pressured Truman into a November 1947 ruling directing the FBI to conduct all loyalty investigations.

HUAC and the CIA

May 1947 saw the House Committee on Un-American Activities (HUAC) begin hearings on alleged Communist infiltration of Hollywood's motion picture industry. Unofficially, HUAC worked closely with the FBI, which supplied it with extensive background information on witnesses both hostile and friendly. Friendly witnesses included actors Gary Cooper and Robert Taylor and studio heads Walt Disney and Jack Warner. The Unfriendly Ten, a group of ten prominent Hollywood writers and directors who took the Fifth Amendment to avoid testifying about their suspected communist links, wound up serving jail terms for being in contempt of Congress.

Another notable event took place in late summer 1947, when Congress passed the National Security Act, which transformed the interim Central Intelligence Group into the Central Intelligence Agency (CIA). Answering to the president and operating through the National Security Council, the CIA's mission was intelligence collecting, analysis, and the integration of domestic, foreign, and military policies. FBI SIS operations in Latin America were officially discontinued, although the Bureau continued to run operations in Mexico City. The CIA charter officially forbade the organization from conducting operations or investigations on U.S. soil, such operations falling under FBI jurisdiction. As far as Hoover was concerned, the only bright spot was that William J. Donovan hadn't been appointed head of the CIA.

The presidential election year of 1948 featured a race between Truman and his Republican opponent, New York Governor Thomas E. Dewey, the former racket-busting New York City district attorney whose prosecution had sent Lepke to the electric chair. Internationally, the Soviet consolidation of power in East Europe and the encirclement of Berlin, civil war in Greece and Albania, and violent communist-inspired labor unrest in Western Europe were bringing East-West tensions to a boil.

Official and Confidential

The freshman crop of Congressmen taking office for the first time in 1947 included at least three notables: Representatives Richard M. Nixon (Republican) of California and John F. Kennedy (Democrat) of Massachusetts; and Senator Joe McCarthy (Republican) of Wisconsin. All three were ex-servicemen: Nixon and Kennedy were Navy veterans, while McCarthy had served in the Marines.

Keeping up the pressure on the home front, in July 1948, J. Edgar Hoover arranged for Elizabeth Bentley and Whittaker Chambers to testify before HUAC, where the names of alleged Communist secret agents Harry Dexter White and Alger Hiss surfaced at Committee hearings. Testifying before the Committee, White vehemently denied the charges. Three days later, he was dead of a heart attack.

Alger Hiss: American Spy?

A newly appointed HUAC member was California Congressman Richard Nixon, who took an instant dislike (the feeling was mutual) to the Eastern establishment, State Department luminary Alger Hiss. In the time since the first postwar allegations had been made against him, Hiss had left the government to find employment as president of the Carnegie Endowment for International Peace. His testimony before the Committee was a smooth performance, in which he denied all charges, offhandedly allowing that he vaguely recollected having once met Chambers years ago, in an unrelated nonpolitical matter.

Hiss dared Chambers to repeat his charges outside the Committee hearing room. Chambers did so on *Meet the Press* (then a radio program), prompting Hiss to sue him for libel. But Hiss had played into Chambers's trap. On November 17, 1948, Chambers led FBI agents to a cache of secret documents he'd hidden in the dumbwaiter shaft of a Brooklyn building where his sister-in-law lived. The 1938-era material, which Chambers said he'd laid away long ago as a "life preserver" against Communist vengeance, included stolen government documents and some of Harry Dexter White's handwritten memoranda.

Early in December, exploding his second bombshell, Chambers led the FBI and HUAC Committee members to his Maryland farm, producing material which had been stashed away in a hollowed-out pumpkin. These soon-to-be-famous "Pumpkin Papers" included photographs of confidential State Department documents which Chambers said he'd given to Hiss to retype on Hiss's Woodstock-brand typewriter for transmission to their Soviet control.

In December 1948, a grand jury indicted Hiss on two counts of perjury. A key witness against Hiss was a 1929 Woodstock typewriter, serial number N230099, which he had owned and which FBI Laboratory document examiners proved had typed the incriminating Pumpkin Papers documents. His first trial, in July 1949, ended in an eight-to-four hung jury. His second trial, in January 1950, ended with Hiss's conviction for perjury and a five-year prison sentence.

Congressman Nixon, who'd publicly staked his credibility on Hiss's guilt, achieved national prominence thanks to the case, using it as a springboard for his successful Senate run in 1950.

Bu Stats

Since 1946, the CPUSA had been working under not-so-deep cover to promote former Vice President Henry A. Wallace's 1948 run for president on the Progressive Party ticket. The party had no expectation of a win; rather, it hoped to launch a new, leftist third political party. To achieve this goal, Wallace had to win about 5,000,000 votes. Instead, Wallace garnered barely a million votes, ending the party's dream of influencing the system through electoral politics.

President Harry S Truman squeezed out a surprise win over Dewey. Much as he would have liked to, he lacked the clout to fire J. Edgar Hoover. For the next four years, as the Cold War heated up, Truman and Hoover were stuck with each other, like two scorpions in a brandy glass.

The Battle of Foley Square

In the summer of 1948, a New York City grand jury indicted twelve top Communist Party leaders for violating the Smith Act. Originally passed in 1940, the Smith Act made it illegal to advocate the overthrow of the U.S. government by force or violence. The New Deal Justice Department was cool to the law, using it only twice during the war. One of the prosecutions, targeting the Socialists Workers Party, had been hailed by the Communist Party because the Socialists Workers Party was pro-Trotsky.

Now, it was CPUSA's turn to come under scrutiny. On July 20, 1949, FBI agents arrested five top party leaders, rounding up seven more in the next two weeks. At their trial in 1949 (minus William Z. Foster, whose case was severed from the others' due to ill health), the prosecution argued that the postwar deposition of Earl Browder and the Popular Front meant that the party had reverted to its traditional strategy advocating the violent overthrow of the U.S. government.

Held at New York's Foley Square Courthouse, the trial, which ran from January to October 1949, soon became known as the Battle of Foley Square. Manifesting a new, post–Popular Front belligerence, the party's defense lawyers used every procedural and rhetorical trick to disrupt and de-legitimize the proceedings. The prosecution was not without tricks of its own. Paramount among them was the revelation that for years, the FBI had placed a number of informants and double agents deep in the CP hierarchy.

Taking the stand for the prosecution were FBI double agents Herbert Philbrick and Angela Calomaris, who testified about the party inner circle's deepest secrets. Further hammering the defendants was the testimony of Louis Budenz, former managing editor of the party's *Daily Worker* newspaper, who asserted that Communist denials of violent intent to overthrow the government were just so much "window dressing."

Cops and Robbers

One of the most important and best-known FBI double agents in the CPUSA was Herbert Philbrick, who'd been a Bureau informant since 1940. Originally disenchanted with the party, Philbrick had been persuaded by FBI agents to remain in place, feeding them information about CP machinations. Philbrick's first-person account of his undercover adventures, *I Led Three Lives*, was a national bestseller, also serving as the basis for a hit TV show of the same name.

The jury found all eleven defendants guilty, all but one of them (a war veteran) being given the maximum five-year sentence. The judge also found their lawyers guilty of contempt of court for their disruptive tactics and disorderly conduct, sentencing them to serve jail terms.

The Foley Square trial destabilized, demoralized, and decimated the CPUSA. The revelation that the FBI had infiltrated the party triggered mass paranoia in the ranks, with members denouncing each other as Bureau agents. Stoking their fears, the FBI used disinformation to throw suspicion on "loyal" party members.

On the heels of the Foley Square trial came the prosecution of the "second echelon" Communists. From 1949–1954, Smith Act prosecutions resulted in the indictments of 126 top Communists, with 93 convictions.

Crime of the Century II

On September 23, 1949, the Soviet Union detonated its first atomic bomb. This came as a dismaying surprise to U.S. military intelligence specialists, who'd calculated that it would take Soviet science about ten years to build one, and to the American public, until then secure in the knowledge that only the United States possessed the super-weapon. In October, Mao Tse-tung's Communists took control of mainland China. While this took place independently of the Soviet development of the atom bomb, it was still disheartening to Free World partisans. The global Communist movement had momentum.

What seemed more credibly linked to Soviet mastery of the A-bomb was the July 1950 invasion by communist North Korea of South Korea. Without it, it seemed unlikely that the Kremlin would have given their North Korean allies the go-ahead for the invasion. The Cold War turned hot, and before the year was out, American soldiers were fighting and dying in Korea.

The search for the atomic spies who'd passed nuclear secrets to Russia was arguably the FBI's greatest spy hunt. The real damage had already been done back in 1944–1945, when the top-secret Manhattan Project under the aegis of the U.S. Army Corps of Engineers sought to create an atomic bomb. The defection of Soviet code clerk Gouzenko had led British Intelligence to Allan Nunn May, the first loose thread in the network of double agents and Red atom spies.

Justice Jargon

Cryptography, literally "secret writing," is the gnarly, mind-bending art and science of code-making and code-breaking. Experts in the field are **cryptanalysts.** To put text into its coded form is to **encrypt** it; to decode it is to **decrypt** it.

A Briton, Nunn May had worked in the Canadian component of the Manhattan Project. In 1950, the spy hunt focused its attention on the American part of the project. A top-secret *decrypted* Soviet military intelligence message indicated that Dr. Klaus Fuchs, a German-born nuclear physicist who'd served with the British contingent of scientists who'd worked at the A-bomb assembly site in Los Alamos, New Mexico, was a Red spy. If not for the FBI, Fuchs might never have been exposed and could have remained in place indefinitely, continuing to pass atomic secrets to the Soviets.

In late January, 1950, Fuchs confessed to British interrogators, fingering his contact in the spy ring who'd passed the information on to the Soviets. Fuchs knew the contact only as "Raymond," but clues he'd provided to the FBI helped them piece together the puzzle, identifying the courier as Philadelphia chemist Harry Gold. Fuchs pleaded guilty and received a 14-year sentence.

On May 22, 1950, while under arrest, Gold confessed that there'd been a second spy at Los Alamos: young U.S. Army machinist David Greenglass. Greenglass had helped build lens-shaped devices designed to focus the A-bomb's explosive energies.

Enter the Rosenbergs

In June 1950, FBI agents arrested Greenglass, who named as ring members his wife, Ruth; his sister, Ethel; and Ethel's husband, Julius Rosenberg. On July 17, 1950, FBI agents arrested Julius Rosenberg; wife Ethel was arrested on August 11. These four—David and Ruth Greenglass and Julius and Ethel (Greenglass) Rosenberg—were the heart of the atom spy ring, with Julius the ringleader.

When Greenglass was arrested, a handful of lesser members of the ring disappeared, going underground. Morton Sobell fled to Mexico but was apprehended by Mexican police, who delivered him across the border to U.S. lawmen. Joel Barr and Alfred

Sarant escaped to the Soviet Union, where they became computer scientists. William A. Perl and Max Elitcher were arrested.

Ethel and Julius Rosenburg were U.S. citizens who were convicted in 1951 of passing information concerning the construction of nuclear weapons to the Russians during World War II. Despite questions concerning the fairness of their trial and international pleas for clemency, they were executed in 1953.

(Courtesy of Corbis)

The trial of Ethel and Julius Rosenberg for conspiracy to commit espionage took place in New York City from March 5–28, 1951. David and Ruth Greenglass testified for the prosecution, as did Max Elitcher. Evidence showed that the Rosenbergs were longtime dedicated Communists. In 1942, while working in a civilian capacity for the U.S. Army Signal Corps, electrical engineer Julius Rosenberg had walked into the Russian consulate, volunteering his services as a spy. He was recruited by GRU, Soviet military intelligence. Rosenberg roped in other like-minded engineers working on defense projects, collecting stolen information and passing it on to his control. In this period, Rosenberg's signal achievement was the passing of a detailed scale model of a top-secret anti-aircraft proximity fuse to the Soviets. Ethel Rosenberg, also pledged to the cause, acted as a go-between and facilitator of the espionage efforts.

In 1943, Julius recruited brother-in-law David Greenglass into the ring, along with wife Ruth Greenglass, who served a function similar to Ethel's, including typing up handwritten notes. In 1944, Greenglass was brought into the technical support side of the Manhattan Project, traveling to Los Alamos to work on the bomb's high-explosive lenses. While on leave in 1945, Greenglass passed information and sketches about his work to Julius Rosenberg and Harry Gold. A belated security check revealed Julius's

Communist Party membership, leading to the revocation of his security clearance and bouncing him from his Signal Corps job. Greenglass went back to Los Alamos with his wife and kept on spying.

Julius Rosenberg was the hub of a major espionage operation whose membership had been only partly identified. Justice Department prosecutors sought the death penalty in the case, hoping that the pressure would cause Rosenberg to crack and name the rest of his co-conspirators in a deal to escape execution. On March 29, 1951, the defendants were found guilty.

Bu Stats

In addition to atomic secrets, the Rosenberg spy ring, from 1943 to 1946, furnished Soviet military intelligence with more than 20,000 pages of technical documents, plus a 12,000-page complete design manual for the first U.S. jet fighter, the P-80 Shooting Star. Julius Rosenberg also supplied a complete working model of the top-secret anti-aircraft proximity fuse.

On April 5, charging that their betrayals had "altered the course of history to the disadvantage of our country," Judge Irving R. Kaufman sentenced Ethel and Julius Rosenberg to death. Morton Sobell was given a 30-year prison sentence and David Greenglass a 15-year sentence. Harry Gold, who'd pleaded guilty, had already received a 30-year sentence.

The Rosenberg Legacy

In leftist circles, the Rosenbergs became an international cause célèbre, generating petitions and protest marches in the United States and Europe. The appeals process delayed their execution until 1953, by which time Eisenhower was president. He refused to commute the death sentences, and the double execution at Sing Sing prison in Ossining, New York, was scheduled for 11:00 p.m. on Friday, June 19, 1953.

Up to the last moment, FBI agents stood by in the death house, ready to halt the execution if Ethel or Julius decided to cooperate. J. Edgar Hoover had been against executing Ethel, arguing that putting to death the mother of two small children would hand the Communists a propaganda club that they'd use to pound the U.S. government. Ethel was tough and wouldn't crack, buttressing the defiance of Julius, whom FBI investigators regarded as the weaker of the two.

Execution was by the biggest Big Heat of them all, the electric chair. Julius Rosenberg was executed first, expiring after two minutes of electrocution. Ethel, tougher, took five minutes to die.

Two Gentlemen from Venona

In 1944, a partially burned Soviet codebook was discovered in a battlefield in Finland. OSS chief William Donovan bought the codebook from the Finns. Learning of the purchase, and viewing with abhorrence the fact that the United States was spying on its wartime Soviet ally, Secretary of State Edward Stettinius demanded that the codebook be returned to the Russians—who immediately changed codes. Still, copies of the codebook had been made and turned over by OSS to the Army Security Agency, where cryptanalyst Meredith Gardner labored over it for three years, trying to break the code. In 1948, he succeeded.

During the war, the FBI had routinely acquired copies of all cable traffic going back and forth between Moscow and the Soviets' Washington embassy and New York City consulate. The texts, of course, were encrypted, rendering them meaningless to anyone who did not have the key. But now Gardner had the key, and began using it to decode some of the thousands of messages sent in 1944 to 1945, when that particular code was in use. The result was a treasure trove of secret documents revealing the extent of Soviet espionage against the United States during the period.

The ultra top-secret decryption program, codenamed Venona, immediately began paying off. Operatives discovered a cable relating to a process involved in making Uranium 235 and revealing the presence of a Soviet spy in the Manhattan Project. Gardner and his FBI contact, counterintelligence expert Robert Lamphere, were ultimately able to identify the spy as Klaus Fuchs. Fuchs' treason (but not the secret of Venona) was made known to British Intelligence. Confronted by his interrogators, Fuchs confessed, later pleading guilty in court. Had he kept silent, or fought the case, he might well have been found not guilty, for the Venona intercepts were judged too valuable to be revealed in court. Fuchs's confession, as noted above, led to the FBI's uncovering of the Rosenberg atomic spy ring.

Cops and Robbers

One of the top counterintelligence officers of the Cold War was FBI agent Robert Lamphere. In 1947, heading an FBIHQ Soviet Espionage Section counterintelligence office, Lamphere began working with Army Security Agency code-breaker Meredith Gardner. Using information from the Venona decrypts, Lamphere cracked the Coplon espionage ring in the Justice Department, identified Klaus Fuchs in the Manhattan Project atom secrets theft, and pinpointed the 1944 British embassy spy, among many other outstanding investigations.

An early Venona decryption revealed that there was a highly-placed spy in the Justice Department. Lamphere followed this lead to Judith Coplon, 28, a political analyst in the department's Foreign Agents Registration Section, where she had access to FBI reports on known or suspected Soviet spies. The trail stretched from Coplon to Amtorg, Russia's U.S. trading company and a vehicle for Soviet espionage. In 1950, a legal technicality resulted in the overturning of Coplon's conviction and 15-year sentence for espionage, but at least the spy ring had been broken.

Another Venona intercept revealed the explosive fact that a spy had been in place in Britain's Washington embassy from 1944 to 1948, passing high-level information to the Soviets. The investigation would ultimately reveal the existence of one of the most incredible espionage operations of the twentieth century, the Cambridge Ring.

But it wasn't easy. Lamphere briefed liaisons from British Intelligence's two main components, *MI-5* (domestic security) and *MI-6* (foreign intelligence), but couldn't seem to get any results from the other end. Months passed with no follow-up on the urgent leads given by the FBI to British Intelligence. Lamphere suspected incompetence—or worse.

Justice Jargon

British Intelligence is divided into two components. **MI-5,** responsible for domestic security, is similar to the FBI. **MI-6,** charged with foreign security and intelligence, is similar to the CIA.

Noticeably cool if not outright hostile to the spy hunt was Harold A. R. "Kim" Philby, in August 1949, a senior officer who'd been appointed MI-6's man in Washington, serving as official liaison to both the CIA *and* the FBI. A joint CIA/MI-6 operation headed by Philby, involving the infiltration of rebels to fight Albania's Communist government, soon came to grief, with the infiltrators being rolled up and executed almost as soon as they were parachuted into the country. Philby blamed lax security at the other end in the Mediterranean staging area.

In August 1950, the British Foreign Office (similar to the U.S. State Department), posted Guy Burgess as second secretary to its Washington embassy. Burgess was dissolute, disheveled, drunk, and often aggressively insulting—traits that should have made him unsuitable even for a diplomatic corps that prided itself on a tolerance for eccentricity. He and Philby seemed to be great friends, with Burgess rooming in the Philby family home, though not without frequent threats of eviction from his long-suffering host.

As the hunt for the 1944 embassy spy intensified, Burgess's behavior grew steadily more erratic, culminating in his May 1951 recall in disgrace to Britain. On the weekend beginning Friday, May 25, Burgess met with Foreign Office diplomat, Donald

Maclean. An influential member of the Establishment, Maclean was also the prime suspect in the embassy spy case. Together, he and Burgess disappeared, fleeing the country, ultimately surfacing in Moscow. In 1953, Maclean's wife defected to Russia, taking her young children with her.

Decades would pass before the full story would be known; no doubt parts of it are still classified. It turned out that Burgess and Maclean were members of the Cambridge spy ring, one of Soviet Intelligence's all-time master stratagems. As in the United States, a marked number of college undergraduates displayed communist sympathies in Britain during the Depression. Soviet spymasters developed a plan to infiltrate the upper ranks of the British government by recruiting idealistic young misfits of promise as deep cover penetration agents, who would burrow into the hierarchy from within, rising to positions of power and prestige while secretly serving Moscow Center's controllers.

The ring, founded in the 1930s at England's prestigious Cambridge University, included such celebrated alumni as Burgess and Maclean, both of whom had been continuously working for Moscow since before World War II. By lineage and position, both had impeccable upper-class credentials that protected them from suspicion. Yet Maclean had been the British embassy spy, while Burgess had committed espionage at his Foreign Office posts.

Their defection sent British officialdom into shock, but that was not the end of it. A persistent rumor indicated the presence of a "third man," an as-yet-unrevealed traitor who had tipped off Burgess and Maclean that the spy hunters were closing in. FBI counterintelligence officers believed that the traitor was MI-6 senior officer Kim Philby. British Intelligence scoffed at the charges, calling them "McCarthyist," a reference to Senator Joe McCarthy, the demagogic Red-baiter whose accusations of treason in high places were usually flat-out wrong.

The FBI insisted, however, freezing out Philby and keeping up the pressure until he was recalled from his Washington post. Even then, the British not only refused to charge him with espionage, but Philby continued on in other duties in the organization. Not until his defection to Russia in 1963 was Philby unmasked as the Third Man and a linchpin of the Cambridge spy ring.

There was more information to come, including the existence of a Fourth Man publicly revealed in the 1980s by British Prime Minister Margaret Thatcher. Thatcher identified the Royal Family's official art appraiser, internationally renowned art historian and scholar Sir Anthony Blunt, as a Cambridge ring Soviet spy and traitor. It has been credibly argued that, at the very least, Blunt had compromising information and a degree of control over wartime-and-after MI-5 head Sir Guy Liddell.

The Least You Need to Know

- The FBI's long-running program to plant informants and double agents in the CPUSA hierarchy culminated in the 1949 Foley Square trial convictions of the party's leadership.

- Crime of the Century: Nuclear physicist Klaus Fuchs stole U.S. atomic bomb secrets, passing them to the Rosenberg-Greenglass spy ring, which passed them to the Russians.

- The decoding operation codenamed "Venona" supplied FBI counterintelligence agents with numerous leads to Soviet espionage.

- FBI efforts led to the exposure of Burgess and Maclean and helped uncover Soviet double agent British intelligence official Kim Philby.

Chapter 9

The Mob

In This Chapter

- Modern origins of Underworld, USA
- Senate syndicate probes
- Apalachin: the last major Mafia convention
- Kennedy justice: JFK makes his brother attorney general
- Dangerous liaisons: CIA, Mafia, and the White House

During the twentieth century, organized crime consolidated itself on a nationwide basis, controlling both the vice trade and legitimate businesses. This chapter explores FBI Director Hoover's longtime policy of avoiding Bureau involvement in what he regarded as a local police matter and how he was forced to adapt to counter the syndicate's post–World War II high-profile inroads throughout American society. Appointed by President John Kennedy, Attorney General Robert Kennedy was a zealous anti-Mob crusader, even as his brother in the White House was conducting dangerous sexual and political liaisons with shady underworld characters.

Underworld Origins

In America, *organized crime* was in existence long before the twentieth century. In fact, by the Civil War era, New York City was infested by a multiplicity of violent criminal gangs sporting such picturesque names as the Hudson Dusters, the Dead Rats, and the Plug Uglies. There was nothing picturesque, however, about the intimidation, beatings, and killings dispensed wholesale by these groups. While the concentration of population, money, and power in the big cities provided an optimal growth medium for organized crime, rural areas were by no means immune to its spread.

Justice Jargon

Organized crime is criminal activity that runs on a systematic, businesslike basis. Generally, the driving engine of most organized crime is vice operations such as gambling, prostitution, and narcotics, while labor racketeering and extortion are also highly profitable. The chasm between what the law forbids and at least part of the public desires is the space where organized crime thrives.

By the start of the twentieth century, organized crime was well established throughout the United States. Two factors operated to expand it from a localized basis, where each city and town had its individual vice rackets, into a nationwide, interlinked crime syndicate. The first was the advent of the Mafia, an unfortunate byproduct of the wave of Southern Italian emigration to the United States, which began in the late 1800s. The criminal confederation known as the Mafia was a specifically Sicilian phenomenon, originating several hundred years earlier as a nativist response to various foreign occupation armies. Another Italian organization, the extortion racket called the Black Hand, came from the Italian mainland and used terrorist methods to exact tribute.

It must be stressed that organized crime is by no means a phenomenon solely associated with Italian Americans or Sicilian Americans, the overwhelming majority of whom are hardworking, law-abiding citizens. Today's national crime syndicate is made up of representatives of every ethnic group in America.

What the Mafia provided was an organizational template, a time-tested infrastructure and operating mode for a secret criminal fraternity securely embedded in a host society. It became the nucleus, the dominant central command and control structure of the national crime syndicate (NCS). For example, with his Neapolitan roots, Al Capone was unable to join the Mafia, yet his Mafia associates and allies were vital in his rise to the top of the Chicago rackets.

The second factor contributing to the explosive growth of organized crime was Prohibition. Against the law or not, alcohol consumption appealed to a majority of the American public, which wanted its alcohol and meant to have it. The public's need was eagerly filled by legions of bootleggers, speakeasies, and gangsters who had lots of help from corrupt cops and public officials. The immense profits generated by the illegal alcohol trade acted like steroids on the crime mobs, ballooning them to Goliath-like stature.

As early as 1929, top leaders of organized crime held a summit meeting in Atlantic City, New Jersey, to stem the headline-grabbing gang violence stemming from jurisdictional disputes. The repeal of Prohibition saw mobdom's finances take a major hit. In order to make up for lost bootleg revenues, the mob increased its extortion, labor racketeering, narcotics, and prostitution activities. In a kind of grotesque parody of the tendency of monopolies to arise in the business sector, the 1930s saw the Mafia-dominated national crime syndicate absorb other ethnic crime mobs and eliminate independent operators.

The founders of the national crime syndicate were New Yorkers Charles "Lucky" Luciano and Jewish gangster Meyer Lansky, who organized the rackets and put them on a businesslike basis. Ultimate enforcement of their dictates was provided by their murder-for-hire arm, nicknamed Murder Incorporated, headed by Lepke Buchalter and Albert Anastasia. Other important associates were Frank Costello, Abner "Longy" Zwillman, and Lansky's lieutenant, Benjamin "Bugsy" Siegel.

Official and Confidential

Starting with Courtney Ryley Cooper's early to mid-1930s articles in *American Magazine*, J. Edgar Hoover put forth the proposition that big-time organized crime was actually a local law enforcement problem, one that occurred when local police failed to suppress the Dillingers and Capones in their towns. By this logic, the national crime problem was not a federal responsibility, except when federal laws were violated.

In the mid-1930s, the FBI gained its fame by taking down Midwest bandits, bank robbers, and kidnappers, such as Dillinger, Machine Gun Kelly, and Ma Barker's killer brood. During the second half of the decade, the key racket-buster was not Bureau Director Hoover but rather crusading New York City District Attorney Thomas E. Dewey, who in 1936 jailed top mobster Luciano for profiting from prostitution rackets. Ironically, a few years earlier, Luciano had saved Dewey's life by ordering the execution of gangster Dutch Schultz, who planned to have Dewey "hit." (This was done not out of tender-heartedness, but from fear that Dewey's murder would generate a law enforcement counterattack which would take down the Mob.)

During the prewar period, the only really significant action taken by the FBI against the national crime syndicate was in 1939, when Hoover accepted Lepke's surrender, a deal that the Mob had brokered behind the scenes to alleviate the Big Heat that Dewey was applying to them.

The burning by saboteurs of the ocean liner *Normandie* in New York harbor, which had been intended to serve as a troop ship, led to the founding of a shadowy alliance between U.S. military intelligence and the underworld. Known as Operation Underworld, it came about when go-betweens for the imprisoned Luciano contacted the Navy's ONI, offering to put their resources to work for the war effort in return for a reduction of Luciano's prison term. Similar contacts were made with Donovan's OSS. Gotham hoodlums guarded the waterfront from spies and saboteurs, while Mafia contacts paved the way for the Allied forces' successful invasion and occupation of wartime Sicily. In return for his services, Luciano was quietly released and deported to Italy at war's end.

Mob Baloney

World War II provided a much-needed shot in the arm for the Mob, restoring big-money revenues unseen since Prohibition. This increase in profits was due to wartime rationing of such vital items as red meat, gasoline, tires, nylon stockings, and the like. While the average citizen was given a limited quantity of ration cards and points toward the legitimate acquisition of such goods, gangsters reaped fortunes in black-market dealings of the commodities.

A prime syndicate component was the Chicago organization, known locally as the Outfit, whose power was revealed in the disturbing Ragen affair. In 1946, James Ragen owned a national wire racing service, which provided current, real-time information about the lineup and gambling odds at all major U.S. race tracks, an invaluable service to illegal off-track betting bookmakers ("bookies") who subscribed to the service. The Outfit moved in on the operation, demanding that he sell.

Cops and Robbers

Continental Wire Service boss James Ragen's three assailants, initially identified as Chicago gunmen Lenny Patrick, Dave Yaras, and William Block, were never brought to trial. Regarded as mobdom's killer elite of the period, the trio are also believed to have been the killers of Lansky lieutenant Benjamin "Bugsy" Siegel in June 1947. Siegel was the man who "invented" Las Vegas as the nation's premier gambling capital.

Ragen contacted the FBI, whose agents confidentially interviewed him over a period of weeks, obtaining important information not only about the Chicago Outfit, but about national crime-syndicate personalities and operations. Once Ragen had been wrung dry, however, J. Edgar Hoover refused to supply him bodyguards. Somehow, mobsters learned that Ragen had been cooperating with the FBI and shot him down on a Chicago street. Surviving the attempt, Ragen was fatally poisoned while later recovering in a police-guarded hospital room. FBI investigations into Chicago mobdom ceased.

Around Christmas 1946, a horde of top mobsters traveled from Miami to Havana to show obeisance to deported chief Lucky Luciano, who'd sneaked into Cuba. Holding court at the Nacional hotel, Luciano met with his underlings to lay plans for an accelerated program of smuggling narcotics into the United States. Providing entertainment at the conclave was singer Frank Sinatra.

Learning of the meeting were Federal Bureau of Narcotics agents, whose boss, Harry J. Anslinger, acknowledged the existence and strength of the national crime syndicate as vigorously as J. Edgar Hoover publicly belittled it. Using his own U.S. newspaper contacts, Chief Anslinger publicized the summit, which forced the Cuban government to arrest Luciano and deport him back to Italy.

Still, for the next decade (as he'd done for the previous two), Hoover continued to proclaim the nonexistence of the national crime syndicate, declaring that no "coalition of racketeers" dominated organized crime. One government report postulating the existence of a nationwide Mob was labeled by a publicly scoffing Hoover as

"baloney." Another time, he characterized believers in a national crime syndicate as people "who spend too much time watching 'Mister District Attorney'" (a then-popular TV crime program).

Truman administration Attorney General McGrath also held this position, stating that the Justice Department had no evidence of the existence of said syndicate. He made this statement on the eve of the May 1950 Senate Special Committee hearings to investigate organized crime in interstate commerce.

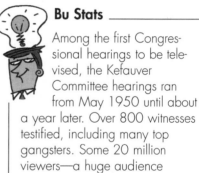

Bu Stats

Among the first Congressional hearings to be televised, the Kefauver Committee hearings ran from May 1950 until about a year later. Over 800 witnesses testified, including many top gangsters. Some 20 million viewers—a huge audience share—watched the proceedings.

Known as the Kefauver Committee after its chairman Tennessee Democratic Senator Estes Kefauver, the probers were forced to proceed without FBI help, instead relying on the cooperation and detailed files of Anslinger's Federal Bureau of Narcotics, as well as on a number of big-city Crime Commissions. Two Committee witnesses were murdered shortly before they were due to testify. J. Edgar Hoover told the committee that organized crime was a problem for local police, not the FBI.

The electrifying hearings concluded, "There is a nationwide crime syndicate known as the Mafia" that controls the most lucrative rackets through political influence, bribery, intimidation, and murder. As much as two years later, FBI Assistant Director Alan Belmont wrote in a 1953 memo that the Mafia was an "alleged organization" whose existence in the United States was "doubtful."

In 1954, a Senate investigating committee began investigating irregularities in the procurement of military uniforms. A tip on Mob infiltration of the mighty Teamsters Union led to the formation of a special Senate Permanent Subcommittee on Investigations. Popularly known as the Senate Rackets Committee, chaired by Senator John McClellan, and with anticrime crusader Robert F. Kennedy as its general counsel, the committee conducted a long-term investigation of labor racketeering. The McClellan Committee found that the Mafia, organized under military lines, and run by a national commission, generated an annual income of billions of dollars.

Kennedy's efforts led to the jailing of Teamsters President Dave Beck, a fate which Kennedy fully intended for Beck's successor, James R. Hoffa. The feud between the self-righteous Senate counsel and the tough Teamsters' proxy quickly reached white-heat and stayed there throughout their long duel into the 1960s.

Yet Justice Department prosecutions were few, and convictions fewer, as the FBI continued to maintain its laissez-faire policy toward the syndicate. Then and now, the Bureau's hands-off attitude toward organized crime remains one of the enduring mysteries of Hoover's directorship. Why this puzzling ineffectuality?

One reason may be that fighting the syndicate was a tough, dirty job that would yield no easy victories or headlines. In every major U.S. city, the Mob was (and is) an integral part of the power structure. To take it on meant trying to effect a change in the basic fabric of American society, as well as making a horde of powerful enemies in the business, law enforcement, and political sectors. It entailed the possible risk of agents being suborned and corrupted with big Mob money. Failing in a public effort to eradicate a possibly ineradicable social problem might negatively affect the FBI's public image. And the Bureau's crime stats would go down.

It's understandable that Hoover might shirk from the task, but to maintain for so long and in the face of such massive evidence to the contrary that there was no such thing as the syndicate seems at best counterproductive and at worst perverse.

Apalachin Outing

The year 1957 was turbulent for the New York City branch of the Mafia, the tumult largely caused by crime boss Vito Genovese's bid for supreme power. Rival Frank Costello was shot in the lobby of his Central Park apartment, sustaining only a grazing head wound. Albert Anastasia, former "Lord High Executioner" of Murder, Incorporated, brutal boss of the docks, and Costello's protector, was executed by gunmen as he sat in a barber's chair in the Park Sheraton Hotel.

On the morning of Saturday, November 14, 1957, in the outskirts of bucolic Apalachin, New York, a village located near the Pennsylvania state line, New York State Trooper Edgar Croswell noticed a number of black limousines arriving at the isolated estate of Joseph Barbara Sr. The appearance of one such vehicle in the little country town would have been unusual; a convoy of such was bizarre. Running a check on Barbara, Croswell learned that the soft-drink distributor had a gun permit and had been arrested (though not convicted) twice in Pennsylvania on murder charges.

No laws having been violated, Croswell was unable to enter the property. He staked out the entrance to the estate, joined by a backup unit of three local deputies. A deliveryman making a stop at the premises remarked that the police were setting up a roadblock outside. This triggered a mass exodus of about 60 of the estate's hundred-odd guests, while another 40 remained safely inside.

Those who fled were stopped by police and detained until they identified themselves, whereupon they were released. The list of those in attendance read like a Who's Who of mobdom, although each maintained that they were respectable businessmen who'd come to enjoy a barbecue thrown by their mutual friend, Joe Barbara. What it looked like to law enforcement personnel was a top-level Mafia convention. It was the last such massive Mob gathering ever held, not surprisingly, in view of the outcome.

> **Cops and Robbers**
>
> Among those detained and identified at Apalachin (63 in all) were representatives of New York City's five top crime "families," including Vito Genovese and Joe Bonanno; and other top Mafiosi such as Stefano Maggadino (Buffalo), Joe Zerilli (Detroit), Joe Civello (Dallas), Santos Trafficante (Miami), and many others.

In the aftermath of Apalachin, no one, not even J. Edgar Hoover, could continue to deny the existence of the Mafia. To say that the revelation/exposure was an embarrassment to the Bureau would be an understatement. It was a public relations debacle. Worse, the nimble spin-doctoring services of longtime FBI publicity chief Lou Nichols were no longer available. Not long before the Mafia meeting, Nichols had retired from the FBI to become the publicity chief of Schenley's whiskey distillery, owned by multimillionaire Lewis Rosenstiel (whom a 1970 New York State Crime Commission linked to organized crime).

McClellan Committee chief counsel Robert Kennedy barged into the Bureau, demanding everything they had in the files on those identified at Apalachin. Deriding the lack of information on the top mobsters, he went to Anslinger's Federal Bureau of Narcotics, where he received massive dossiers on each hoodlum.

With brother Bobby (second from right) and J. Edgar Hoover (center) looking on, President John F. Kennedy signs Anti-Racketeering Bill.

(Courtesy of Corbis)

William Sullivan, then-chief of Research and Analysis, was put in charge of preparing a study on the Mafia. In late 1958, the two-volume monograph was completed, its readership restricted to members of the FBI.

Within ten days of the Apalachin incident, the FBI instituted its Top Hoodlum Program, requiring each field office to identify the top ten hoodlums in its jurisdiction. Information collected by agents soon began streaming, then flooding, into headquarters.

Much of that information was collected via electronic surveillance devices, microphonic "bugs" and telephone taps. One of the most productive bugs in law enforcement history was that installed by a Chicago FBI anti-Mob squad led by Special Agent William F. Roemer. A surreptitious entry allowed agents to plant the single-microphone bug in a second-floor tailor shop where Chicago's top mobsters such as Sam "Momo" Giancana, Murray "the Camel" Humphreys, and Tony "Tuna" Accardo met to hatch out their schemes. The nicknames may sound comical but there was nothing funny in the way the Outfit had its tentacles deep into every corner of the city's business, political, and police infrastructure. In the five years in which the bug was operational, the listeners amassed an encyclopedic amount of knowledge about how the Mob ran Chicago.

Other highly productive bugs were installed in a favorite Mob eatery, a political ward headquarters building, even Giancana's home. A particularly valuable session was one in which Giancana held forth to his associates about the make-up and membership of The Commission, the national crime syndicate's ruling board, a subject on which Giancana could speak with some authority, being himself a Commission member.

Bu Stats

Internal sanitizing of the appropriate documents make it difficult to calculate how many of the FBI's electronic intelligence bugs on the Mafia were in use. The best estimate is that there were at least a thousand bugs operating at one time, and probably more.

Information gained from the Chicago bugs would ultimately play a major role in a high-stakes showdown between J. Edgar Hoover and President John F. Kennedy, but that would come later.

High Rollers

The post-Apalachin anti-Mob onslaught ran out of steam as the 1950s straggled to their end, resulting in few if any major convictions against syndicate bosses or any real curtailment of their operations. In New York City in 1959, four hundred agents were assigned to monitor communists, while only four were assigned to cover organized crime.

In official Washington, D.C., and not least in the upper ranks at FBIHQ, attention focused on the upcoming 1960 Presidential election. Having served two terms, Eisenhower was leaving office. The prime GOP contender was Vice President Richard M. Nixon, while the leading Democratic candidates were Massachusetts Senator John F. Kennedy and Texas Senator (and Senate Majority Leader) Lyndon Johnson. J. Edgar Hoover's interests would best be served by Nixon's election. If it had to be a Democrat, he preferred that it be Johnson, who was Hoover's neighbor and more than friendly acquaintance.

Leaving nothing to chance, former Ambassador Joseph P. Kennedy used his longtime Mob connections to better Senator Kennedy's chances of winning the Democratic nomination. Transcripts of FBI wiretaps and eyewitness statements confirm that he carried out this strategy.

The Mafia hated Robert Kennedy, and would have cause to do so in the future. No reformer himself, John F. Kennedy lacked his younger brother's zeal for prosecuting mobsters and labor racketeers. Old Joe Kennedy, with his high-level syndicate connections, stood as surety against any such inclination his older son might have had, assuring them that all would be well if JFK were elected. He met with his son Robert's pet enemy, Teamsters boss Jimmy Hoffa, thereby attempting to ease Hoffa's misgivings about a Kennedy presidency.

Most important to clinching the party's presidential nod was money. That was something the elder Kennedy had plenty of, but there was a limit to how much he could legitimately funnel to JFK's campaign. An FBI wiretap of a conversation between Chicago mobster Sam Giancana and associated Mafioso Johnny Rosselli caught the two complaining about how much money they'd had to "contribute" to a JFK vote-buying operation during the West Virginia primary (which JFK won).

At the 1960 Democratic convention, John Kennedy won the presidential nomination on the first ballot. In a compromise bid to avoid alienating the south, he chose as his vice presidential running mate, Texas Senator Lyndon B. Johnson.

Official and Confidential

John F. Kennedy, who disliked Lyndon Johnson, told family retainer Kenneth O'Donnell, "I'm 43 years old. I'm not going to die in office. So the vice presidency doesn't mean anything." For his part, Johnson observed to Claire Boothe Luce, "One out of every four presidents has died in office. I'm a gambling man, and this is the only chance I got."

Election night was a real nail-biter, going down to the wire. The two candidates were neck-and-neck, until late returns from Chicago's Cook County nudged JFK past Nixon into the winner's columns. FBI wiretaps monitored unsuspecting Chicago vote-fixers in the process of tilting the election. A second wave of suspect Kennedy votes materialized in Texas, home of vice presidential candidate Johnson, whose first election to the Senate in 1948 had similarly been clinched by suspect balloting.

Many of those in the GOP's upper hierarchy urged Nixon to contest the election on the basis of these suspect returns. Nixon declined to do so, fearing that a prolonged and acrimonious court challenge would dangerously divide the country at a critical time in the Cold War, threatening the national security. Not until 15 years later, when Theodore White, respected political reporter and author of the acclaimed *Making of the President* series, documented the facts in his book *Breach of Faith*, was the American public made aware of the fact that JFK stole the 1960 election. The much-maligned Nixon's statesmanlike act of not

Bu Stats

In the 1960 presidential election between John F. Kennedy and Richard M. Nixon, 68 million votes were cast, with Kennedy winning with a margin of fewer than 120,000 votes.

contesting that theft has thus far earned him zero credit with his media detractors and Camelot standard-bearers.

Nixon conceded. The day after the election, President-elect Kennedy announced that his first two appointments (reappointments, actually) of his administration would be Allen Dulles as Director of CIA and J. Edgar Hoover as Director of the FBI.

Mr. Attorney General

Obeying the urgings of Joe Kennedy, President Kennedy made the controversial decision to appoint his brother Robert Kennedy as attorney general. Before accepting the appointment, Robert Kennedy went through the motions of visiting J. Edgar Hoover and asking him for his advice. Hoover told him that it was a good job and that he should take it, though later confiding to his lieutenant William Sullivan, "I didn't like to tell him that, but what could I say?"

Kennedy took the job of attorney general, becoming Hoover's (nominal) boss, a relationship marked by friction from Day One, swiftly ripening into mutual animosity and deep hostility on both sides. Exacerbating the tension was Kennedy's determination to put the Justice Department back full-tilt into the racket-busting business, which Hoover took as a slap against the credibility and competence of the FBI and its director. Kennedy quadrupled the staff and budget of the department's Organized Crime Section. The FBI's New York City field office's complement of a dozen agents covering organized crime was boosted to 115 men, while the Chicago office's anti-Mob squad jumped from six agents to 80.

Attorney General Robert Kennedy attacked the national crime syndicate with the energy, imagination, and righteous fury with which young J. Edgar Hoover had attacked communists, anarchists, and subversives back in 1919. Statistics told the tale. In 1960, the Justice Department had indicted 19 members of organized crime. In 1961, 121 were indicted, with 96 convictions.

Official and Confidential

During a July 12, 1961, encounter with FBI agents at Chicago's O'Hare Airport, Sam Giancana (accompanied by his girlfriend, singer Phyliss McGuire) unleashed a profanity-drenched tirade, telling Special Agent William Roemer, "I know all about the Kennedys, and Phyliss knows more about the Kennedys, and one of these days we're going to tell all. F— you! One of these days it'll all come out!"

A prime target was Chicago crime boss Sam Giancana, who became the recipient of the Justice Department's own version of the Big Heat. In addition to being bugged and wiretapped at his headquarters and home, he was also put under high-profile "lockstep" surveillance, with FBI agents literally following on his heels, day and night. Claiming that agents were tailing him so closely that his golf game was suffering, Giancana got a court order mandating that agents shadowing him on the golf course must remain at least two foursomes behind him.

Whether he knew it or not, Robert Kennedy's moves against Giancana were directed against a powerful, violent hoodlum who believed that his efforts had put the attorney general's brother, John Kennedy, into the White House. More, Giancana and the president shared not only a mistress, but also the deadly secret of an assassination plot against the leader of a foreign country. As Giancana had threatened, it would all come out—with potentially lethal consequences.

The Least You Need to Know

- The Sicilian-born Mafia is the controlling element of the national crime syndicate, whose total membership includes criminal gangs representing all ethnic groups in American society.

- FBI bugs and wiretaps on Chicago's Giancana-headed Outfit generated massive information on the national crime syndicate, including the existence and membership of its ruling Commission.

- The 1957 gathering of the nation's top crime bosses in Apalachin, New York, conclusively proved the existence of the Mafia.

- Mob money and vote-fixing directly led to the 1960 election of President John Kennedy.

- Attorney General Robert Kennedy's zealous anticrime crusade put him on a collision course with the Mafia.

Chapter 10

Coming Apart: The 1960s

In This Chapter

- ◆ The FBI learns of CIA/Mafia assassination plots
- ◆ J. Edgar Hoover versus the Kennedys
- ◆ Mobster Joe Valachi's televised tell-all Mafia testimony
- ◆ President Kennedy is assassinated in Dallas, Texas
- ◆ Lone nut or conspiracy?—the Warren Commission versus House Special Assassination Committee

From 1960 to 1963, high-level elements of the CIA and the Mafia conspired to assassinate Cuban communist dictator Fidel Castro. FBI electronic surveillance operations discovered that President Kennedy shared a girlfriend and more with Mafia crime boss Sam Giancana. At the same time, Attorney General Robert Kennedy was trying to send Giancana to jail. Confronting the president, Hoover convinced him to sever his Mob liaisons.

This chapter reveals how white supremacists, Mafiosi, and anti-Castro Cuban extremists threatened JFK's life in the months leading up to November 22, 1963, when Kennedy was assassinated. Appointed by President Johnson, the Warren Commission found that Lee Harvey Oswald was the lone assassin. Others aren't so sure.

Hoover–Kennedy Capers

Hoover was used to getting his way with attorneys general. The last one he'd had serious trouble with was FDR's Attorney General Robert Jackson back in the early 1940s. He'd had his differences with Truman's attorneys general, but he'd always held the upper hand. His relations with Eisenhower's two AGs, Herbert Brownell and William Rogers, couldn't have been more cordial or mutually harmonious.

Robert Kennedy was something else. Neither Hoover nor anybody else had worked for an AG whose brother was the president; the arrangement was unprecedented in the history of the Republic. (Since then, antinepotism laws have been passed to prevent such a repeat occurrence, which is why Jeb Bush is unable to serve in brother George W.'s cabinet.) Multiplying the tension between Hoover and Kennedy was the latter's personality, described by admirers as "hard-charging" and by detractors as "abrasive."

Official and Confidential

Attempting to assert his dominance, Attorney General Robert Kennedy installed a "hot-line" phone in Hoover's private office, insisting that it be placed on Hoover's desk. Kennedy harrumphed, "When I pick up this phone, there's only one man I want to talk to." The phone remained in place throughout the administration's tenure.

Add to that the generation gap: Hoover, 66, had become Bureau director in 1924, one year before Robert Kennedy, 35, was born, a fact that FBI tour guides liked to point out to visitors until the AG's office prohibited them from doing so. A major theme of John Kennedy's presidential campaign was the derisive comparison of Eisenhower's "old, tired" administration with the youth and vigor of the Kennedy team.

Like other Presidents before (and after) him, JFK wanted to replace Hoover with his own man, but lacked the power to do so. Hoover had too much detrimental information on the entire Kennedy clan. In addition to his knowledge of how vote fraud had affected the outcome of the 1960 Presidential election, and his extensive files on Joseph P. Kennedy's Nazi appeasement and Mob business ties, Hoover had plenty of material on JFK's amatory indiscretions.

John Kennedy liked women and vice versa. The first of his indiscretions to become a matter of national security dated back to the early years of World War II, when as a lieutenant posted to Naval Intelligence in Washington, D.C., young Kennedy conducted a sexual liaison with Inga Arvad, a Danish beauty contest winner who'd been the toast of what passed for Third Reich high society, friendly with the likes of Hitler and Göring. FBI-bugged hotel rooms caught Kennedy discussing military matters during pillow talk with his paramour. No evidence was found indicating Arvad was passing information to German intelligence, but she still qualified as a security risk. Not long after, Kennedy was transferred to the Pacific, where he gained fame for his exploits as the commander of PT-109, the only PT-boat ever to be rammed and sunk by the Japanese navy.

During his postwar political career, Kennedy's marriage proved no impediment to his numerous extracurricular affairs. What raises these sexual interludes from being mere bedroom gossip is that several of them affected not only Kennedy's administration, but the course of American history (and by extension, world history) itself.

President Kennedy's most potentially explosive dangerous liaison was with Judith Campbell. In February 1960, at Las Vegas's Sands Hotel, then-Senator Kennedy was introduced to Campbell by none other than superstar singer (and then–JFK booster) Frank Sinatra. Campbell, whose several White House visits and frequent phone calls (70 between 1960 and 1962) are documented on official logs, also appears on FBI bugs and wiretaps of Chicago's Mafia Commission kingpin, Sam Giancana.

> **Cops and Robbers**
>
> Divorced wife of a mid-level Hollywood actor, Judith Campbell was a strikingly attractive brunette who in the early 1960s carried on simultaneous affairs with Chicago's top mobster Sam Giancana, Mob-connected singer Frank Sinatra, and President John Kennedy. Campbell also served as a go-between for the two men during the abortive CIA-Mafia plot to kill Cuban communist dictator Fidel Castro.

To Kill Castro

Located 90 miles offshore from the United States, Cuba had been a centerpiece of Mafia activity for decades. By the mid-1950s, the Mafia controlled Havana's high-rolling casinos and the lucrative vice trade in narcotics and prostitution. In 1959, after toppling Mafia-friendly dictator Fulgencio Batista, triumphant insurgent Fidel Castro revealed his true colors as a devout Marxist-Leninist, transforming Cuba into a communist tyranny and client state of the Soviet Union. Among the American businesses he nationalized were the Mob's casino and vice holdings, inflicting losses of hundreds of millions of dollars on the syndicate's balance sheets.

Reasoning that the Mafia certainly had reason to want Castro dead, top CIA officials entered into a kill-Castro plot with top Mafiosi. Super-*spook* Robert Maheu, a former FBI agent who'd served in the Bureau's SIS division in World War II and had later formed his own private investigations agency, made overtures to Giancana, West Coast mobster Johnny Rosselli, and Miami crime lord Santos Trafficante, who'd suffered the indignity of being jailed by Castro for a few months.

The CIA/Mafia plot to kill Castro is best seen as a linchpin of U.S. efforts to liberate Cuba by landing an invasion force of anti-Castro Cuban exiles. Begun late in the Eisenhower administration, the secret invasion plan was continued by JFK. The assassination of Castro on the eve of the invasion would have destabilized and demoralized the Cuban communists, creating conditions favorable to the seaborne invaders establishing a beachhead in the critical opening hours of the operation.

Justice Jargon

In the argot of the intelligence community, a **spook** is a spy or similar clandestine operator. The ghostly, elusive nature of secret agents notwithstanding, one theory of the term's origin is that it derives from the Yale University secret society, Skull and Bones, a number of whose members held top posts in OSS and CIA. (George H. W. Bush and George W. Bush are both Bonesmen.)

Official and Confidential

On December 11, 1961, J. Edgar Hoover presented Attorney General Robert Kennedy with transcripts of mobster Sam Giancana discussing his buying of pro-JFK votes in West Virginia's presidential primary. On December 19, patriarch Joseph P. Kennedy suffered a debilitating stroke that paralyzed his right side and left him unable to speak. He would live like this for another eight years.

The CIA/Mafia dealings peaked during the period from August 1960 through April 1961, as part of the run up to the scheduled invasion. While there's no doubt that the Mafia wanted Castro dead, the seriousness of their efforts on behalf of the plot is open to question. However, totally committed do-or-die efforts by anti-Castro Cuban exiles were uniformly foiled by Castro's intelligence service, resulting in execution or long prison terms for the conspirators.

The April 17, 1961 invasion of Cuba has become known as the Bay of Pigs, taking its name from the landing site (Playa de Giron) where the anti-Castro Cuban freedom fighters of Brigade 2506 fought to establish a beachhead. Castro had not been assassinated and directed the island defenses. A key component of the plan called for U.S. air strikes to take out Cuba's Soviet-supplied MIG jet fighters. After green-lighting the invasion, however, President Kennedy got cold feet, canceling the second wave of air strikes. This left Castro's air force standing, freeing it to wreak havoc on the invasion force, sinking its boats and strafing and bombing Brigade 2506's troops which were already on the beach.

The result was one of the most disgraceful episodes in modern U.S. history. Several thousand anti-Castro Cuban patriots, who had trusted the U.S. government, were betrayed and left to die. Those not killed outright on the beaches were taken prisoner, with hundreds being executed within the next 48 hours and hundreds more locked up in Castro's political prisons.

Ultimately, responsibility for the debacle lay with President Kennedy, who instead hung the blame on the CIA, firing the agency's director Allen Dulles. More determined than ever to eliminate Castro, Kennedy continued the assassination conspiracy and his affair with Judith Campbell. Perhaps because he'd lost confidence in the CIA, Kennedy dealt directly with Giancana, using Campbell as a courier to deliver at various times some 20 sealed envelopes to Giancana. This at the time when his brother, the attorney general, was doing his best to put Giancana in jail.

Oval Office Showdown

An eyeball-to-eyeball stare down between two superpowers who loathe and have the power to destroy each other. No, that's not a description of the face-off between the United States and the Soviet Union during the Cuban Missile Crisis of October, 1962, though it could be. Here, though, it pertains to the March 22, 1962, showdown between J. Edgar Hoover and President Kennedy.

For several months, rumors had been buzzing that Kennedy intended to fire and replace Hoover. On March 22, answering Kennedy's summons to the White House, Hoover arrived for a lunch with the President that stretched into a four-hour meeting. Hoover went into the meeting armed with the knowledge of Kennedy's affair with Judith Campbell and his dealings with Sam Giancana, including the ongoing kill-Castro plot. These were merely the big guns in his arsenal of documented Kennedy infidelities and improprieties.

What transpired between the two of them at that meeting is unknown. What is known, however, is that when a visibly distressed Kennedy ended the meeting, so ended all talk of replacing Hoover during this term.

Cops and Robbers

Born in Hoboken, New Jersey, superstar singer Frank Sinatra had career-long links to the Mob. A big JFK booster (he sang the campaign's theme song), Sinatra had a helicopter landing pad built at his West Coast house, anticipating frequent presidential visits. When JFK abruptly canceled his March 1962 weekend visit, an enraged Sinatra, in one of the most hyperbolic real-life scenes in American show business history, took a sledgehammer to the helipad, demolishing it.

After that March 22 meeting, Kennedy ended all telephone calls from the White House to Campbell, though the affair continued through the summer of 1962. Kennedy also canceled a planned weekend visit with Frank Sinatra, using his actor brother-in-law Peter Lawford to deliver the bad news. Adding insult to injury, JFK instead stayed at the home of rival crooner Bing Crosby (a Republican). The Kennedys subsequently cut off contact from Sinatra, wounding and embittering the cast-off crooner.

Run-Up to Dallas

In 1963, serious threats to kill President Kennedy were being voiced by three groups being monitored by the FBI: Southern white supremacists, the Mafia, and anti-Castro Cuban exiles living in the Miami area.

JFK and Civil Rights

Despite their bold public rhetoric on the subject, the Kennedy brothers had no great desire to rock the boat when it came toward pushing for full civil rights for black Americans. Black people, though, weren't taking direction from the White House but instead were forging ahead to secure their constitutionally guaranteed rights. Using sit-ins, protest marches, and similar nonviolent protest tactics, the civil rights movement confronted the white Southern power structure to demand voting rights and desegregation.

This triggered a counter-reaction of raw violence, race hatred, and terrorism. In the states of the deep South, the Ku Klux Klan and related hate groups physically attacked civil rights demonstrators while local police looked on approvingly, moving in afterward to arrest the beaten, brutalized victims. Police violence in Birmingham and Selma, Alabama, antiblack riots at the University of Mississippi, and other outbursts caused President Kennedy to call in the FBI and federal troops to restore order. Seeing their white supremacist way of life being threatened by the man in the White House, violent Southern extremist hate groups seethed and plotted.

Mob Pressure

Long accustomed to federal law enforcement indifference to its activities, the Mafia was first stunned, then enraged by the pressure suddenly being exerted against it by Robert Kennedy's newly energized Justice Department. Led by former FBI agent Walter Sheridan, the Attorney General's "Get Hoffa" squad of lawyers and investigators hit Teamsters boss Jimmy Hoffa hard. In the summer of 1962, Hoffa complained to a close associate that Robert Kennedy "has got to go," then described how he could be murdered while riding in an open car by a sharpshooter armed with a high-powered scoped rifle. The associate, Grady Partin, became an FBI informant.

Justice Department agents hustled New Orleans Mafia chief Carlos Marcello on to an airplane that took a one-way trip to Guatemala, marooning him there, leaving him to his own devices to return to the United States. Although the deportation was of questionable legality, the fact that he was not a native-born U.S. citizen paved the way. Marcello told an intimate that Robert Kennedy would be taken care of: not by an attempt made on his life, but by assassinating his brother, the President.

Notoriously short-tempered Sam Giancana fumed and writhed under relentless FBI surveillance of him, his family, and his associates, making it impossible for the mobster to make any money. Especially galling to Giancana was his belief that he'd helped put John Kennedy in the White House, and that his kill-Castro efforts should have brought him a certain amount of immunity from federal law enforcement "harassment."

Beginning in June 1962, Joseph Valachi, a drug dealer, killer, and member of Vito Genovese's New York City crime family, turned federal informant. FBI SA James P. Flynn convinced Valachi to tell all about his life and times in the Mafia. Valachi detailed Mob doings since the early 1930s, including descriptions of taking a blood oath when he became a "made" member of the Mafia, which means given full membership in the organization. In September 1963, Valachi's testimony at the Senate's McClellan Committee hearings were televised, creating a national sensation.

Wiretaps and bugs on top mobsters showed that they were paying close attention to the hearings. The most universal complaint made by his colleagues was not Valachi's testimony about the business of organized crime, but rather his depiction of the *mafia* initiation and the blood vows. A Florida mobster was overheard declaring, "There's going to be a lot of killings over this hearing."

Official and Confidential

In April 1963, New York City's Gambino crime family members badly beat FBI SA John P. Foley. J. Edgar Hoover stated, "For every man we lose, we make certain, through legal means of course, that the hoodlums lose the same number or more." The FBI put the Big Heat on mobdom in general, and the Gambino family in particular. Organized crime offered no further acts of violence against Bureau agents.

Justice Jargon

As revealed by the 1962 to 1963 testimony of Joe Valachi, members rarely use the term **mafia** to designate their organization. Generally, they refer to it as "our thing," or more formally, "this thing of ours"—in Italian, "La Cosa Nostra," often abbreviated in FBI reports as LCN.

Cuba Libre?

The October 1962 Cuban Missile Crisis between the United States and Soviet Union ended with an agreement by the Soviet Union to withdraw its missiles from Cuba. In return, the United States agreed not to invade Cuba. Efforts to keep the latter half of the agreement a secret failed when the anti-Castro exile community learned of it in the most direct way possible, as joint U.S. government–exile ventures against Cuba began to wither on the vine from lack of money, weapons, and the logistical support needed to sustain the venture.

When it came to prosecuting the struggle against Castro, the Cuban exile community wasn't taking direction from a White House that they saw as having "sold out" the cause. Centered in Miami's "Little Havana" community, the anti-Castro movement produced such gutsy freedom fighters as Tony Varona, Felix Rodriguez, Eugenio Martinez, Bernard "Macho" Barker, Tony Cuesta, and many others, aided by a colorful cadre of American adventurers including soldier of fortune Gary Patrick Hemming, oddball aviator Dave Ferrie, tough guy Frank Fiorini Sturgis, and New Orleans–based former top FBI agent Guy Banister, who'd formerly headed the Bureau's Chicago Red Squad. Risking imprisonment and death, paramilitary Cuban "*Gusano*" exile groups like Alpha 66 and Commandos L made daring nighttime motorboat runs and raids against Castro's Cuba.

Justice Jargon

Fidel Castro scorned the opposition anti-communist Cuban exile action groups, once publicly dismissing them as **gusanos,** a Spanish word meaning "worms." Taking the term to themselves as a badge of honor, anti-Castro activists proudly refer to themselves as Gusanos.

Fearing an international incident should the raiders target Soviet ships in Cuban harbors, the White House tried to suppress action-oriented anti-Castro groups. Seeing the power of the U.S. government being turned not against Castro, but rather against those who fought to free Cuba from communist tyranny, extremist exile leaders grew bitter, focusing their rage on President Kennedy. Undercover agents caught rumblings of an anti-JFK bomb plot planned for Kennedy's December 29, 1962, address to the Cuban community at Miami's Orange Bowl station. Under the hard glare of federal investigators' scrutiny, the plan evaporated.

In 1963, White House antipathy to the Gusanos hardened, with President Kennedy setting the FBI on the Cuban exile groups, breaking them up and closing them down. An FBI raid on an anti-Castro camp near New Orleans's Lake Pontchartrain unearthed a massive cache of CIA/Mafia-supplied weapons and explosives that had been stockpiled for use against Cuba's communist Fidelistas.

Crime of the Century III

In the fall of 1963, plans were made for President Kennedy to make an official visit to Texas, home state of Vice President Lyndon Baines Johnson. The trip was designed to help shore up Democratic support in the Lone Star State and to mend fences between top state Democrats Johnson, Governor John Connally, and Senator Ralph Yarborough. With the presidential election year of 1964 just over the horizon, it was a good time to start solidifying support in electoral vote–rich Texas, which had been narrowly prevented from going Republican in the last election by the vice presidential nomination of native son LBJ.

In addition to the forthcoming election, the imminent retirement of J. Edgar Hoover also loomed large. On January 1, 1965, at age 70, Hoover would have reached the mandatory retirement age for federal employees. President Kennedy would avoid the political heat that Hoover's firing would generate, simply by letting the process play out and easing him into retirement, allowing the second-term president-elect to nominate his own man for the supremely powerful post of FBI director.

Bu Stats

The FBI investigated three crimes (and solved two) considered by their contemporaries to be the Crime of the Century: the Lindbergh baby kidnapping, the theft of atom secrets by Soviet spies, and the JFK assassination.

Kennedy's Texas trip was scheduled for the latter part of November, one week before the Thanksgiving Day Weekend. On Friday, November 22, 1963, at midday, JFK and his wife Jacqueline Kennedy were taking part in a ceremonial motorcade in downtown Dallas, Texas. The president and first lady were riding in an open-top convertible Lincoln limousine with Texas Governor John Connally and his wife, Nelly. Vice President Johnson and his wife were riding in another limo several car lengths back in the procession.

Rounding the city's Dealey Plaza, at about 12:30 P.M. the motorcade turned off Commerce Street, making a left on to Elm Street. Cheering crowds lined the sidewalks.

Mrs. Connally turned to Kennedy, saying, "You can't say Dallas doesn't love you, Mr. President."

Shots rang out, unleashing the original American nightmare on Elm Street. Kennedy was shot in the throat, a follow-up shot causing the top of his head to explode. Governor Connally was also shot, sustaining multiple wounds. Connally cried, "My God, they are going to kill us all!"

Cops and Robbers

Originally from New Orleans, where his family had organized crime connections, Lee Harvey Oswald enlisted in the Marines, serving in Japan. Postservice, he defected to the Soviet Union in 1959, returning to the United States in 1962. While in custody at the Dallas police station as a suspect in the murder of JFK, Oswald said, "I'm just a patsy!"

Not long after, while lunching at home, an unsuspecting Robert Kennedy received a call from J. Edgar Hoover. Hoover said, "I have news for you. The president has been shot." Shaken, stunned, Kennedy inquired about the seriousness of the injury. "I think it's serious," Hoover said, promising to call back when he had more details.

At about that same time, in a New Orleans federal courtroom, crime boss Carlos Marcello was present at deportation hearings, as Justice Department lawyers argued for his expulsion from the United States. (Ultimately, the inconclusive proceeding ran out of steam and expired—Marcello was never deported.)

President John F. Kennedy was rushed to the emergency room of Dallas's Parkland Hospital, where he was pronounced dead at 1 P.M. Within a few hours, Dallas police arrested Lee Harvey Oswald, 24, as a suspect in the same-day shooting of police officer James Tippett. Initially charged only with the Tippett shooting, Oswald swiftly emerged as the prime suspect in the assassination of JFK.

Oswald was a strange bird, a high-profile oddball, a misfit. In the months before the assassination, his dealings and double-dealings with pro- and anti-Castro groups, and U.S. and Soviet intelligence agents, had been many and murky. At the time of JFK's death, he'd been working as an employee at the Texas School Book Depository building, which overlooked Elm Street. On the building's sixth floor, searchers had found what was believed to be the murder weapon, an Italian-made Mannlicher-Carcano rifle, which was later identified as belonging to Oswald.

Oswald had been arrested as a fugitive in connection with the slaying of Dallas patrolman Tippett, who'd been shot dead when stopping to question a suspicious person in the immediate aftermath of the presidential assassination. Within hours, evidence linking Oswald to the Kennedy killing began to emerge.

Oswald never went to trial. On Sunday morning, November 24, during his transfer from Dallas police headquarters to the County Jail, Oswald was shot dead by Jack Ruby, proprietor of the local Carousel Club, whose lineup of exotic dancers was much appreciated by the many Dallas police officers who frequented the place. Gambler, political fixer, and pay-off man, Ruby was originally from Chicago; among his chums were Dave Patrick, Lenny Yaras, and William Block, the syndicate's killer elite team believed to have murdered wire service owner James Ragen, gangster Bugsy Siegel, and many others.

Formed by President Lyndon Johnson to investigate the assassination, a high-level fact-finding commission headed by U.S. Supreme Court Chief Justice Earl Warren ultimately concluded that Lee Harvey Oswald was the lone assassin, that there had been no assassination conspiracy, and that Jack Ruby had killed Oswald out of a deluded attempt to "cleanse" the honor of Dallas.

In 1978, however, the House Select Committee on Assassinations decided that at least two persons had been involved in the killing of JFK. The conclusion was based on recordings of Dallas Police Department radio transmissions made in Dealey Plaza, which picked up the sound of two rifles being fired at the time of the assassination.

A leading proponent of the Oswald-acted-alone scenario, within 48 hours of the assassination, President Johnson expressed his fear of being killed and was grateful for the squadron of FBI agents temporarily assigned to augment his Secret Service guards. After his term as President, Johnson later told an interviewer that he thought Kennedy's death was the result of a conspiracy, a side effect of "some kind of damn Murder, Incorporated we were running in the Caribbean." He did not further expand on this cryptic reference, which may have alluded to the CIA/Mafia kill-Castro plots.

After the assassination, Robert Kennedy continued as LBJ's attorney general for another nine months, in a vastly diminished capacity. The next time the AG's hotline to Hoover rang, Hoover ignored it, saying, "Put that damn thing back on Miss Gandy's desk, where it belongs."

"Those people don't work for us anymore," Kennedy observed sadly to Justice Department intimates.

On May 8, 1964, in a ceremony honoring J. Edgar Hoover's fortieth year as head of FBI, President Johnson issued Executive Order 10682, waiving the compulsory retirement age and allowing him to continue as Bureau director. In the event, Hoover's tenure would outlast Johnson's, for within four years events would force Johnson to vacate the office without serving a second term.

The Least You Need to Know

- Elements of the CIA and the Mafia conspired to assassinate Cuban communist tyrant Fidel Castro.

- President Kennedy maintained dangerous connections with Chicago Mafioso Sam Giancana at the same time that his attorney general brother was trying to jail the mobster.

- On November 22, 1963, while in a motorcade in Dallas's Dealey Plaza, President Kennedy was fatally shot and Governor John Connally seriously wounded.

- The Warren Commission ruled that President Kennedy was shot by lone assassin and self-proclaimed Marxist Lee Harvey Oswald.

- In 1978, the House Select Committee on Assassinations concluded that at least two riflemen had been shooting at Kennedy in Dealey Plaza.

Chapter **11**

Civil Rights and Wrongs

In This Chapter

- ◆ FBI COINTELPRO operations apply wartime counterintelligence tactics to domestic foes
- ◆ J. Edgar Hoover's bitter personal feud with Martin Luther King Jr.
- ◆ The FBI's secret war against the KKK
- ◆ FBI responses to nationwide urban riots and antiwar protests
- ◆ War in Vietnam wrecks the presidency of Lyndon Johnson

The 1960s saw a major shift in FBI strategy and tactics, as the emphasis changed from investigations to counterintelligence programs aimed at domestic foes. The initial operations were applied to the Communist Party with great success. As the war in Vietnam expanded, America was rocked with urban rioting and civil disturbance. Some FBI operations were of dubious legality and they expanded to include such targets as the KKK, black militants, and the New Left. The Vietnam War brought down President Lyndon Johnson, while leaving J. Edgar Hoover in place as FBI Director.

All the Way with LBJ

Like Hoover, Democrat Lyndon Baines Johnson was a flawed giant. A consummate politician, a real-life incarnation of the back-slapping, deal-making power broker, masterful in the arts of flattery and arm-twisting, Johnson had been an extraordinarily successful Senate majority leader, adept at forging compromises needed to get legislation passed.

Official and Confidential

When he'd agreed to take the vice presidential spot on JFK's ticket, the move hadn't exactly been a blind leap of faith into the dark. Johnson was aware of Kennedy's chronic weakness, a case of Addison's disease (which affected the adrenals), which was kept secret from the voters lest it compromise the candidate's image of youth and vigor. LBJ knew there was a good chance that the disease would render JFK incapable of finishing out his term.

As things worked out, Kennedy's assassination made Johnson the 36th President of the United States. Johnson and FBI Director Hoover had a solid relationship as friends and neighbors, dating back almost 20 years. Both shared a mutual detestation for Robert Kennedy who, after serving for nine months as LBJ's lame-duck attorney general, left Washington to run for and win election as a New York senator in 1966.

Many Kennedy partisans (nicknamed New Frontiersmen), a number of them in cabinet-level positions, remained in the Johnson administration. Unsure of where their loyalties lay, Johnson was eager for each bit of information brought to him by Hoover.

Unlike his predecessor, Johnson had no overriding obsession about Communist Cuba. Under him, residentially-sponsored assassination plots against Castro ceased, though efforts continued to be unsuccessfully launched by elements of the intelligence community and anti-Castro Cubans.

The rock on which Johnson's presidency was wrecked was not Cuba but Vietnam. North Vietnam's communist government sponsored the Viet Cong insurgency that labored to overthrow the government of South Vietnam, a U.S. client state. In 1964, President Johnson, the Pentagon, and most congressmen believed that if South Vietnam was allowed to fall to the Communists, it would create a "domino" or spillover effect, causing the other governments in the region to also fall under communist regimes.

Congress's 1964 Tonkin Gulf resolution paved the way for massive U.S. military involvement in the Vietnam War, ultimately including the posting of hundreds of thousands of U.S. combat troops to the area. The war in Vietnam and racial conflicts at home would present the U.S. government in general and the FBI in particular with unprecedented challenges in the field of internal security, leading to official abuses with revelations that would rock the Bureau and nation.

COINTELPRO

By the mid-1950s, the FBI attacked the Communist Party USA by planting informers in the organization and decimating the leadership's upper and second-level echelons with Smith Act prosecutions and prison terms. These attacks brought the party to one of, if not the lowest, ebbs in its history.

At this time, certain Supreme Court decisions seemed to challenge the constitutionality of the Smith Act, ruling that party membership alone was not grounds for conviction, unless it was conjoined with an actual plan for violent revolution. With potential Smith Act convictions negated, and the party seemingly on its last legs, a plan to finish it off was devised by FBI leadership.

Thus was born the Counterintelligence Program, *COINTELPRO*. This proactive operation moved far beyond investigation to active disruption, to neutralize the targeted organization. Essentially, it used the active counterintelligence measures taken against the Nazi Party and other subversive groups during wartime, applying them against peacetime domestic foes.

Bu Stats

In 1955, CPUSA membership numbered about 22,000 members. In 1956, the Kremlin's revelation of Stalin's excesses, Soviet anti-Semitism, and the brutal suppression of the Hungarian revolt, brought party rolls down to fewer than 5,000 members, of whom about 1,500 were FBI informants.

Authorized by Hoover in August 1956, the initial program, COINTELPRO–CPUSA, aimed to create chaos and internal disruption of the CPUSA through a variety of harassment techniques, some of questionable legality. Among them were the use of anonymous phone calls and letters to set factions and members against each other. As always, sex was a weapon, and accusations of real (or imaginary) adulterous affairs helped poison members' feelings against each other. Other actions for sowing dissension and distrust included punitive IRS audits; high-profile questioning of co-workers, friends, and neighbors to establish that the suspect party member was under investigation; and the use of "snitch jackets," smearing loyal party members as FBI informants.

COINTELPRO–CPUSA, the original COINTELPRO operation, was also the longest lived (1956–1971) and the most extensive. During the Eisenhower administration, it was the sole such program up and running. After 1960, there would ultimately be some 12 FBI Counterplots, launched against such varied groups as the Socialist Workers Party and the KKK. But tactics that could be applauded when used against the likes of the KKK and the Black Panthers would prove less defensible when applied to nonviolent civil rights and antiwar protesters. In late June 1964, three civil rights workers, Goodman, Chaney, and Scherer, vanished under suspicious circumstances in Mississippi, triggering a national furor. President Johnson sent former CIA head Allen Dulles to the area on a fact-finding mission. Dulles came to two key conclusions: The Klan must be suppressed and the FBI presence in the area strengthened.

Justice Jargon

COINTELPRO (Counterintelligence Program) was an FBI operation using wartime counterintelligence techniques against peacetime domestic foes. Not an investigation, it was a pro-active operation designed to disrupt, harass, and ultimately neutralize the targeted operation from within.

Bu Stats

The FBI's COINTELPRO targeting the KKK averaged roughly 40 major anti-Klan actions per year through 1971, developed 2,000 informants (20 percent of Klan total membership), and penetrating the top 14 Klan organizations, preventing planned Klan violence and discovering numerous weapons caches.

Hoover personally appeared at the opening of the Bureau's field office in Jackson, Mississippi. The FBI's investigation, codenamed MIBURN (for "Mississippi Burning"), broke the case with an informant, leading agents to the dead bodies of the missing men and identifying 19 Klansmen as conspirators in the killing. Eight were convicted. Later that summer, the FBI launched a COINTELPRO to "expose, disrupt, and otherwise neutralize the KKK." Using the same tactics of deception, disinformation, and anonymous denunciations that had proved successful against the CPUSA, the FBI continued its secret war against the Klan, the American Nazi Party, and other white-hate groups through 1971.

Civil Wrongs

Despite the Klan-crushing operations of the Johnson presidency and beyond, the rude fact is that at best, J. Edgar Hoover was noticeably unsympathetic to the aspirations of black Americans. Bluntly, he could be called a racist. A product of turn-of-the-century Washington, D.C., when it had been a segregated Southern town, he had always viewed with suspicion black Americans' struggle for civil rights. For most of his career, his attitude had not been too far removed from the majority of his white fellow citizens, but from the mid-1950s on, Hoover was increasingly out of step with the rest of the country.

In 1957, Hoover successfully resisted Eisenhower's Attorney General Herbert Brownell's attempt to involve the FBI in enforcing voting rights laws and protecting nonviolent desegregation protesters. His policy of active disengagement met with less success during the Kennedy administration, when the president and the attorney general demanded protection for civil rights protesters victimized by conspiracies of local white racists, Klansmen, and corrupt local law enforcement agents. Hoover's interests lay more in trying to prove that the civil rights movement was a Communist front.

A Communist King?

Seeking to raise the profile of blacks in the Bureau, Robert Kennedy was dismayed to learn that there were only five black FBI agents and unaware that even those agents all served Hoover in some personal capacity as chauffeurs, butlers, and domestic servants. Hoover grudgingly agreed to double the total (to 10) by the end of 1962.

The FBI had been aware of Atlanta preacher's son and apostle of Gandhiesque nonviolence Martin Luther King Jr. from the time he'd first come into prominence as a civil rights leader in the mid-1950s. Not until the fall of 1962 did he incur J. Edgar Hoover's active enmity, when King gave an interview to *The New York Times* where he opined that the FBI was not doing enough to protect civil rights protesters in the South. Increased surveillance on King discovered that one of his key friends and advisors, Stanley Levison, was an ex-member of the CPUSA. Preying on the Kennedys' fears that their prestige would suffer if King should be proved to be Communist-influenced, Hoover got the attorney general to sign warrants authorizing the wiretapping of King in October 1963. In later years, these signed warrants would prove to be an embarrassment to Robert Kennedy's liberal supporters.

Official and Confidential

J. Edgar Hoover said that the three men he hated the most in the world were Quinn Tamm (nondeferential head of the International Association of Police Chiefs, and brother of the Bureau's former Number Three man, Ed Tamm), Robert Kennedy, and Dr. Martin Luther King Jr.

Extensive monitoring of King and his associates failed to find any evidence of secret Communist influence in the civil rights movement. This created tension between Hoover and the Bureau's Number Four man (after Hoover himself, Associate Director Tolson, and Crime Records head Cartha "Deke" DeLoach), Domestic Intelligence Division head William C. Sullivan. When Sullivan's division issued a

67-page report on Communist subversion of the civil rights movement, saying that they couldn't find any, Hoover was so angry that he stopped talking to Sullivan.

When All Else Fails ... Sex

Within a week, Sullivan reversed his field, memoing Hoover that King must be revealed to the nation as a "fraud, demagogue, and moral scoundrel." Hoover wrote that he was glad Sullivan's division had "seen the light," and resumed talking to Sullivan. In place of the Communist angle, a new club with which to beat King had presented itself: sex. Like JFK, King liked women and conducted a number of extra-marital affairs and liaisons, evidence of which appeared on Bureau wiretaps and bugs.

FBI agents close to Hoover circulated the material to their press contacts but the media refused to touch the story. In Fall 1964, it was announced that King would be the recipient of the Nobel Peace Prize. In Washington, during a group interview with 18 female reporters, Hoover denounced King as "the most notorious liar in the country." A fence-mending meeting in December between King and Hoover went nowhere.

A more sinister twist to the affair developed when Sullivan read a magazine profile stating that during his teens, a depressed King had considered suicide. In January 1965, the minister's wife, Coretta Scott King, received at the family home an anonymously mailed package, the contents of which included a reel of tape containing audio recordings of several of her husband's bedroom encounters with other women. The package also held an unsigned, typed note to the reverend which concluded, "You are done. There is but one way out for you. You better take it before your filthy, abnormal fraudulent [sic] self is bared to the nation."

King went into a depression that lasted for some months before he was able to shake it off. A decade later, a Senate investigating committee determined that the tape was made of several of the King sex tapes spliced together in the FBI Laboratory. Later during his post-FBI career, Associate Director William Sullivan said that the mailing had originally been planned to scare King off from accepting his Nobel Prize in Oslo, but that it had not reached him until after the event. He also maintained that the idea had been hatched by Hoover and Tolson.

In this matter, as in many others involving Hoover, Sullivan's statements must be viewed with skepticism. The two had a relationship that had become very distorted. It was Sullivan who oversaw the Domestic Intelligence Division's post-Apalachin report on the Mafia, which contradicted Hoover's long-term denial of its existence by proving that the Mafia had existed for decades. Sullivan's initial conclusion that the

CPUSA had no real role in the civil rights movement had put him in the doghouse with Hoover, a condition that ended only with Sullivan's fervent memo agreeing that King must be neutralized as the movement's head. The question is, how much of King's harassment was Hoover-directed, and how much was devised by Sullivan in an attempt to anticipate and curry favor with his boss?

As you'll see, Sullivan was ambitious to replace Hoover as director, and when he finally broke with him during the Nixon era, his version of the events that occurred when he'd been one of Hoover's trusted lieutenants tend to have a self-serving quality.

The Supreme Court's mid-1950s decisions disallowing Smith Act prosecutions had forced the FBI to change its strategy and tactics, replacing investigations of domestic subversive groups with extralegal harassment and disruptive actions. Sullivan's abilities and ambitions made him the key man in this sea-change. His masterstroke was to harness the World War II counterintelligence techniques used against pro-Axis groups to peacetime domestic foes. He was instrumental in 1956 in shaping the FBI's initial COINTELPRO targeting the CPUSA. Subsequently, he oversaw the 1961 COINTELPRO against the Socialist Workers Party, the 1966 anti-KKK COINTELPRO, the 1967 Black Militants COINTELPRO, and the 1968 COINTELPRO targeting the New Left.

It was Sullivan who authored the anonymous note urging King to kill himself, Sullivan who had handed over the note and sex tape to another agent to mail to King. But one thing is certain: when Sullivan used COINTELPRO techniques against Martin Luther King Jr., he could not have done so without the approval of J. Edgar Hoover.

> **Cops and Robbers**
>
> One of the FBI's crop of WWII-era agents, William C. Sullivan, 29, joined the Bureau in 1941. As head of the Research and Analysis Section of the Domestic Intelligence Division, in 1956 Sullivan helped design the COINTELPRO–CPUSA operation. In 1961, he was made head of the Division, a post he held until 1971 when he broke with Hoover and resigned from the FBI amid controversy.

Exit LBJ

Reelected in 1964 by a landslide victory over GOP opponent Senator Barry Goldwater, President Lyndon Johnson enacted an ambitious domestic agenda (the Great Society) that featured the passage of historic civil rights legislation and a federal "war on poverty." Thanks to Johnson's stewardship, the landmark 1965 Civil Rights Act was passed by Congress, becoming the law of the land. The war on poverty was ultimately less successful, expiring in a welter of big-spending government boondoggles, fraud, and corruption. By 1968, in response to national demand, LBJ was proclaiming a hard-line "war on crime." During the Johnson years, the number of FBI agents would grow from 6,000 to 7,000.

But it was a real shooting war, the war in Vietnam, that was LBJ's undoing. Postelection, Johnson had basically given the Pentagon a blank check to do what it thought needed to be done to prevent South Vietnam from falling to the Communists. The Pentagon plan involved sending hundreds of thousands of young U.S. soldiers, many of them draftees, to fight in Vietnam. Ultimately, the war would take its toll of over 50,000 American lives. Adding to a sense of rancorous injustice was the 2-S Selective Service deferment, which allowed college students to avoid going into service and ensured that the draft (and wartime casualties) would fall primarily on minorities and poor whites unable to go to college.

Justice Jargon

J. Edgar Hoover described the **New Left** as "a new style in conspiracy... a conspiracy reflected by questionable moods and attitudes ... rather than by formal membership in specific organizations." Elsewhere, he characterized those "moods and attitudes" as "new-style subversion that is erupting in civil disobedience and encouraging young people to mock the law."

Pentagon disinformation assuring the public that the United States was winning the Vietnamese war clashed with the reality of ever-greater troop deployments and mounting casualty tolls. This reality generated a nationwide antiwar protest movement which helped midwife the emergence of the *New Left*.

The term "New Left" was something of a misnomer. At its heart were the offspring of the Old Left, the so-called "red diaper" babies whose parents had been communists, socialists, or leftist ultra-liberals. Coming of age, the new generation became involved in the civil rights and student protest movements, which mutated into more aggressive, activist operations as the antiwar furor heated up.

Where it differed from the Old Left, however, was that the new movement had few if any links to CPUSA or Socialist Workers Party–type organizations, which had been moribund since the mid-1950s in any case. The new breed took its inspiration not from Trotsky or the Kremlin, but rather from Communist Cubans Fidel Castro and especially his lieutenant, Che Guevara, as well as Red China's Chairman Mao. Also worth noting is that these militant leftists represented a minority of the antiwar movement, on to which they had piggybacked in an attempt to hijack the cause.

Seeing the streets of major American cities filled with thousands of peace protesters, LBJ sincerely believed that they gave aid and comfort to the enemy, stiffening the North Vietnamese resolve to fight. Try though they might, however, Hoover's FBI could unearth no credible evidence of any kind indicating that the antiwar movement was being secretly directed by Moscow—or, for that matter, Peking.

The same applied to the riots which from the mid-1960s on flared up in the black communities in virtually every major U.S. city, including Los Angeles, Chicago, Newark, Cleveland, Baltimore, Detroit, and many more. Hoover reported to Johnson that the riots were unplanned, spontaneous, with no proof of any conspiratorial militant or communist-inspired organization behind them. No foreign power or entity was to blame; all by itself, America was tearing itself apart.

Bu Stats

Begun in October 1967, the FBI's Ghetto Informant Program developed a network of 4,000 contacts who provided the Bureau with a steady stream of information about persons, groups, and activities in the nation's black communities.

In the summer of 1967, Hoover authorized Sullivan's proposal for a COINTELPRO targeting black militants, ultimately unleashing some 360 "disruptive actions" at such radical leaders and groups as Stokely Carmichael, H. Rap Brown, and the paramilitary Black Panther Party. At the same time, the FBI was also running a COINTELPRO against the KKK and related white-hate groups.

FBI monitoring of antiwar groups turned to active measures in 1968, with the launching of COINTELPRO–New Left. A prime target was the militant group Students for a Democratic Society (SDS), who had agitated a student strike at New York City's Columbia University into a violence-drenched debacle. Their 1968 membership totaled 80,000. Also monitoring student protest groups were the CIA (in violation of its charter prohibiting it from domestic operations) and military intelligence. No evidence of foreign control of such groups was found.

The year 1968, a presidential election year, was marked by a watershed event in the Vietnam War, the Tet Offensive, a massive Viet Cong military campaign launched against the South Vietnamese government. The March 1968 offensive took its name from the Vietnamese month of Tet, in which it was launched. Initially, the thrust won great gains, including a high-profile attack on the U.S. embassy in Saigon. Eventually, the offensive was beaten back, inflicting tremendous casualties on the Viet Cong.

In hindsight, Tet was ultimately a clear-cut military defeat for the Viet Cong and their North Vietnamese patrons. But other forces were at play in this, the first war televised into U.S. homes on the six o'clock news. Tet ripped off the fig leaf of disinformation efforts by U.S. generals and politicians, who had depicted the war as a smooth, steady flow of U.S. victories marked by ever-higher enemy body counts.

Instead, the war was revealed as a tough, dirty, bloody business that was a long way from being won by the United States, if such an objective could indeed be achieved.

Within weeks of Tet, on March 31, 1968, the nation was stunned by President Johnson's announcement that he would not be seeking another term. Few had labored as long and hard as LBJ had to reach the White House, only to see it turn so memorably sour. (One of those few would be Johnson's immediate successor, Richard M. Nixon.)

After Johnson's abdication, things happened fast. On April 4, 1968, while helping to lead a city-workers strike in Memphis, Tennessee, Martin Luther King Jr. was shot dead by an assassin with a rifle. Identified as the killer was petty career criminal and white racist James Earl Ray, the subject of the FBI's most intensive manhunt ever, which two months after the murder arrested him in London, England. Ray's shadowy background, overseas travel while a fugitive, and other particulars indicate that he may not have acted alone, a viewpoint he maintained over the decades while serving out his sentence in a Tennessee prison, where he died.

On June 4, 1968, at the Ambassador Hotel in Los Angeles, while celebrating his win in the California Democratic Presidential primary, Robert F. Kennedy was shot dead. Crowd members wrestled down the gunman, Sirhan Bishara Sirhan, a Palestinian immigrant who later claimed he shot Kennedy because of his pro-Israel stance. Evidence at the shooting scene indicated that some 12 or more bullets were fired, yet Sirhan's gun held only eight bullets, and he had no time for reloading. Employed at several racetracks, Sirhan had links to organized crime. As of this writing, he is still in jail and almost certainly will die there.

The big winner of 1968 was Richard Nixon, elected 37th President of the United States. Another winner was J. Edgar Hoover, whose reappointment as FBI Director, with a corresponding raise in salary, was announced shortly before Christmas by the president-elect.

Official and Confidential

During a transitional courtesy call to the White House, the president-elect was told by outgoing President Johnson, "If it hadn't been for Edgar Hoover, I couldn't have carried out my responsibilities as Commander in Chief. Period. Dick, you will come to depend on Edgar. He is a pillar of strength in a city of weak men. You will rely on him time and again to maintain security. He's the only one you can put your complete trust in."

The Least You Need to Know

- In the 1960s, American society was destabilized by the Vietnam War, urban rioting, and civil disturbances.

- During the same period, COINTELPRO counterintelligence programs became the FBI's primary vehicle against domestic foes.

- The FBI's anti-KKK COINTELPRO was highly successful in suppressing the Klan.

- J. Edgar Hoover's personal enmity toward Martin Luther King Jr. led to the harassment and persecution of the civil rights leader.

- FBI investigations found no evidence of Communist party or foreign manipulation of the antiwar and civil rights movements.

Death of a Legend

In This Chapter

- ◆ Hoover's FBI clashes with the Nixon White House
- ◆ Hoover kills plan for increased domestic intelligence operations
- ◆ The Pentagon Papers
- ◆ Sullivan's FBI takeover bid
- ◆ The passing of J. Edgar Hoover

As you'll see in this chapter, Hoover's reluctance to involve the FBI in illegal domestic operations during his final days clashed with the Nixon White House's demands for increased surveillance of political foes. For instance, Hoover shut down the administration's Huston Plan, which would have mandated intensified domestic operations by the nation's intelligence agencies. Hoover's 1971 curtailment of all illegal counterintelligence programs targeting domestic groups and individuals (COINTELPROs) triggered a challenge to his leadership by his heir apparent William Sullivan, a challenge that Hoover defeated. The White House Special Investigations Unit was established to provide political intelligence the FBI refused to supply. On May 2, 1972, J. Edgar Hoover died in his sleep, ending an era.

White House Wiretaps

In March 1969, the United States began secretly bombing North Vietnamese bases in the neighboring country of Cambodia. Officially neutral, Cambodia's Prince Sihanouk had agreed to the bombing as long as it was kept secret. But on May 9, 1969, an article in *The New York Times* described the bombing and Sihanouk's failure to protest. President Nixon and his national security advisor Dr. Henry Kissinger were outraged, believing that this *leak* of the news item imperiled their strategy to bring the North Vietnamese to the negotiating table.

Justice Jargon

News **leaks** are a way of life in official Washington, D.C. When a government official wants to anonymously surface some information in the national news media, the item is "leaked" to friendly press contacts, who protect the anonymity of the tipster by ascribing the item as having come from an unidentified "inside source," "high-level official," and so on.

Believing that the leak had come from a dissident staff member of the Kissinger-chaired National Security Council, Nixon and Kissinger authorized J. Edgar Hoover to wiretap the phones of the main suspects. Hoover agreed to install the taps as a matter of national security, but insisted on receiving written authorization for them from Attorney General John Mitchell. The operation was closely held, with Hoover delegating responsibility for it to his lieutenant, William Sullivan. Kissinger's deputy, General Alexander Haig, served in the matter of the taps as liaison between his chief and Sullivan.

Ultimately, the FBI ran some 17 wiretaps on National Security Council, Defense Department, and State Department staffers, as well as on four prominent national reporters. Logs of material from the taps were kept separate from other FBI files, first held in a safe in Hoover's office and later in Sullivan's office. The leaker was never identified, though the taps yielded much confidential information about the private lives of those under surveillance.

Nixon and Hoover's longtime, mutually profitable, alliance reached back to the days when the FBI had provided hot tips on the Alger Hiss case to the freshman California congressman. Now President Nixon and especially some of his close aides began to complain that the FBI director was no longer willing to take the necessary risks to order electronic surveillance operations against domestic foes.

They were right. In recent years, Hoover had grown more cautious. In 1966, Hoover had officially discontinued black-bag surreptitious entry break-ins. That is, they were no longer officially authorized. Although they continued, the SACs who ordered such operations would be on their own if caught, with the Bureau disavowing any responsibility for their illegal actions.

Over four decades of FBI directorship had given Hoover a unique long view of American history and the parameters of power. He knew that it had become politically risky to authorize illegal operations against the mainstream leadership of the antiwar movement. While he personally might have favored such surveillance, he was increasingly reluctant to assume all the risk. No doubt he recalled how the Palmer Raids, even with a national mandate to crack down on Reds, had ultimately nearly brought him to professional grief.

Huston Plan

Like LBJ, President Nixon and his inner circle of White House aides were ever-more infuriated by antiwar activists and the peace movement. That fury peaked in the spring of 1970, during a wave of student protests against the U.S. invasion of Cambodia, protests that culminated in the May 1970 shooting death of four students by National Guardsmen during a demonstration at Ohio's Kent State University campus. Nixon and his associates felt unduly hampered by Hoover's unwillingness to give them the complete coverage on domestic foes that they craved.

Further fueling what the White House had come to see as a domestic intelligence impasse was a schism that had developed between the CIA and the FBI. Part of the problem was Hoover's deep-dyed antagonism to any other federal intelligence agency operating on what he considered his turf. Since 1966, the CIA had been running Operation CHAOS, the codename for the agency's 1966 to 1974 domestic intelligence efforts to detect foreign influence in the U.S. antiwar movement.

Worse, CIA and FBI counterespionage operations had come to a parting of the ways, largely inspired by competing claims and countercharges of each group's own set of Soviet defectors and double agents. (This important topic will be covered in depth later in the book.) The CIA's refusal to identify an FBI source of information led to Hoover's February 1970 decision to end all cooperation with the agency. Shortly after, Hoover cut off cooperation with all other U.S. intelligence agencies, except through the White House. He refused to carry out any electronic surveillance jobs (apart from those he controlled) unless they were authorized in writing by the attorney general. This refusal effectively put a stop to them, since the other agency heads were unwilling to sign their names to such illegal requests.

This development had potentially devastating consequences, since the FBI was authorized to conduct domestic security investigations, but the CIA's charter specifically forbade it to conduct such investigations. The CIA continued such domestic operations (as did various branches of military intelligence), but should the risky, illegal actions ever be made public, those who had authorized them would be vulnerable to prosecution.

Chafing under what it saw as Hoover's inability to take risks, the White House longed to remove him from his central position in domestic intelligence. But Nixon would soon learn, as had his predecessors before him, that it was near-impossible to pressure a man whose files documented the dirty secrets of his nominal superiors.

Ambitious young White House staffer Tom Charles Huston made no secret of his longing to occupy in the domestic intelligence field a fiefdom similar to that held by Henry Kissinger over the administration's foreign policy. In the spring of 1970, he was tasked with the designing of a new, improved domestic security program. He forged a close alliance with FBI Domestic Intelligence Division head William Sullivan.

Cops and Robbers

Originally from Indiana, Tom Charles Huston was a "conservative libertarian" who aimed to be the Nixon administration's domestic security czar. After a short stint in Army intelligence, speechwriter Huston, 29, was recruited in 1969 to serve on a White House internal security committee. His "Huston Plan" mapped out a wide-ranging plan for unprecedented coordination of all agencies carrying out domestic intelligence operations.

On June 5, 1970, a summit conference of U.S. intelligence agency heads was called by President Nixon. Present were CIA Director Richard Helms, the Defense Department's General Donald Bennett, the National Security Agency's Admiral Noel Gaylor, and FBI Director Hoover. Demanding improved, streamlined, and coordinated domestic intelligence, Nixon put Tom Huston in charge of the interagency group. The Huston Plan called for dramatically increased surveillance operations (mail opening, break-ins, bugs, and wiretaps) against domestic radical and antiwar organizations, with Huston himself as the White House's secret domestic intelligence czar.

The other intelligence chiefs, all in favor of the newly expanded capabilities, balked at the single-handed resistance of Hoover, who professed himself content with the current state of affairs in domestic intelligence and refused to rubber-stamp the plan. Disrupting a planned signing ceremony by reading aloud his footnoted objections to every page of the 43-page report, Hoover treated Huston with no small contempt, repeatedly referring to him by the wrong name: "Any comments, Mr. Hoffman? Any comments, Mr. Hutchinson?"

Huston, furious, memoed the White House that "[t]he only stumbling block was Mr. Hoover … [he] refused to go along with a single conclusion drawn or support a single recommendation made." Huston fumed that Hoover was only interested in "possible embarrassment to the intelligence community (i.e., Hoover) from public disclosure of clandestine operations."

When Nixon gave his approval to the plan, Hoover made an end-run around him, teaming with Cartha DeLoach to inform Attorney General John Mitchell (heretofore kept out of the loop) what was afoot. Hoover's position was that if the administration's demands should endanger him or the Bureau, he'd force Nixon and Mitchell to sign off on it, thus implicating themselves.

Huston protested, claiming that "[w]hat Hoover is doing here is putting himself above the President." Which, ultimately, was the point. By August 1, 1970, the Huston Plan was dead, killed by Richard M. Nixon. Authority over domestic security concerns was taken from Huston and given to newly appointed White House counsel John Dean, while Huston went into a kind of bureaucratic limboland, the equivalent of an FBI agent's being posted to the field office in Butte, Montana. Details of the Huston plan remained secret until 1973 and the aftermath of Watergate.

Carefully playing both ends against the middle, Huston's erstwhile ally (and co-creator in drafting the plan) William Sullivan emerged even more strongly established in Hoover's favor. Cartha DeLoach retired from the FBI in July 1970 (one year short of his 30-year mark), becoming a Pepsi Cola executive. His spot was filled by William Sullivan, later promoted to FBI assistant director, third in the hierarchy after Hoover and Tolson. With Tolson elderly and ailing, Sullivan was in position to potentially succeed J. Edgar Hoover as Bureau director.

Hoover's fastidiousness toward potentially illegal domestic intelligence operations undertaken for other agencies or the White House failed to extend to such actions that were under his complete control. FBI COINTELPRO operations against political extremism of the right and left, the Klan, black militants, and the New Left continued through 1971.

Heir Unapparent

Like a younger J. Edgar Hoover, FBI Assistant Director William C. Sullivan was ambitious, inventive, and tirelessly resourceful in promoting his personal and professional objectives. Unlike Sullivan, however, Hoover hadn't had a figure like J. Edgar Hoover standing between him and the top job he coveted.

From the mid-1950s on, Sullivan had been Hoover's top lieutenant. As the architect and overseer of the COINTELPRO operations, the FBI's primary vehicle against domestic foes, Sullivan wielded extraordinary power. With Cartha DeLoach's exit from the Bureau, Sullivan seemed poised to claim the Directorship. But Hoover showed no sign of readiness to retire and Sullivan grew impatient.

In the Nixon White House, Sullivan had forged strong alliances with Kissinger's deputy, Al Haig, and Justice Department Internal Security Division chief Robert Mardian, as well as with the CIA's counterintelligence wizard, James J. Angleton. It was Sullivan who'd guided Tom Huston through the brainstorming of the Huston Plan, which in effect was really the Sullivan Plan to put the FBI back in the intensive domestic surveillance operations which Hoover had curtailed back in 1966.

Bu Stats

In the spring of 1971, a Gallup poll asked the question, "Should J. Edgar Hoover resign as head of the FBI?" Of the respondents, 50 percent answered yes, 41 percent said no, and 9 percent were undecided. Asked if Hoover had done an excellent or good job as FBI head, 70 percent said yes, with only 17 percent responding in the negative. A Harris poll had an even 43-43 percent split on the question of Hoover's retirement.

Turnabout was not considered fair play in March 1971, when a band of antiwar activists executed their own black-bag job on an FBI resident agency in the Philadelphia suburb of Media, Pennsylvania. The intruders stole hundreds of documents, which they began selectively surfacing for maximum impact over the next few weeks. Documents detailing illegal FBI surveillance of college campus groups and individuals were leaked to politicians and the press. Despite intensive investigation, the culprits were never identified.

A single document on campus radicals contained the word COINTELPRO. On April 28, 1971, Hoover officially directed all SACs to discontinue all COINTELPRO operations. A side-effect of this directive was that it radically undercut Sullivan's power base, adding to his mounting unhappiness. By early summer of 1971, Sullivan was ready to force the issue. He did so in the most overt way possible: by directly disagreeing with J. Edgar Hoover. Worse, he did so on paper, through a series of memoranda challenging some of Hoover's recent policy decisions.

In response, Hoover promoted Assistant Director Mark Felt, head of the Inspections Division, to the position of deputy associate director, giving him authority over Sullivan. Realizing that the axe was about to fall, Sullivan contacted the Justice Department (and Nixon man) Robert Mardian, arranging for the transfer of some sensitive materials to White House custody. These "sensitive materials" comprised the transcripts, summaries, and logs of the Kissinger-ordered wiretaps that had begun in 1969 and only recently discontinued.

Some months earlier, worried about the security of that material, and to further hide it from Congressional snoopers with subpoenas, Hoover had moved the documents to the safe in Sullivan's office. In mid-July, without the director's knowledge, Sullivan passed the documents to Mardian, who ultimately passed them to H. R. Haldeman and John Ehrlichman, Nixon's top lieutenants.

The linchpin of Sullivan's strategy was the belief that Nixon was about to fire Hoover, although not so crudely, because Nixon genuinely liked and admired Hoover and didn't want to hurt the old man's feelings. Hoover would retire as director emeritus, heaped with honors. The meeting between Nixon and Hoover was scheduled for sometime in mid-July, at ten o'clock in the morning. When it was done, Hoover was still FBI director. For whatever reason, Nixon hadn't been able to fire him.

After some tense cat-and-mouse games and an explosive final confrontation with Hoover, William C. Sullivan resigned on October 1, 1971, ending a thirty-year career in the FBI. After cleaning out his desk, he left behind only one item: a personally autographed framed photograph of the director.

Official and Confidential

On November 9, 1977, while walking in the woods outside his New Hampshire cabin, William Sullivan was fatally shot by a local youth, a hunter who said that he'd mistaken Sullivan for a deer. Coming one week before he was scheduled to testify before the House Select Committee on Assassinations investigating the deaths of the Kennedys and Martin Luther King, the timing struck some as suspicious. However, no evidence of foul play was found and the death was ruled an accident.

It wasn't until Sullivan was gone that Hoover learned he'd taken the only copies of the Kissinger wiretap materials. The White House gave Sullivan a job, making him director of the Justice Department's Office of National Narcotics Intelligence. Sullivan continued sniping at Hoover, keeping the duel alive by peppering him with negative stories leaked to friendly press contacts and using his connections in the Bureau to keep abreast of key developments.

The Plumbers

Nixon-era administration ire at unfriendly leaks took a quantum jump on June 13, 1971 (one day after Nixon's daughter Tricia's wedding), when the Sunday edition of *The New York Times* published the first excerpt of what would be called the *Pentagon Papers*, a lengthy and classified series of Defense Department documents probing the origins of the Vietnam War.

Justice Jargon

What came to be known as the **Pentagon Papers** was a 7,000-page, 47-volume study originally entitled "United States–Vietnamese Relations, 1945–1967." Prepared in the last days of the Johnson administration in 1968, the classified Defense Department study documented the history of U.S. involvement in the Vietnam War.

Initially, President Nixon was not overly worried about the disclosures. While resenting the *Times*'s "disloyalty" in publishing the Pentagon Papers, Nixon felt that the onus of the revelations would fall on the preceding Johnson and Kennedy administrations, Democratic administrations, where the escalation had taken place. But national security advisor Henry Kissinger went ballistic. Kissinger argued that secrecy was necessary to conduct foreign policy. Involved in highly sensitive and secret negotiations intended to pave the way for Nixon's historic opening to Communist China, Kissinger feared that the exposure of U.S. government secrets would cause the Red Chinese leadership to lose confidence in the White House's ability to keep secrets, thus destabilizing the planned overture. Such security breaches might also deter the North Vietnamese from continuing secret negotiations to stop the war.

The Pentagon Papers had been leaked by Daniel Ellsberg, 40, a Harvard graduate, former Defense Department planner, and architect of America's involvement in the Vietnam War. Turning against U.S. involvement in the war, he clandestinely made copies of the documents and disseminated them to the *Times* and other newspapers. Cannily comparing Ellsberg to Alger Hiss, Kissinger warned Nixon that he would look like a "weakling" if he failed to move hard against the antiwar dissenter. Also, discrediting Ellsberg would discredit the peace movement itself with the voters, thereby helping Nixon's upcoming reelection efforts.

Reflecting unhappiness with Hoover's perceived "timidity," as well as a desire to operate his own domestic political intelligence operations, Nixon formed a Special Investigations Unit in July 1971 headed by two White House lawyers in their early thirties, David Young and Egil "Bud" Krogh. Established next door to the White House in Room 16 of the Executive Office Building, the SIU's mission was to "stop leaks." As a humorous note, Young hung a sign outside his office reading "Mr. Young—Plumber." And so the SIU came to be called the Plumbers.

Cops and Robbers

A World War II OSS veteran who joined the CIA early, Everette Howard Hunt simultaneously pursued two careers: CIA agent and prolific writer of more than 50 novels (mostly spy thrillers). A key Agency liaison to the Cuban exiles' anti-Castro movement, Hunt was attached to U.S. embassies in Mexico City and Montevideo, Uruguay, and later served in the CIA's domestic operations division.

In the months to come, the administration was bedeviled by other leaks. Unlike the Pentagon Papers, these leaks concerned ongoing Nixon foreign policy initiatives. Special Counsel to the President Charles "Chuck" Colson, once the youngest company commander in the U.S. Marines and a hardcore Nixon loyalist, headed the effort to find a professional investigator to head the anti-leaking efforts. Reaching out to a fellow Brown University alumnus, in the summer of 1971 Colson hired retired CIA agent E. Howard Hunt.

A veteran anticommunist clandestine operator in some of the Cold War's hottest back-alley rumbles, Hunt had officially retired from the CIA when Colson hired him. That didn't stop Hunt from calling on the Agency for technical support when carrying out White House assignments. Among these tasks were the forging of diplomatic cables to highlight JFK's role in the 1963 assassination of South Vietnamese strongmen, the Diem brothers; and the investigation of Mary Jo Kopechne's death by drowning in the back seat of Senator Edward M. "Ted" Kennedy's car at Chappaquidick, Massachusetts.

Also hired in midsummer 1971 was former FBI agent G. Gordon Liddy, 40, a pro-gun, Second Amendment absolutist and rightwing political extremist with a yearning for intrigue and an unsettling admiration for the Third Reich. Leaving the Bureau in the early 1960s, Liddy had been elected assistant district attorney in upstate New York, where he'd once famously busted LSD guru Timothy Leary. A stint in the Treasury Department led to Liddy's being scouted for the Plumbers unit.

> ### Cops and Robbers
>
> Originally from Caldwell, New Jersey, G. Gordon Liddy was an FBI SA from 1957 to 1962, ultimately working for the Crime Records (publicity) division. Famously described by a colleague as a "super-klutz," Liddy's Bureau career was noteworthy for his having run a background check on his future bride and his having been caught by local police while pulling a black-bag break-in job—a prophetic foreshadowing of his later Watergate woes.

In the nuclear reactor that was the Nixon White House, Liddy and Hunt were a pair of graphite rods whose insertion would ultimately bring the whole atomic pile to critical mass. The shorthand name for that subsequent explosion remains "Watergate."

Hoover's Last Bow

In October 1971, Plumber G. Gordon Liddy authored a memorandum weighing the pros and cons of removing J. Edgar Hoover, coming down on the side of easing him into an honorable retirement. The memo was greeted with general approbation at the White House, from Nixon on down. A prominent dissenter was Attorney General John Mitchell, who pointed out that Hoover had his own sizeable constituency among the voters, who might well be alienated by his removal during the upcoming election year. That constituency would have somewhere to go, to register their protests: by voting for third-party candidate and populist race-baiter, former Alabama governor George Wallace.

A meeting that month between Nixon and Hoover to discuss the latter's future ended as had the summer one, with Hoover emerging from the Oval Office still firmly entrenched in the directorship.

Over at the Plumbers unit, Hunt and Liddy found plenty of work to keep them busy. The White House demanded derogatory background material on Pentagon Papers leaker Daniel Ellsberg, to use against him in his forthcoming trial and against the Democrats in the upcoming 1972 presidential election year. Nixon was upset by what he felt was the FBI's desultory pursuit of those facts, suspecting that Bureau foot-dragging was the product of Hoover's friendship with Ellsberg's father-in-law, toy-making magnate Louis Marx.

White House pressure caused the Plumbers unit to go operational, with a plan to burglarize the office of Ellsberg's psychiatrist and acquire confidential material from the Ellsberg files. Hunt and Liddy handled the operation with the assistance of some of Hunt's Miami Cuban anti-Castro associates. In September 1971, on Labor Day weekend, Hunt, Liddy, and the Cubans performed a black bag job on the California office of Ellsberg's psychiatrist, Dr. Henry Fielding. Attempting to create the impression that the break-in was a burglary committed by a thief looking for drugs, they tore up the office, but not before photographing documents from Ellsberg's files.

Justice Jargon

The primary vehicle of President Nixon's campaign for a second term was the Committee to Reelect the President, whose initials formed the unfortunate and universally used acronym, **CREEP.**

That burglary would ultimately result in a number of jail terms for highly placed White House aides. But that unhappy denouement wasn't even a blip on the radar screen as the White House's focus turned to the upcoming presidential election. Heading that effort was John Mitchell, who resigned his post as attorney general to head the President's reelection campaign.

In December 1971, *CREEP* hired G. Gordon Liddy as its general counsel. In late January 1972, Liddy presented Operation Gemstone, his comprehensive plan to unleash total surveillance and dirty tricks on the Democrats at their summer political convention. The plan, budgeted at a million dollars, was turned down by John Mitchell, who told Liddy to come up with something less ambitious.

In Fall 1971, CREEP hired James McCord as its security director. McCord was a former FBI agent who'd spent most of his subsequent career at CIA. His former director, Allen Dulles, had once referred to McCord as "my top man." In February, Special Counsel to the President Chuck Colson arranged for Howard Hunt to join Liddy at CREEP. Before long, Hunt and Liddy were seriously discussing plans to assassinate syndicated newspaper columnist Jack Anderson, whose revelations of secret foreign policy decisions had enraged the White House.

Anderson alleged that international communications giant ITT had made a $400,000 campaign contribution to the Nixon reelection effort in return for a favorable settlement of an antitrust lawsuit. Buttressing Anderson's case was the existence of a memo said to have been written by ITT lobbyist Dita Beard, which linked the contribution with the settlement.

In an effort to take some of the heat off in March 1972, White House counsel John Dean took the memo to Hoover, who said he was willing to submit the memo to the FBI Laboratory to determine whether it was a forgery, as Dita Beard and the White House claimed. After lab technicians concluded that the memo was not a forgery, Hoover duly reported this fact to the White House. Enraged by the finding, Nixon and his inner circle put heavy pressure on Hoover to "cooperate" by at least "modifying" the report so it wouldn't totally contradict their (and ITT's) position.

The finding went unchanged. Hoover had protected the integrity of the FBI Laboratory and, by extension, the Bureau which he'd headed for almost 48 years.

It was his final bow. On May 2, 1972, at age 77, J. Edgar Hoover was found at home, dead of a heart attack. On May 3, by order of a House resolution, Hoover was honored by having his body lay in state in the Rotunda of the Capitol Building. By order of President Nixon, Hoover was given a state funeral with military honors. His remains were interred in the Congressional Cemetery.

Almost all of Hoover's estate, valued at over half a million dollars, was bequeathed to his longtime companion, Clyde Tolson. On April 10, 1975, at age 74, Clyde Tolson died of kidney failure.

Official and Confidential

At Hoover's funeral, Senate Chaplain Pastor Edward L. R. Elson's eulogy contained this quote from Ephesians 6: "For we wrestle not against flesh and blood, but against principalities, against powers, against the rulers of the darkness of this world, against spiritual wickedness in high places."

Another autocrat, France's Sun King, Louis XIV, once famously observed, "After me, the deluge." So it would be at the FBI, soon to be imperiled by the chain reaction detonated by the June 1972 arrests of the Watergate burglars.

The Least You Need to Know

- Hoover's unwillingness to authorize illegal FBI domestic operations clashed with the Nixon White House's demands for increased political intelligence.

- In 1971, Hoover ended all COINTELPRO operations, leading to a final break with his ambitious lieutenant, William Sullivan.

- Leaks of White House secrets to the press caused the Nixon administration to set up the clandestine Plumber's unit.

- The Plumbers illegally broke into the office of the psychiatrist of Pentagon Papers leaker, Daniel Ellsberg.

- Hoover's last official act was to refuse White House demands to compromise the integrity of the FBI laboratory.

- On May 2, 1972, J. Edgar Hoover died.

Part 3

Cold War Climax

The post-Watergate era of Congressional investigating committees and public disillusionment with key American institutions resulted in reforms at the FBI instituted by Directors Clarence M. Kelley and Judge William Webster. The 1980s saw the rise of a new kind of mercenary traitor, trading top-secret data not for ideological causes, but for the money. FBI counter-intelligence operations apprehended double agents and broke up spy networks, but still more dangerous traitors sprang up to take their place.

Chapter 13

Line of Succession

In This Chapter

- Intrigue over Hoover's "secret files"
- Deepening Watergate woes
- Using the CIA to thwart the FBI
- "Tough cop" and FBI veteran Clarence M. Kelley
- Nixon forced to resign

Hoover's immediate successor was Nixon political appointee L. Patrick Gray, installed as acting director of the FBI to avoid Senate confirmation hearings during the 1972 presidential campaign. Hoover's "secret files" containing derogatory information on top politicos and power brokers were denied to the White House and held by the FBI. Burglars apprehended while breaking into Democratic National Committee headquarters at the Watergate building were linked to the White House, panicking the administration. Gray's nomination as FBI permanent director was abandoned.

This chapter reveals the spreading Watergate scandal that decimated Nixon's staff and caused his resignation from the office of the presidency. However, Nixon didn't leave before appointing veteran law enforcement professional Clarence M. Kelley as FBI director.

Secret Files

The director was dead, long live the new director! But that would be—who? The unique historical and personal circumstances that had allowed J. Edgar Hoover to exert near-absolute control of the FBI for nearly a half-century were unlikely to be duplicated in the foreseeable future. During his tenure, Hoover had been mythologized into a crimebusting icon. Those who followed would be not living legends but mere mortals, and sometimes flawed ones at that.

Cops and Robbers

A World War II Pacific submarine captain, 20-year Navy man, and dedicated Nixon supporter, Louis Patrick Gray III was a high-level Justice Department appointee, serving as assistant attorney general (where early on he managed to irritate J. Edgar Hoover). On May 3, 1972, the day after Hoover died, Gray was installed as acting director of the FBI, serving until April 27, 1973.

Such a flawed mortal was Hoover's immediate successor, L. Patrick "Pat" Gray III, a friend and political supporter of President Nixon, who'd selected him to fill the vacant directorship at the FBI. Attorney General Richard Kleindienst installed Gray as acting director, a bureaucratic ploy that allowed Nixon to fill the office without having to first undergo a process that would be something new for the FBI: a Senate confirmation hearing to vote aye or nay on the nominated FBI director. Nixon intended to handle the confirmation after the upcoming 1972 presidential election.

Of paramount interest to Nixon and his aides (and many others) was the fate of Hoover's secret files. These were the files accumulated over the course of a lifetime, containing derogatory material on national figures and specifically, Washington power players and their families, friends, and co-workers: material documenting substance abuse problems, arrests, marital infidelities, suspect political allegiances, shady business dealings, sexual proclivities, and so on.

In his Justice Department lair, Hoover's main office opened on to a suite of eight rooms. In these rooms were held filing cabinets containing two sorts of files: the Official and Confidential files and the Personal files. The Official/Confidential files held the concentrated political dynamite documenting the foibles of the high and mighty, while the Personal files held material relating to Hoover himself. The latter could include anything from copies of licenses for his dogs to ultra-sensitive material. Certainly the Personal files overlapped some of the Official/Confidential material.

In the weeks before his death, Hoover had made a small attempt to sanitize the files, but the handful that he'd reviewed and destroyed were only a drop in the bucket. On May 2, 1972, within hours of his death, L. Patrick Gray III appeared at the office of

FBI assistant director for administration John P. Mohr, a Hoover sub-lieutenant. Gray demanded the "secret files." Mohr said there weren't any. (Technically, he was right. There were no "secret files," only Official/Confidential and Personal files.) Tempers flared, leading to a shouting match between the two. Gray left the office minus the files.

On May 4, 1972, Hoover's longtime executive assistant and personal secretary, Helen Gandy, 78, turned the Official/Confidential files over to Deputy Associate Director Mark Felt, who stored them in a basement vault. According to her own sworn testimony before a Congressional investigating committee, Gandy oversaw the destruction of Hoover's Personal files. It took two and one-half months to destroy enough documents to create a 105-foot pile.

However, what happened to Hoover's most explosive files has been a matter of longtime speculation, fueled by the belief that the cream of them had been skimmed by high-level insiders before the remainder was turned over to official channels. Told in 1975 that then-Attorney General Edward H. Levi had Hoover's Official/Confidential files, former FBI Number Three man William Sullivan said, "Yeah, but he didn't get the gold." Sullivan said that the secret political files had just "disappeared," he knew not where. Evidence exists to suggest that some of the most top-secret national security files were passed to CIA counterintelligence chief James Angleton.

One thing seems certain: while the inner circle of Nixon White House aides lusted to get their hands on Hoover's secret files, they were unable to do so. Had they been in possession of that explosive potential blackmail material, their fates in the aftermath of the Watergate burglary might have been quite different.

The Big Break-In

In January 1972, Hoover had given an interview to a friendly journalist on condition that his remarks would not be made public until after his death. In addition to some scathing appraisals of the Nixon White House staff, Hoover also made an observation that would turn out to be eerily prophetic. "By God," he said, "Nixon's got some former CIA men working for him that I'd kick out of my office. Someday that bunch will serve him a fine mess."

Two former CIA men were working for the political intelligence/dirty tricks component of the Committee to Re-elect the President (CREEP): James McCord and Howard Hunt. Indeed, as Hoover prophesied, they did indeed serve the President "a fine mess." Still open is the intriguing question of whether Hoover was also referring to other as yet unidentified CIA men who might have been working in other parts of the Nixon White House—and for whom they might have ultimately been working.

Political Maneuvering

After Hoover's death, things moved fast. The May 15, 1972, shooting of George Wallace relieved the administration of the threat of a third-party candidacy. In the Democratic presidential race, centrist Senator Edmund Muskie faded, replaced by front-running ultraliberal George McGovern.

Official and Confidential

On May 15, 1972, during a campaign rally in suburban Washington, D.C., maverick third-party presidential candidate Governor George Wallace was shot by assailant Arthur Bremer, 22, a classic "lone nut" gunman. Wallace survived but was paralyzed for life. His withdrawal from the race freed the Nixon campaign from the fear of Wallace's third-party votes tilting the presidential election to the Democratic candidate.

The White House Plumbers unit had been formed because of the administration's dissatisfaction with the level of political intelligence being supplied by Hoover's FBI. With summertime national political conventions looming, the Nixon crew was eager to set in motion CREEP's clandestine component comprising Hunt, Liddy, and McCord. Illegal surveillance of the rival Democratic party had been part of the plan from its inception, but in May 1972, pressure came down from above for the Plumbers to mount an operation against the Democratic National Committee headquarters.

Cops and Robbers

Lawrence F. "Larry" O'Brien was a famously skillful Democratic political strategist and Kennedy loyalist who'd served as JFK's postmaster general. After the 1968 assassination of Robert F. Kennedy, O'Brien was hired as a consultant by reclusive billionaire and then–Las Vegas impresario Howard Hughes. Hughes's shady associations with Richard Nixon—and what O'Brien knew of those associations—may have been the motive behind the Watergate break-in.

Who gave the order to activate the operation is one of the great unanswered mysteries of Watergate. Jeb Magruder, Liddy's boss at CREEP, claimed that the order had come down from CREEP head, former attorney general John Mitchell, an accusation which Mitchell dismissed as a "palpable, damnable lie." A leading theory is that the order came down from President Nixon, and that the obfuscation was designed to shield his role in the operation.

This much is known: In mid-May, Liddy was ordered to mount an operation against the offices of the Democratic National Committee, located in the Watergate office building in Washington, D.C. Specifically targeted was the office of DNC chairman and longtime political nemesis Lawrence F. O'Brien.

O'Brien's previous employment with "eccentric" (i.e., cracked) billionaire Howard Hughes was a source of profound unease to President Nixon, who had a long, checkered history with the phantom tycoon, who was notorious for having sealed himself away from the outside world in a controlled, sanitized penthouse environment in Las Vegas. In 1960, late-breaking revelations about an unsecured loan that Hughes had made to one of Nixon's brothers had hurt the GOP candidate at the polls. Looming closer was an illegal $100,000 campaign contribution that Hughes had "skimmed" from one of his Vegas casinos and passed along to Nixon confidante and money conduit Bebe Rebozo.

Released from the Hughes organization and installed as DNC head, O'Brien was in a position to hold damaging information on Richard Nixon. Whatever he had, Nixon wanted to know what it was.

Liddy's clandestine unit was charged with accessing DNC headquarters and O'Brien's office, planting bugs, and photographing documents. The team was made up of Liddy, Hunt, McCord, and a half-dozen or so anti-Castro Cubans, action operatives which Hunt had brought into the show.

The Most Famous Break-In of All

In the early morning hours of Saturday, June 17, 1972, a security guard making his rounds in the Watergate building noticed that certain connecting doors had been rigged with pieces of tape over the locks, neutralizing them—a burglar's trick. Police were called and the investigating officers discovered five intruders, whom they apprehended at gunpoint at two A.M. The suspects, wearing business suits and rubber gloves, were equipped with sophisticated cameras and tripods, burglary tools, and electronic bugging devices. No ordinary burglary, this!

Those arrested were James McCord, soldier-of-fortune Frank Sturgis, and anti-Castro activists Bernard "Macho" Barker, Rolando Martinez, and Virgilio Gonzalez. A mysterious "*sixth man*" eluded capture, exiting the building. His identity remains unknown.

Official and Confidential

The unknown **sixth man** of the Watergate burglars is theorized to be Louis James Russell, a former HUAC investigator, private investigator, and wiretapper. Prior to the break-in, Russell had worked for the security service which guarded the building. An associate and sometime employee of ex-CIA agent James McCord, Russell was a deep player in the murk of Watergate. Declaring his conviction that he'd been poisoned, Russell died of a heart attack in July 1973.

Outside the building, team members Howard Hunt and Gordon Liddy were still at large, though not for long. A police acquaintance recognized the pseudonymous leader of the burglars as Jim McCord, CREEP's security director. A notebook belonging to one of the Cubans held Hunt's name, along with a note identifying him as being associated with the White House. White House–connected burglars bugging the opposition DNC headquarters was political dynamite.

News of the arrests sent the White House into full crisis mode, with key Nixon staffers sending their paper shredders into overdrive and kindling document bonfires in their home fireplaces. Publicly, the administration downplayed any connections to the burglars, arguing that they were minor-level personnel who'd gone off and done something stupid on their own.

FBI Versus the White House

For seasoned clandestine operators, the Watergate burglars had been incredibly sloppy about maintaining security. Found on the intruders and in their hotel rooms was $4,500 in $100 bills. FBI investigators focused on those bills, back-checking along the money trail. Within a week of the arrests, agents had determined that the bills had come from an Atlanta bank after first having been surfaced through a Mexican money laundering operation.

At the head of the money trail lay more than $100,000 in illegal campaign contributions that CREEP's Finance Committee had collected to fund Liddy's political intelligence operations. It was only a matter of time before the FBI discovered that fact, which caused intense anxiety among Nixon's inner circle of John Mitchell, White House counsel John Dean, and the President's top aides, H.R. Haldeman and John Ehrlichman.

The Watergate burglars' CIA connections caused FBI investigators to wonder whether the Agency was running the Mexican money-laundering operation. Gray made inquiries along those lines to CIA Director Richard Helms, who insisted that there was no Agency involvement.

But had there been CIA involvement, it would have provided a perfect pretext to shut down the FBI probe, because the White House could claim that the probe endangered an operation vital to the national security. Such at least was the thinking at the White House, which set about trying to lay down a phony smokescreen of CIA involvement to derail the FBI investigation. Handling that effort was slick, cocky presidential counsel John Dean, who managed to stall the probe for several weeks.

On the July 4th weekend, a mini-revolt blossomed at FBIHQ, as high-level Bureau professionals pressed Gray to move forward aggressively with the money chain probe. His spine stiffened, Gray ordered the probe to continue. Even so, John Dean later bragged that he'd been "totally aware of what the bureau was doing at all times."

Not quite. Throughout the summer and fall of 1972, FBI investigators had found clues that connected the money laundering operation to top CREEP staffers, weaving a net which would ultimately be cast over the Oval Office itself (including Dean).

During the presidential campaign, follow-up features on the Watergate burglary were largely absent from the nation's major newspapers and TV news shows. The issue itself failed to make an appreciable dent in the landslide victory won by President Nixon over challenger George McGovern.

Bu Stats

As the fall 1972 presidential campaign raged, a Gallup poll showed that only half of the respondents had even heard of the Watergate burglary. On Election Day, carrying every state but Massachusetts, Republican Richard Nixon beat Democrat George McGovern with more than 60 percent of the national vote. Of those identifying themselves as Democrats, one-third voted for Nixon.

Every Tree in the Forest

The Watergate affair had not ended, it had merely gone underground for the duration of the presidential campaign. Since the arrests, Nixon's cadre had been paying some of the expenses of the five jailed burglars, such as legal fees and family support. An expensive proposition, it called for more fancy money-handling of the type that triggered FBI curiosity. The pay-offs were disbursed through private investigators working for the president, who passed the payments to Dorothy Hunt, Howard Hunt's wife, who then distributed the funds to the burglars' lawyers and families.

Then there was the matter of Hunt's safe in the Executive Office Building. Soon after the burglary arrests, the White House moved to secure the materials in the safe by having John Dean take possession of them. The safe contained, among other things, a pistol, electronic eavesdropping equipment, operational notebooks, Pentagon Papers documents, memos from Hunt to Colson about Plumbers' operations, and copies of diplomatic cables relating to the deaths of South Vietnamese Diem brothers, including two cables faked by Hunt.

Wanting to rid himself of this red-hot material, yet unwilling to destroy it (Secret Service agents had witnessed the opening of the safe and the inventorying of its contents), Dean came up with what he thought was an ingenious solution. The "non-sensitive" material from the safe would be turned over to FBI agents, while the "sensitive" material would be turned over to Acting Director Gray. That way, Dean could truthfully say that all the safe's contents had been turned over to the FBI.

Stating that the documents related to national security matters unrelated to Watergate, Dean turned folders of the most sensitive materials over to Gray. Gray took them home for a few weeks, then returned them to his office safe. After holding them for six months, Gray burned the documents at his Connecticut home a few days after Christmas 1972.

After the election, Howard Hunt had been pressing the president's men hard, demanding that they live up to their obligations to financially and legally support the burglars, or else they might have to break silence and start talking to prosecutors. On December 8, 1972, his wife Dorothy Hunt was on board Chicago-bound United Airlines Flight 553. Making its mid-afternoon approach to Midway Airport, the 737 nosedived, crashing, killing 43 of the 55 people on board. Among them was Dorothy Hunt, who was found to have been carrying $10,000 in $100 bills. Crash investigators were unable to discover any evidence that the plane had been sabotaged.

Hard-hit by his wife's death, Hunt lost the will to fight. One whose pugnacity had only increased was ex-CIA man James McCord. Contacting his friends at the Agency, he warned that the White House was conspiring to hang Watergate on the CIA. Sending a message to the White House, he warned one of the President's privately retained private investigators that if the CIA was blamed for the burglary and CIA Director Richard Helms forced out of office, "every tree in the forest will fall."

Official and Confidential

Writing his friend and White House contact Jack Caulfield (former "presidential private eye" for President Nixon), Watergate burglar James McCord stated, "If [CIA Director Richard] Helms goes and the Watergate operation is laid at CIA's feet, where it does not belong, every tree in the forest will fall. It will be a scorched desert ... Just pass the message that if they [the Nixon White House] want it to blow, they are on exactly the right course ...."

In January 1973, Richard Helms left his post as CIA director to accept a new job as ambassador to Iran. Sure enough, the trees began to fall. One of the first to topple was FBI Acting Director L. Patrick Gray. In February, Richard Nixon decided to nominate Pat Gray as the FBI's permanent director. During his year-long tenure,

Gray had made some changes in the Bureau, including opening it to women agents and relaxing strict dress code and weight strictures.

But Gray was an outsider, with no real law-enforcement experience, and dependent on his aides, notably acting associate director Mark Felt. His frequent absences from FBIHQ to make partisan pro-Nixon speeches had won him the nickname of Two Day Gray. He'd stalled the money chain probe, destroyed documents from Hunt's safe, and allowed White House counsel John Dean near-unlimited access to FBI investigatory materials.

Now appearing before the Senate judiciary committee, nominee Gray ran into trouble. Accidentally or on purpose, he volunteered the information that he'd allowed John Dean to sit in on interviews with Watergate figures. Now the spotlight was on Dean, too, and committee members began clamoring for him to testify.

Deciding that the hearings had compromised Gray, Nixon decided to abandon the nomination. On March 6, speaking of Gray to John Dean, White House aide John Ehrlichman said, "I think we should let him hang there. Let him twist slowly, slowly in the wind." On April 5, Nixon withdrew the nomination; on April 27, Gray resigned as acting director.

Toward the end of March, McCord decided to cooperate with the prosecution. Now the trees fell faster. On April 30, 1973, President Nixon announced the resignations of Attorney General Richard Kleindienst, H.R. Haldeman, John Ehrlichman, and John Dean. That same day, he appointed former Environmental Protection Agency head William Ruckelshaus as acting director of the FBI. Ruckelshaus's 70-day tenure was marked by the discovery that evidence against Daniel Ellsberg had been picked up on the Kissinger-ordered wiretaps, which tainted the case against Ellsberg because Ellsberg was not a subject of the taps and thus the evidence gathered was not admissible against him. This led to the dismissal of all charges against Ellsberg in the Pentagon Papers case. Another notable event was the downfall of the man widely believed (certainly by himself) to be in line for the next directorship, Mark Felt, who was caught leaking to the press and forced to submit his resignation to Ruckelshaus.

Selected as permanent Bureau director was a solidly credentialed law-enforcement professional, former FBI agent turned Kansas City

Official and Confidential

During his FBI stint, when G. Gordon Liddy was arrested during a surreptitious black bag job in Kansas City, his release was obtained by the efforts of Chief Kelley. Years later, Liddy's botched Watergate break-in set in motion the chain of events ultimately resulting in Gray's resignation and Kelley's appointment as FBI director.

police chief, Clarence M. Kelley. Kelley had been an FBI agent from 1940 to 1961, and for 12 years after that, the police chief of Kansas City, Missouri. Described as a "tough cop" and strict but fair disciplinarian, Kelley moved swiftly to get the FBI back on track.

Endgame

On March 21, 1973, John Dean told President Nixon that the Watergate scandal was a "cancer on the presidency." In April, Dean began cooperating with prosecutors, telling all he knew in return for immunity. Now the trees began falling in all directions, decimating the Nixon cadre with arrests, convictions, and prison terms. The Watergate burglars generally drew light sentences of a year or two, except for the uncooperative G. Gordon Liddy, who was sentenced to serve a minimum of at least six years.

The break-in at the office of Daniel Ellsberg's psychiatrist, Dr. Henry Fielding, generated many arrests and convictions. Plumbers' head Egil Krogh was convicted of violating Fielding's civil rights. John Ehrlichman was convicted of violating Fielding's civil rights and lying to a grand jury. Charles Colson pled guilty to obstruction of justice in the case.

Nixon associates who served time for other offenses included Liddy's boss at CREEP, Jeb Magruder, for obstruction of justice; former attorney general and CREEP head John Mitchell, for conspiracy to obstruct justice and perjury; presidential counsel John Dean, for conspiracy to obstruct justice; and former White House chief of staff, H.R. Haldeman, for charges including obstruction and lying under oath.

A key threshold was crossed on Friday, July 13, 1973, (Friday the 13th) when former Haldeman aide Alexander Butterfield told Senate probers of the existence of a White House taping system. In the Oval Office and Executive Office Building, sets of voice-activated microphones automatically recorded conversations between the President and his advisors. Nixon's stated reason for taping himself and his associates was to assist himself in compiling his future memoirs someday.

Resisting demands by investigators that he surrender the tapes, Nixon brought the nation to the brink of tumult and disorder. On July 24, 1974, the Supreme Court ordered Nixon to surrender 64 subpoenaed tapes. On August 5, transcripts of the tape of June 23, 1972, recorded just days after the Watergate arrests, were made public. On the tape, Nixon is heard telling Haldeman that it would be "fine" to use the CIA to pressure the FBI to halt its investigation into the money-laundering chain linking illegal campaign contributions to CREEP and the burglars.

That was the smoking gun, proof that the President had authorized a cover-up. Faced with the threat of impeachment, on August 8, 1974, Richard M. Nixon resigned from office.

The Least You Need to Know

- Hoover's explosive political files were denied to the Nixon White House and retained by the FBI.

- Political appointee L. Patrick Gray served as FBI acting director from 1972 to 1973.

- Five burglars caught breaking into Democratic National Committee headquarters at the Watergate building were linked to the White House, triggering a national crisis.

- Twenty-year FBI veteran and Kansas City, Missouri, police chief Clarence M. Kelley was appointed permanent director of the FBI.

- Nixon's failed attempt to use the CIA to impede FBI money-laundering probes was caught on tape, forcing his August 8, 1974, resignation.

New Brooms: The Chief and the Judge

In This Chapter

- The 1970s: an era of scandal and reform
- FBI Director Kelley: A key transitional figure
- President Carter picks a new director
- Judge Webster's way
- Shootings, stings, and crime-busting successes
- The FBI gets back in the political monitoring business

The 1970s was an era of upheaval for virtually all American governmental institutions, and the FBI was no exception. Under the stewardship of Director Clarence M. Kelley (1973–1978), the Bureau successfully transited into the post-Hoover era. The election of President Jimmy Carter led to Kelley's retirement and the search for a successor. The new director, Judge William H. Webster, completed the work that Kelley had begun, remaking the FBI and restoring public confidence in the organization.

Scandal Time

"Don't embarrass the Bureau"—that had been the watchword of the Hoover-era FBI. But the "top cop" was no more and the political climate was defiantly different. The 1970s was a time not only of embarrassment but of sheer mortification for heretofore untouchable major American institutions, moving beyond the FBI to include the CIA, Pentagon, Congress, and the presidency. Nixon's resignation, his pardon by successor President Gerald R. Ford, and the U.S. defeat in Vietnam all contributed to creating a climate of national cynicism, muckraking, and reform. In a kind of political exorcism, reputations were made and unmade overnight, as Congressional investigating committees such as the *Church and Pike committees* probed past governmental misdeeds and abuses of power.

Justice Jargon

In early 1975, the Senate's Select Committee to Study Government Operations with Respect to Intelligence Activities and the House's similar Select Committee on Intelligence were formed to probe CIA and FBI abuses. Named for their respective chairmen, the Senate's **Church Committee** and the House's **Pike Committee** investigations resulted in the creation of House and Senate intelligence oversight committees to monitor the Agency and the Bureau.

Justice Jargon

Located at Pennsylvania Avenue between 9th Street NW and 10th Street NW in Washington, D.C., the new FBI building was first occupied in late 1974 and officially dedicated in September 1975 by President Gerald Ford. Named the J. Edgar Hoover Building, encompassing some 2.5 million square feet, the structure's unusual 7-story front and 11-story slab rear was mandated by local zoning regulations.

Such a climate was dangerous to the FBI, which over the decades had performed countless illegal wiretaps, buggings, and break-ins, not to mention harassing domestic political foes with COINTELPRO operations. The danger lay in the very real possibility that in its reformist zeal, Congress would throw out the baby with the bathwater, straitjacketing the FBI with revisionist rules and regulations that would hamper it from effectively carrying out vital law enforcement and national security duties.

That this did not happen may largely be credited to Director Clarence M. Kelley, who headed the FBI during the critical years 1973–1978. Under Kelley's stewardship, the FBI made a successful transition into the post-Hoover era, restoring public and legislative branch trust in the integrity of the organization.

The Chief

Kelley had performed a similar role in the 1960s as the Kansas City, Missouri, police chief, when he'd revitalized a scandal-ridden department, restoring morale and fostering the use of such then-novel technologies as helicopters and computers. Confirmed as FBI Director by a 96–0 Senate vote on July 9, 1973, Kelley moved quickly to put the Bureau back on track.

Early on, Kelley ended the "cold war" that had existed between the FBI and other intelligence agencies during the final years of Hoover's tenure, closing a dangerous window of vulnerability in the national security sector. The Domestic Intelligence division, author of most of the past illegalities, was downsized, its activities strictly curtailed. Former police chief Kelley also reestablished good working relations with various local and national law enforcement agencies.

Bu Stats

Under Director Clarence M. Kelley, FBI domestic security investigations dropped from 21,000 to fewer than 300.

Cleaning House

Even at the height of the mid-1970s national malaise, the FBI still retained a solid bedrock of public support, thanks in large part to its sterling performance in investigating the complex criminal-political offenses grouped under the label of "Watergate." With the exception of acting director Gray, who destroyed evidence from Howard Hunt's safe and who tried to impede the investigation of illegal Mexican-based money-laundering, the FBI performed with admirable integrity. The Criminal Investigations Division, whose personnel numbered about 80 percent of the FBI's SAs, performed cleanly and effectively throughout the period.

However, problems lingered in the Administrative Division and particularly in the upper echelons of FBIHQ in Washington, D.C., where unreconstructed Hooverites continued to hold sway. High-level administrators continued Hoover's questionable uses of Bureau facilities and personnel for private ends, such as having Exhibits Section craftsmen build costly improvements to their private residences, the improper use of Bureau cars ("Bucars"), and cozy arrangements with suppliers that violated federal competitive bidding guidelines.

At the start of his term, Kelley himself was unwittingly burned by such practices. For one thing, unbeknownst to him, some improvements to his apartment were made by the FBI's Exhibits section, and he also was the recipient of a pair of free TVs, and free airline tickets to an FBI alumni meeting in New York City. The gifts slipped under

Kelley's radar while he was distracted by taking care of his wife, Ruby, ill with terminal cancer. Learning the details of the arrangements, Kelley paid for the cost of the carpentry and the New York City trip and returned the two TVs.

Official and Confidential

On March 10, 1976, Attorney General Edward H. Levi established FBI intelligence guidelines; on April 5, 1976, he set down FBI domestic security activities guidelines. The guidelines stated that the FBI had to have evidence of a criminal act, or intent to commit a crime, before it could place an individual under surveillance or infiltrate a suspected criminal or subversive organization.

Kelley then set about methodically cleaning up Administration Division corruption. Operating in conjunction with a Justice Department investigation, Kelley put an end to such questionable practices. He instituted a host of administrative and procedural reforms, putting in new inventory, auditing, and accounting controls, and reorganizing the Inspection Division.

The FBI's longtime reliance on and touting of often-inflated crime statistics (especially at appropriations time) to quantify its work product and appear to outdo the previous year's quota, was de-emphasized.

Shadows of the Past

In a speech at a Missouri college, Kelley admitted that "wrongful abuses of power" had occurred at the FBI, a statement that created much controversy among FBI alumni associations.

Over the years, the FBI had generated so much paperwork that there was no possibility of completely sanitizing the files. A case in point involved the March 1976 discovery that New York field office SAC John Malone's safe contained lists of illegal break-ins conducted by the office from 1954 to 1973, comprising some 25 volumes in all. A Hoover favorite, square-jawed Malone (nicknamed by associates "Cement Head") had disobeyed the late director's orders not to retain such documentation.

Official and Confidential

On April 15, 1981, President Ronald Reagan pardoned FBIHQ administrators Mark Felt and Edward S. Miller, finding that they had approved the break-ins in good faith while pursuing radical fugitives, and praising them for having served the country with "great distinction."

FBI investigators turned the lists over to President Carter's attorney general, Griffin Bell. Focusing on an early-1970s series of break-ins and mail openings of friends of radical Weather Underground fugitives, Bell found that those responsible for ordering the actions were former acting Director L. Patrick Gray, acting associate director Mark Felt, and assistant director for domestic intelligence Edward S. Miller.

In April 1978, the three were indicted by a federal grand jury. Ultimately, charges against Gray were dropped for lack of evidence, whereas Felt and Miller were prosecuted for the illegal break-ins. The defendants argued national security justifications for the acts, and claimed that Gray told them to do it. On November 6, 1980, they were found guilty, the judge fining Felt $5,000 and Miller $3,500.

An important innovation was the reforming of the promotion process, with career boards composed of FBI officials making recommendations on personnel advancement. L. Patrick Gray had hired the first women agents. Under Kelley, recruitment of women and minorities increased.

Bu Stats

In February 1978, the FBI had 7,931 agents, of whom 147 were women, 185 were black, and 173 were Hispanic.

Kelley tried to bring the FBI into the techno age, using computers and video surveillance tactics that foreshadowed later successes such as Operation Abscam (see below). After Nixon resigned, Kelley actively pursued the war on organized crime and official corruption. During the Hoover era, wary of treading on touchy territorial and jurisdictional matters, the FBI had shied away from investigating state and local corruption. In 1974, a new proactive policy began with an FBI probe into Oklahoma construction-industry graft, resulting in the conviction for bribe-taking of the state's governor. Other successful corruption investigations followed.

Dangerous Doings

In 1975, radical activist Native Americans fomented demonstrations and disturbances at Pine Ridge Indian Reservation near Wounded Knee, South Dakota. On June 26, 1975, FBI agents Ronald A. Williams and Jack R. Coler, attempting to arrest fugitive James "Jimmy" Eagle, spotted him and some associates in a fleeing vehicle and gave chase. During the pursuit, Eagle's associates fired on the Bucar. In the subsequent shootout, both agents were killed with .223 rounds.

It was later determined that the rounds could only have been fired by an AR-15 assault-type weapon owned by Native American activist Leonard Peltier, riding in the murder car. Found guilty of the murders, Peltier was sentenced to serve two consecutive life sentences. Peltier became a leftist cause célèbre, the object of movie stars and literati who sought (and continue to seek) a pardon for him, at least in part because they felt sympathy for the plight of the Native Americans. On a September 1991 segment on an episode of the *60 Minutes* TV show, Peltier admitted to the shootings, a confession that has not affected by one whit his followers' blind faith in his innocence. FBI personnel, both active duty and retired, remain resolute in their determination that Peltier remain behind bars.

In 1972, at the Munich Olympics, the Palestinian terrorists' slaughter of hostage Israeli athletes generated the swift founding of FBI Special Weapons and Tactics SWAT teams attached to various field offices. The SWAT teams were paramilitary units assigned to hostage-taking incidents, stand-offs, sieges, and similar situations requiring heavy firepower and military assault tactics. The ugly shape of things to come was made manifest in 1977, when 12 Hanafi Muslim radical terrorists took 149 hostages at three Washington buildings, including the headquarters of the Anti-Defamation League of the Jewish organization B'nai B'rith. A potential bloodbath was averted when the siege was peacefully resolved, but the incident ultimately helped lead to the creation of the FBI's Hostage Rescue Team, to be covered in Chapter 18.

Mr. Peanut

In the 1976 presidential election, incumbent President Gerald Ford was defeated by self-described Democratic party outsider candidate, ex-Navy submariner and Georgia peanut farmer turned Governor, James Earl "Jimmy" Carter. Carter's election prompted FBI Director Kelley's 1977 announcement of his imminent retirement, setting off a search for his successor. Potential candidates associated with COINTELPRO were removed from consideration. A blue-ribbon panel unanimously recommended Buffalo SAC Neil J. Welch for the director's job.

Cops and Robbers

Highly respected by his colleagues, Buffalo SAC Neil J. Welch pioneered the use of video surveillance, a powerful law enforcement tool that impressed juries, helped win cases, and led to such video-based operations as Abscam. Welch was appointed New York field office SAC by Director William Webster.

With a campaign pledge of "I'll never lie to you," President Jimmy Carter was elected as a reformer. Attorney General Griffin Bell convinced Carter that a judicial appointee, chosen from outside the Bureau, would have the necessary independence to generate public confidence in the FBI's making. Of the candidates from the judiciary, Carter chose former prosecutor and federal appeals court judge William Hedgecock Webster.

Here Comes the Judge

Born on March 6, 1924 in St. Louis, Missouri, William H. Webster served as a U.S. Navy lieutenant in World War II and the Korean War. In 1960, he was appointed

U.S. attorney for the Eastern District in Missouri. 1970 saw his appointment by President Nixon as judge for the U.S. District Court; in 1973 he was named by Nixon to the U.S. Court of Appeals for the Eighth Circuit. A Republican, he was appointed FBI director by President Carter, a Democrat, and was arguably one-termer Carter's most successful appointment. Webster served as director from 1978 to 1987. Fifteen years would pass before the director was once again one of the FBI's own.

Confirmed by a Senate vote of 90–0, Webster took the oath of office as FBI director on February 23, 1978. He quickly let it be known that he preferred to be called "Judge" rather than "Director," perhaps to emphasize his independence and quasi-outsider status. A figure of imposing rectitude, Webster insisted that the FBI operate according to the dictates of the Constitution and the law.

Kelley was a key transitional figure who'd successfully midwifed the Bureau into its post-Hoover incarnation, while Webster successfully refurbished the luster on the laurels of the FBI. Kelley's tenure had been touched by Hoover's long shadow, while Webster's regime saw the mandatory retirement age effect the disestablishment of the last of the high-level Hooverites. Webster restructured the organization's top level by replacing the post of associate director with three executive associate directors.

Death of a Different Judge

Early in Webster's tenure, the first assassination of a federal judge in the twentieth century took place in 1979, when Texas U.S. District Court Judge John H. Wood was shot dead by a marksman who used a high-powered, scoped rifle. Investigation revealed that on the day he was killed, the tough-minded judge, known for handing out long prison terms, had been scheduled to sentence drug kingpin Jamiel "Jimmy" Chagra. Although he was already behind bars, imprisonment would have been no impediment to Chagra's ordering the high-level contract killing.

> ### Cops and Robbers
>
> Like previous Director Clarence Kelley, William H. Webster was from Missouri, where he'd been a former prosecutor and trial and appellate court judge with a reputation for uncompromising, iron-clad integrity. In 1987, Webster left the FBI to become director of the CIA, earning the unique distinction of having headed both organizations.

> ### Official and Confidential
>
> During his arrest for the murder of Judge Wood, a bizarre incident developed when contract killer Charles "Hitman" Harrelson put a gun to his own head, threatening to kill himself. Had his gun been pointed at them, Texas lawmen would have made quick work of him, but by in effect taking himself hostage, the killer managed to delay the proceedings (if only temporarily) with a bizarre and lengthy standoff.

Planting rumors in prison, the FBI fooled Chagra into thinking that it possessed wiretap tapes of him plotting the murder, causing him to make incriminatory statements that were picked up by bugs. Chagra's motive for the murder was the hope that a different judge would give him a lighter sentence. Chagra and the actual assassin, Texas career criminal Charles V. "Hitman" Harrelson, were tried and convicted in a San Antonio court. Presiding over the trials was Judge William S. Sessions, from whom more would be heard at a later date—as a future FBI director.

The Sting

Webster's FBI continued the Kelley concentration on white-collar crime, the corruption of public officials, drugs, espionage, and counterintelligence. A powerful law enforcement tool was videotaped *sting* operations, of which one of the most notable was the one codenamed Abscam.

Beginning as an investigation into art and securities thefts, the operation's focus shifted to political corruption in the fall of 1978. Abscam—codename for Arab oil shiek scam (deception operation)—used a bogus, seemingly deep-pocketed "Arabian oil sheik" to expose corrupt legislators, who were secretly videotaped taking bribes to deliver political favors. Congressional legislators targeted by the investigation were introduced to an agent posing as a wealthy Arabian official willing to pay big bribe money in exchange for legislative favors. The meetings were videotaped, providing irrefutable evidence of malfeasance and bribery.

Justice Jargon

In the argot of confidence tricksters, a **sting** is a successful deception operation carried out on an unsuspecting victim. FBI sting operations apply similar tactics against criminals.

To avoid charges of entrapment, Abscam shunned the use of high-pressure, hard-sell techniques against its intended targets. Besides, they were unneeded, as there proved to be no shortage of greedy grafters eager to jump on the gravy train. The Abscam investigation led to the convictions of New Jersey Senator Harrison "Pete" Williams Jr. and six Congressional representatives.

Another successful sting was Operation Greylord, targeting judicial corruption in the famously dirty political milieu of Cook County, Illinois. The sting resulted in 91 convictions of crooked judges, lawyers, and law enforcement officials.

Hitting hard against organized crime, Judge Webster's FBI launched one of its most successful anti-Mafia ploys, thanks to undercover infiltrator Joseph Pistone who, posing as jewel thief Donnie Brasco, penetrated deep into the heart of the Mafia. The Pizza Connection case busted a Sicilian Mafia plot to use a nationwide chain of U.S. pizza parlors as a front for heroin distribution. The FBI destabilized New York City's ruling Mob commission and Five Families, including the arrest and conviction of Gambino Mafia family boss John Gotti, the well-tailored, recently deceased "Dapper Don" of tabloid headline infamy. Another major arrest was the takedown of Boston Mafia chieftain Raymond Patriarca.

Undone by a flailing economy and the Iran hostage crisis, Jimmy Carter was defeated in the 1980 presidential tilt by ex-governor of California and former Hollywood movie star, Ronald Reagan.

Political Probes

In March 1983, Reagan's new attorney general, William French Smith, revised the FBI's 1976 guidelines on intelligence and domestic security operations, permitting the Bureau to investigate violence-advocating domestic and international terrorist groups. Naturally, the rules for investigating terrorist organizations were looser than those covering domestic political groups.

During the Reagan era, a prime source of contention was the administration's Central American policy, which opposed Nicaragua's pro-Communist Sandinista government and backed the counter-revolutionary Contra insurgent movement. Nicaragua's civil war between Sandinistas and Contras spilled over into neighboring El Salvador. U.S policy in the region generated a fair amount of domestic opposition and political protests.

From 1981 to 1985, the FBI investigated more than 1,300 organizations and individuals opposed to President Reagan's Central American policy. A prime target was the Committee in Solidarity with the People of El Salvador (CISPES), professedly non-violent (and generally held to be so), smeared by a few informants as a pro-terrorist organization. Other left-leaning subjects for investigation included the National Council of Churches, the Maryknoll Sisters, the United Auto Workers union, and the Southern Christian Leadership Conference.

Suspect groups were monitored by FBI agents as they attended political rallies, protest marches, peace demonstrations, and the like, documenting who attended and what was said, and opening files on prominent protestors. Unlike the COINTELPROs, however, these actions were legal, not involving any violations of law.

Bu Stats

In 1987, at the end of Judge Webster's term as director, the FBI had 9,100 SAs, including 650 women, 350 blacks, and 350 Hispanics. Ten percent of the FBI agents were minorities; 8 percent women.

Equally legal and controversial was the FBI's Library Awareness Program. Launched in New York City, the pilot program sought to enlist the voluntary cooperation of librarians in monitoring reading patterns to detect foreign (that is, Soviet) spies. The idea was that the mass of technical information available in scientific and trade journals would be gleaned by foreign agents, allowing our side to spot and triangulate the opposition's intelligence targets. Librarians' reluctance to infringe on First Amendment rights by becoming government informants led to a public outcry that quickly doomed the program.

The Least You Need to Know

- The 1970s was a time of upheaval for American governmental institutions.
- Director Clarence Kelley successfully oversaw the remaking of the post-Hoover FBI.
- Kelley's successor, Judge William Webster, continued the work of his predecessor, restoring public confidence in the FBI.
- Video surveillance "sting" operations like Abscam became a powerful investigative tool.
- Under President Reagan, the FBI resumed monitoring dissident domestic political groups.

Chapter 15

Global Crime

In This Chapter

- ◆ The RICO Act: Hammer of hoodlums
- ◆ New anti-Mob tactics: Sting operations, undercover agents, and enough rope
- ◆ Jackie Presser: Teamsters president and FBI informant
- ◆ The FBI takes down New York City's Five Families
- ◆ Inside dope on the Mob's narcotics trade
- ◆ John Gotti: the last don?

Post-Watergate Congressional investigations triggered a wave of high-level Mafia assassinations, including those of Teamsters ex-prexy Hoffa and Chicago Mob boss Giancana. Enacted by Congress, the RICO Act targeted patterns of racketeering, providing law enforcement with a powerful anti-Mob tool. Despite well-publicized denials, the narcotics trade is an integral Mafia operation. The 1980s saw the FBI's vigorous anti-Mob assault result in massive disruption of the National Crime Syndicate. While the rise and fall of brutal crime boss John Gotti may signal to some the Mob's decline, the Mafia still remains at the center of U.S. organized crime.

Cleaning House

The federal government's post-Watergate reformist investigations produced their own variety of collateral damage. On June 19, 1975, a week before he was scheduled to appear before the Senate's Church Committee's probe into CIA-Mafia plots, Chicago Mafia boss Sam Giancana, who knew much, was murdered Mob execution-style in his own home while cooking a snack. The unknown killer, who must have been someone Giancana trusted, shot him in the back of the head with a .22 pistol, then shot him six more times around the mouth. The message was clear: He'd been silenced to keep from talking.

During the Nixon presidency, former International Brotherhood of Teamsters (IBT) boss Jimmy Hoffa's prison sentence had been commuted, on condition that he stay out of union politics for a number of years—a condition congenial to then-Teamsters president Frank Fitzsimmons, a big Nixon backer. On July 30, 1975, Hoffa vanished, never to be seen again.

Johnny Rosselli, the "all-American Mafioso" who'd been the linchpin in the CIA-Mafia plot to assassinate Cuban communist dictator Fidel Castro, lived to testify to Senate investigators about his dealings with the agency. On August 8, 1976, in Florida's Biscayne Bay, police recovered a floating 50-gallon metal drum to which the top had been welded shut. Inside was Rosselli, strangled to death. In a macabre touch, his legs had been cut off, presumably after rigor mortis had set in, so the body would fit in the drum. Prime suspect but never charged for the kill was Florida Mob boss Santos Trafficante.

The Mafia was cleaning house, too.

FBI Onslaught

This bears repeating: Every ethnic group and nationality has its own organized crime groups. In the United States, the ruling council of the National Crime Syndicate is the Sicilian-born Mafia, whose associates include members of a wide-ranging multi-ethnic spectrum of gangs and organized crime groups.

The FBI's first major assault wave against the Mafia took place during Robert Kennedy's tenure as attorney general. Prosecutions dwindled during the final years of the Hoover era, recommencing in 1975 under Director Clarence M. Kelley. A powerful law enforcement tool for taking on (and taking apart) organized crime was the *RICO Act*, essentially an anti-crime conspiracy statute specifically designed to be used against the Mob.

Aggressive, proactive anti-Mob operations were sparked by new FBI strategy and tactics. In the past, once a targeted subject was caught taking a bribe, an arrest quickly followed. Now, the FBI adopted a long-term strategy toward such cases, the objective being to take down not one or two individual mobsters, but the entire organization. In effect, the corrupt ones were given a longer rope with which to hang themselves, allowing in-depth exposure of the workings of the underworld.

A prime target of Director Kelley's regime was crooked public officials and their corrupters. A prime example of such corruption was New York City's Mafia-dominated construction trades, where pandemic bribery and kickbacks had raised the cost of concrete to twice what it was in nearby Philadelphia.

Justice Jargon

Part of Congress's Organized Crime Control Act of 1970, the Racketeer-Influenced and Corrupt Organizations **(RICO) Act** federalizes the prosecution of two or more people committing two or more crimes in a racketeering pattern. Its stiff sentencing guidelines and asset forfeiture provisions have made it a bulwark of the Justice Department's war on organized crime.

An NYC sting operation using FBI undercover agents posing as members of the coyly named James Rico Construction Consultants company exposed and convicted an unholy triangle of Mob bosses, union leaders, and public officials. Another significant Kelley-era success was the UNIRAC operation, countering Mob control of a Miami-based longshoreman's union.

Three Can Keep a Secret

Key elements of the FBI's success against the mob were (beginning in mid-1970s) the RICO statute itself, particularly those provisions that authorized electronic surveillance in organized crime cases; the use of undercover agents as Mob infiltrators; the federal witness protection program, which protected witnesses and informants from mob retaliation by providing them and their families with new identities and relocating them far from their old haunts; and improved cooperation with state, local, and other federal agencies.

The assault on organized crime begun by Kelley was continued during Judge Webster's directorship. In 1979, the FBI's BRILAB (Bribery-Labor) sting operation focused on New Orleans Mafia boss Carlos Marcello, 70, who'd once boasted, "We own the Teamsters," ("we" meaning the National Crime Syndicate, not Marcello's New Orleans branch of same).

Marcello now conspired with an insurance company to skim millions in commissions from policies written for union members, unaware that the company was a phony, operated by undercover agents. Maintaining round-the-clock electronic surveillance of Marcello at his home and places of business, an FBI break-in succeeded in planting a bug in the mobster's inner sanctum, a private office decorated with a wall plaque bearing the ominous legend, "Three can keep a secret if two are dead."

The most successful sting operation against the Mafia up to that time, BRILAB culminated in Marcello's 1980 arrest and subsequent conviction and imprisonment. He has since died.

The Mighty Brotherhood

Few combinations have proved as potent and deadly as the alliance between the Mafia and the International Brotherhood of Teamsters. Control of the mighty union has furnished mobsters with no-show jobs, kickbacks, bribes, extortion money, and all the cream that can be skimmed from the lucrative trade of labor racketeering. But the IBT's prize plum is control of its massive welfare and pension funds, which have been used to invest many millions in Mafia-controlled businesses and "loans" to top mobsters.

Few men have lived lives so steeped in corruption, betrayal, and just plain playing both ends against the middle than Jackie Presser, who was at once both president of the Teamsters and a top confidential informant for the FBI.

In 1977, while a high-ranking Teamsters official, Presser became an FBI informant. The new recruit was deemed so important that aspects of the arrangement were overseen by Director Kelley himself. Codenamed ALPRO, Presser's file eventually ran to 2,000 pages, and was an integral part of PROBEX, the FBI's Teamster investigation.

Cops and Robbers
Son of a Mob-linked Teamsters fixer, IBT president Jackie Presser was an eighth-grade dropout who'd never driven or loaded trucks for a living. Controlled by the Mafia's Cleveland, Ohio, branch while informing on them to the FBI, Presser was also named to President Reagan's transition team.

The Teamsters was one of only two national labor organizations to endorse the 1980 presidential candidacy of former California governor and Hollywood actor Ronald Reagan. (The other was the Air Traffic Controllers, whose illegal 1981 walkout led to their firing en masse by President Reagan). Postelection, Presser was appointed to the Reagan transition team as "senior economic adviser."

In 1983, Presser became president of the Teamsters, enabling him to make millions of dollars of pension fund loans to Mafia enterprises. At the moment of his ascendancy, FBI Director Webster officially "closed out" Presser as an informant, not wanting to put the Bureau in a position of control over the union. Unofficially, Presser continued to pass information along to FBI contact agents.

One such tidbit was his account of the fate of missing IBT ex-boss Jimmy Hoffa. Presser said that Hoffa had made himself obnoxious by insisting that he be granted a million-dollar IBT Pension fund "loan." The Hoffa murder "contract" was handled by the Detroit Mafia. A close intimate, one he trusted, lured Hoffa to a meeting of Mob associates, where he was killed and his body later disposed of.

Presser's information led to the indictment on labor racketeering charges of Chicago-based Mob-Teamsters financier and fixer Allen Dorfman. Before he could come to trial, Dorfman was murdered by a team of ski-masked hit men who shot him down in a parking lot. Also vital was Presser's information about secret Mafia ownership of Las Vegas casinos.

Official and Confidential

During a speech to a law enforcement conclave, FBI Director William H. Webster observed, "The informant is the, with a capital T, *the* most effective tool in law enforcement today—state, local, and federal."

Ultimately, Presser helped the FBI take down key union-linked mobsters in Cleveland, Chicago, Kansas City, and New York. In 1988, while facing charges of union corruption, the overweight, stressed-out Presser died—of natural causes.

Five Families of Death

Despite the administration's dangerous liaison with the Teamsters, the Reagan era saw the Justice Department's most massive assault yet on the Mafia, with federal prosecutors bringing over 1,000 (mostly successful) indictments against top Mafiosi, hammering the syndicate nationwide.

Spearheading the government's anti-organized crime efforts was assistant secretary of the Justice Department Rudolph Giuliani, who in 1983—operating from the U.S. Attorney's office at One St. Andrews Plaza in Manhattan, behind the Foley Square Federal courthouse—set out to prosecute all of New York City's Mafia Five Families and the national Commission.

Official and Confidential

In most U.S. cities, the underworld is dominated by a single Mafia crime family. In New York City, there are five. NYC's Five Families are the Bonanno Family, the Columbo Family, the Gambino Family, the Genovese Family, and the Lucchese Family.

A Yankee baseball fan while growing up in Dodgers-dominated Brooklyn, New York, Giuliani exhibited that same sense of single-minded purpose in his war against the Mob. He formed the Organized Crime Drug Enforcement Task Force, consisting of elements of the FBI, DEA, Justice Department federal attorneys, INS, IRS, and local and state cops. A dozen such *task forces*, equipped with money, agents, and government backing, were assigned to major U.S. cities.

In 1985, applying the RICO Act against New York City's ruling Mafia Commission, Giuliani brought to trial three of the Five Family bosses and five of their key associates. During the trial, the defense admitted the existence of the Commission. All eight defendants were found guilty of a pattern of racketeering that included murder, loan sharking, and labor corruption.

Justice Jargon

A **task force** is a investigative team whose members are recruited from a variety of law enforcement agencies working toward a single goal. A federal organized crime strike force might typically consist of representatives from the FBI, DEA, Justice Department lawyers, INS, IRS, and local and state agencies.

Inside Dope

Much nonsense has been disseminated about the Mob's policy on drug dealing, a large part of it promulgated by the Mafia itself. The popular myth is that members are or were once forbidden on pain of death to deal drugs. Yet as far back as the 1920s, National Crime Syndicate founding father Lucky Luciano and his cohorts dealt in narcotics. More recently, New York City's Five Families imported 95 percent of the heroin coming into the United States.

The Mafia's public posture was one of shunning the dope business; the reality was quite different. In 1957, one of every three Bonanno and Columbo crime family members had been arrested on drug charges; in the Gambino family, two in five; in the Genovese family, one in two; and in the Luccheses, three in five. That year, which saw the abortive Apalachin debacle, also saw a lesser-known, more successful conclave in Palermo, Sicily. A delegation of U.S. Cosa Nostra members led by Joe Bonanno concluded a historic agreement with their Sicilian counterparts, in which the latter would supply heroin to the former.

Drug trafficking is a dangerous business. Mobster Vito Genovese, renowned for his Byzantine treachery and murderousness, was caught making a 160-kilo heroin buy. Sentenced to serve 15 years in the Atlanta federal pen, he died there, but not before inadvertently setting off a chain of events which would make *Cosa Nostra* a household word. Believing that Genovese meant to have him killed, fellow inmate Joe Valachi killed a convict he thought was his designated executioner. He'd killed the wrong man. To beat a possible death penalty murder rap, Valachi agreed to tell all he knew about the Mafia to federal probers.

Joe Bonanno's successor, Carmine Galante, served a long prison term for trafficking. Galante was the Five Families' contact man with Sicilian Mafia heroin suppliers, responsible for making pay-offs and disbursing heroin money shares to the New York City Families. In 1977, undercover agent Joe Pistone first alerted the FBI to the dimensions of the Five Families–Sicilian narcotics connection. Carmine Galante's increasingly cavalier attitude about fairly sharing out heroin money proceeds led to his murder in the summer of 1979, the first big Mob boss hit in 20 years.

Galante's place in the heroin distribution pyramid was taken by Gambino family and Commission head Paul "Big Paulie" Castellano, who was being troubled by the brash, destabilizing power grab moves of upstart underboss John Gotti.

A massive FBI effort was launched to bust the Sicilian Mafia's heroin dealership infrastructure, which was centered in the Bonanno Family's Brooklyn territory. In what became known as the Pizza Connection case, agents shot a thousand rolls of film; conducted 55,000 wiretaps; and clocked an amazing million man-hours of surveillance on organized crime targets. A startling and sinister component of the traffic was the Mafia's use of a nationwide chain of pizza parlors as fronts for heroin distribution.

The investigation resulted in the narcotics ring's destruction. Leading the effort was a former FBI agent turned assistant U.S. attorney, Louis Freeh, from whom more would be heard later.

> **Cops and Robbers**
>
> FBI undercover agent Joseph Pistone posed as wiseguy jewel thief "Donnie Brasco," infiltrating NYC's Bonanno family, beginning in 1975. He became an associate of the crime family, though not a "made" (inducted) Mafia member. In 1977, Pistone tipped the FBI to Sicilian Mafia heroin trafficking, setting the stage for what became the "Pizza Connection" case.

> **Cops and Robbers**
>
> Crusading U.S. Attorney Rudolph "Rudy" Giuliani was elected two-term New York City Mayor (1984–2002). In the aftermath of the September 11, 2001, terror strikes against the World Trade Center, Giuliani rose to new heights of leadership, rallying the city and inspiring a nation.

Boston Confidential

Great success and ultimate disgrace marked the battle between the FBI's Boston field office and the Mafia family headed by Raymond Patriarca Jr. In a stunning coup, agents learned of an upcoming ceremony to induct new Mafia members and planted bugging devices on-site in advance of the meeting. On October 29, 1989, with Halloween right around the corner, the FBI bugs caught a five-hour ceremony as Patriarca and 15 New England Mafiosi "made" four new members, inducting them into the family.

A mobster was heard enthusing, "This thing you're in, it's gonna be the life of heaven ... It's a wonderful thing, the greatest thing in the world." The inductees agreed that they would kill a brother if so commanded by their bosses. They swore to keep *omerta*, the Mafia code of silence. Each new member's trigger finger was cut with a dagger, the blood was dripped on a picture of a saint, and the burning paper was held in the initiate's hand while he vowed to burn like the saint should he ever betray the secret of Cosa Nostra:

Bu Stats

By the end of the 1980s, some 2,500 Mafiosi and their associates, including the entire national Commission and leaders of every major U.S. city's crime family, had been sent to prison. In 1990, the U.S. Cosa Nostra numbered 1,700 made members. By contrast, Sicilian Mafia members numbered 15,000, one percent of the island's population.

"I want to enter alive into this organization, and I will have to get out dead."

Later, the ritual completed, a mobster was recorded crowing, "Only the [expletive] ghosts knows what really took place here, by God!"

The tape stands as a final refutation for those last few benighted souls who continue their refusal to believe in the existence of the Mafia.

The Boston field office took down Patriarca and his high command, but at what price? We've since learned that the two agents heading the office's Organized Crime squad protected the city's Winter Hill gang, whose top killers were also FBI informants. The killers were tipped off about local law enforcement investigations aimed their way.

Worse, one of the killers falsely accused four innocent men of committing a Mob hit, causing them to be sent to prison. Two died behind bars, while the other two were only recently released, after spending over 35 years in jail. A Justice Department task force found suppressed documents in FBIHQ files proving that some of the Boston agents knew of the false imprisonment.

The Last Don?

In 1985, New York City Gambino Family head Paul Castellano was assassinated while he and a bodyguard were enjoying dinner at Spark's Steakhouse restaurant.

The hit was ordered by ambitious, ruthless underling John Gotti, who succeeded the deceased as head of the family.

> ### Cops and Robbers
>
> A penchant for expensive, custom-tailored suits and daily blow-dried haircuts led to Gambino Family crime boss John Gotti being nicknamed by the tabloids the Dapper Don. For a time in the mid- to late-1980s, Gotti cut a wide swathe through New York City society, carrying himself with the high-profile arrogance of a rock star. His ability to escape prosecution (for a time) generated the sobriquet the Teflon Don. But such publicity only assured his swift downfall. He spent the last decade of his life in a cell in maximum-security federal penitentiary in Marion, Illinois, dying of cancer in summer of 2002.

A brutal street thug and strong-arm enforcer, Gotti had "made his bones" (committed murder) in the killing of James McBratney, who was believed to have been involved in the kidnap-murder of a Gambino nephew. Compared to the shadowy, secretive Castellano, Gotti was a publicity hound, loving the media limelight. But like Al Capone, his headline-hunting ways only certified his status as federal law enforcement's top target.

The Teflon Don was able to elude conviction in one racketeering trial in 1987, followed by two mistrials in 1988. But his luck ran out in May 1989, when his chief executioner Sammy "The Bull" Gravano turned state's witness, testifying against boss Gotti in return for a light sentence and relocation in the federal witness protection plan. Sent to the federal maximum security prison in Marion, Illinois, one of the nation's toughest lock-ups, Gotti was penned in his cell for 23-hour lockdowns, broken only by a daily one-hour exercise period, which he took alone in the prison yard.

Son and successor John Gotti Jr. was subsequently arrested and imprisoned. In June 2002, acting boss Peter Gotti (Gotti Sr.'s brother) and 13 other Gambino family members and associates were busted by the FBI. It is unlikely that the onetime Dapper Don was aware of the event, having at that time slipped into his final, fatal coma. His death from cancer triggered an orgy of tabloid and media coverage.

Bu Stats

In 1991, New York City FBI agents prepared a poster-sized chart of 25 top Gambino crime family leaders and managers. By the June 2002 death of John Gotti and indictment of 14 Gambino associates, 22 of the 25 mobsters were either dead or under arrest. Of the two original members still at large, one was 88 years old and the other, 73—and they may yet be prosecuted.

Is this the end of the American Mafia? History may supply the answer. In Fascist dictator Benito Mussolini's regime, Cesare Mori, the "Iron Prefect," armed with virtually unlimited police powers and unhampered by legal niceties, managed to suppress the Sicilian Mafia from roughly 1925 to 1945. Even before the end of World War II, the Mafia was already resurgent, coming back stronger than ever.

Today, other nationalities' crime mobs are on the rise: the Chinese Triads, Japan's Yakuza, the Russians, Columbians, and Nigerians to name but a few. But for the foreseeable future, the Mafia's unparalleled global drug distribution system will ensure its continued primacy.

The Least You Need to Know

- ◆ The RICO Act's provisions for federal prosecution of patterns of racketeering has proved to be one of law enforcement's most powerful weapons in the fight against organized crime.

- ◆ The late 1970s marked the start of new FBI anti-Mob tactics, such as sting operations, undercover infiltration, and long-term in-depth operations.

- ◆ An alliance dating back to 1957 with the Sicilian Mafia enabled New York City's Five Families to control the traffic of 95 percent of the heroin imported into the United States.

- ◆ By the end of the 1980s, the FBI had seriously disrupted Mafia operations in every major American city.

- ◆ Despite the rise of other ethnic crime mobs, the Mafia's global infrastructure and drug distribution networks ensures it will remain one of organized crime's key players.

Chapter 16

Year of the Spy

In This Chapter

- True believers versus walk-ins
- FISC: America's top-secret court
- John Walker's family of spies
- Ivy Bells: The Pelton Affair
- Edward Lee Howard: The spy who got away

Foreign intelligence officers don't steal our secrets, American traitors do. Post-1960, the demolition of the U.S. Communist Party and the scarcity of Marxist ideologues led to their replacement by a new breed of U.S. spies who traded secrets for cash. The late 1970s saw the establishment of the Foreign Intelligence Surveillance Court, a top-secret judicial process allowing for the wiretapping and bugging of suspected spies. The year 1985 became known as the Year of the Spy due to the arrest and conviction of a number of high-profile Soviet-controlled U.S. spies.

Death of the True Believer

The seven decade–long spy war between the United States and the Soviet Union had two distinct phases.

In the first, lasting from the founding of the Soviet state in 1917 until roughly 1960, the Kremlin's American spy operations were mostly carried out by dedicated U.S. communists, true believers in the world socialist revolution. In the second, American spies mostly sold secrets to the Soviets for pay. Treason's motivation had changed from ideology to greed.

Not all true believer spy recruits were members of the Communist Party USA. In fact, being openly enrolled in Party ranks was a "red flag" to security investigators. But almost all the Kremlin's American spies of this period were passionately devoted to the Communist cause. Besides, to a true Marxist ideologue, any squeamishness about turning traitor and betraying one's country on behalf of the cause was just so much sentimental bourgeois nonsense.

But J. Edgar Hoover had more or less destroyed the CPUSA, and what he hadn't done, time had; Stalin's tyranny, the occupation of East Europe, and the brutal suppression of the 1956 Hungarian uprising had washed up the cause with all but a handful of the most don't-bother-me-with-the-facts diehards. By 1960, the ideologically motivated true believer Communist spy was virtually a vanished species. He was to be replaced by a new breed of spies and traitors motivated by good, old-fashioned American greed.

Official and Confidential

A statute of limitations sets a time limit during which a crime is legally prosecutable. In the United States, only three crimes are unbound by any statute of limitations: tax evasion, homicide, and espionage.

Justice Jargon

A **walk-in** is a volunteer spy, one whom often literally walks-in to the embassy or consulate of the country to which he intends to offer his services.

Not that paid spies were anything new. Soviet intelligence had long made a practice of targeting for recruitment code clerks, secretaries, mid-level bureaucrats, and enlisted military personnel—whomever needed the money. Starting in the 1960s, this became a well-traveled two-way street, with would-be spies from the United States actively seeking out Soviet intelligence officers to make deals.

And yet, as any intelligence case handler knows, spying is rarely just about money. There's a certain psychology involved in betraying one's country. Profiles of traitors highlight such characteristics as narcissism, ego-gratification, the need to show one's "specialness" in outwitting the authorities, a need for intrigue, and lust for revenge against a system that fails to hold the budding traitor in the same sense of exaggerated esteem in which he holds himself. Spy handlers are aware of such needs and know how to expertly play on them to motivate their agents for peak performance.

In modern times, the most dangerous U.S. spies have been the *walk-ins*, who offer their services and knowledge to foreign intelligence services for money.

Eye on Spies

The FBI is the nation's counterintelligence agency, the only one empowered to make arrests. In classic spy tradition, the FBI's deceptively named Intelligence Division, which has little to do with intelligence collecting, is actually its foreign counterintelligence unit.

The two key U.S. cities for spy activity were (and are) New York and Washington, D.C. During the 1980s, FBI counterintelligence operations focused on monitoring KGB officers working under Soviet diplomatic cover. As an international protocol, diplomatic personnel are generally immune from arrest. When a diplomat is caught spying, he's declared persona non grata and expelled from the host country. When a non-diplomat is caught spying, he or she is subject to severe criminal penalties, up to and including execution during times of war.

Soviet intelligence's (*KGB* and *GRU*) top three American targets were the military, federal agencies (especially intelligence agencies), and the defense industry.

A Matter of Judgment

One hurdle the KGB never had to overcome in its dealings with suspected spies was the American legal system. From the mid-1960s until a decade later, virtually no espionage cases were prosecuted by the U.S. government. Instead, deals were made to keep things quiet. Cap-tured spies bartered their way out of being prosecuted with the threat of revealing state secrets in open court, a practice known as *graymail*.

To nullify the threat of graymail, in 1980 Congress passed the Classified Information Procedures Act, which allows judges and lawyers to

> **Official and Confidential**
>
> The **GRU** (Glavnoye Razvedyvatelnoye Upravlenie or Chief Intelligence Directorate of the General Staff) was the Soviet military intelligence service. The **KGB** (Komitet Gosudarstvennoy Bezopasnostie/Committee for State Security), primarily responsible for internal security, was the last incarnation of the secret police apparatus which had been known as MGB, NKVD, OGPU, GPU, and at birth, the Cheka.

> **Justice Jargon**
>
> **Graymail**, a variant on the word *blackmail*, is the threat of exposing government secrets in order to avoid prosecution for espionage.

confidentially view classified materials and information relating to espionage cases without having them divulged in open court.

Like a physician, the primary goal of the prosecution (that is, the U.S. government) is to do no harm. What's important is that the accused reveal no more secrets in open court. Operating on this logic, the government often decided that keeping what secrets were left was more important than prosecuting the spy, leading to the dropping of the case.

Cops and Robbers

For most of the last two decades of the twentieth century, the Justice Department's top prosecutor of spies was John L. Martin. A former FBI agent (1962 to 1968), in 1980 Martin became head of the DOJ's Internal Security Section. By the time of his 1997 retirement, Martin had supervised the prosecution of 76 spies, of whom only one was acquitted.

A second, more self-serving motive of the agencies that had been victimized by the spying was to protect themselves from the institutional embarrassment which comes from having had their foibles publicly exposed.

Beginning in 1977, President Carter's attorney general, Griffin Bell, made a policy decision to vigorously prosecute espionage cases. Henceforth, the government would see that justice was done when it came to prosecuting spies and traitors.

America's Most Secret Court

A product of 1975 reformist legislation was a law creating a mechanism allowing intelligence agencies to run electronic surveillance (or similar measures such as *watch listings*) in foreign espionage or terrorism cases, without violating national security or alerting the targets. Introduced in 1976 by liberal Democrat Senator Ted Kennedy, the Foreign Intelligence Surveillance Act (FISA), entitled "Electronic Surveillance Within the United States for Foreign Intelligence Purposes," became law in 1978.

Justice Jargon

A **watch listing** is the acquisition of telegrams and cables sent by or intended for the person being watched.

FISA established the Foreign Intelligence Surveillance Court (FISC), the most top-secret court in the land. Not only the FBI but all other U.S. intelligence agencies (CIA, NSA, and so on) seeking authorization for electronic surveillance must apply to the FISC court. In 1981, the act was expanded to include break-ins.

This court runs like no other. For one thing, no defense attorneys are allowed within the court. All briefs presented to the court are secret, as are all of its actions and decisions. Records of court proceedings are sealed under procedures established by the chief justice of the U.S. Supreme Court and the attorney general.

The FISC courtroom is located in a secure, bugproof room on the sixth floor of the Justice Department Building. The Supreme Court's Chief Justice designates one of seven alternating U.S. District Court judges to sit in session at the FISC court for several days each month.

Individual applications for electronic surveillance on suspected spies are reviewed by the FBI director, then passed to the attorney general. The Justice Department then coordinates the request with the head of the CIA, the latter operating in his capacity as director of central intelligence (DCI) to exercise final operational approval. In the illusory world of spy-counterspy, the request must be reviewed to determine that the target is actually spying for foreigners and not a U.S. double agent.

The DCI is empowered to halt or initiate an investigation, but is (theoretically) powerless to intercede once prosecution has begun. And again, only the FBI is empowered to make arrests.

Requests for bug or wiretaps are rarely turned down by the FISC court, but an adverse decision may be appealed to a specially vetted three-judge panel from the U.S. Courts of Appeal.

Family of Spies

Various operations and investigations came to a head in 1985, which has been christened by U.S. intelligence professionals as the Year of the Spy.

Perhaps the greediest and certainly the most dangerous spy of the era was U.S. Navy communications specialist John A. Walker Jr., whose activities created a chilling window of vulnerability in America's global and national defense posture against the Soviets.

In the late 1960s, while on active duty with the Navy, Walker ran a stateside bar as a sideline. When the bar business began failing, Walker tried to convince his then-wife Barbara to enter into prostitution to help pay the bills. Failing to persuade her to enter the oldest profession, Walker himself then decided to follow the world's second oldest profession: spying.

In 1968, Walker walked through the front door of the Soviet embassy in Washington, D.C., volunteering to sell his services to the other side. He was quite a catch. A highly rated Navy radioman, Walker's resumé included tours of duty in two strategic missile submarines (SSBNs) and a turn as communications watch officer at the Navy's Atlantic Fleet submarine command headquarters (SubLant), where he supervised the communications center for a fleet of missile and attack nuclear subs.

His top secret cryptographic clearance gave him virtually unlimited access to a treasure trove of ultra-classified material such as equipment manuals, communications documents, and operations plans. Possibly most valuable of all to the Soviets was Walker's access to the daily code keys that encrypted secret message traffic over the Navy's worldwide communication network. Possession of such code keys allowed the Soviets to read encrypted Navy communiqués as easily as reading another person's mail.

Walker knew what he was worth and charged for it accordingly, and the Soviets were happy to pay. They deemed him such an important asset that the KGB took him over from the GRU. The military advantage gained from the secrets he betrayed was priceless. For years, Walker periodically passed thousands of pages of top-secret documents to his Soviet handlers, using the loot to finance a high-living, free-spending lifestyle of fine food and drink, fast cars, and faster women.

Retiring from the Navy in April 1976 to head his own private investigation agency, Walker had no intention of withdrawing from the spy game. Anticipating his future retirement, he'd created his own spy ring, recruiting Navy buddy radioman Jerry Whitworth, brother Arthur Walker, and sailor son Michael Walker into the business of stealing classified documents for sale to the KGB. His attempts to recruit daughter Laura Walker Snyder into the ring were rebuffed.

Most spies are caught when either an associate or a defector from the other side identifies them. Walker had remarked to his son Michael in regard to Walker's long-divorced ex-wife Barbara, Michael's mother, that "She is a problem and can put us away." In late 1984, Barbara Walker did her own kind of walk-in by informing the FBI that John Walker was a Soviet spy. After a delay of some months, her charges were finally taken seriously and the FBI investigation codenamed Operation WIND-FLYER was opened on Walker.

Official and Confidential

An FBI investigation into a suspected spy begins with putting the subject under surveillance; interviewing the suspect's acquaintances, employers and co-workers; and thoroughly checking such relevant records as birth certificates, marriage licenses, divorce hearings, educational records, military service history, financial and credit histories, and police and court records.

Weeks of wiretapping Walker's phones failed to uncover any incriminating statements, but remarks he'd made and his pattern of behavior indicated that he was scheduled for a meeting or exchange with one of his handlers. A face-to-face meeting would be too risky and ran contrary to KGB standard operating procedure. Rather, he would be going to a *dead drop*, a secure and anonymous preselected site. A location is chosen: a park bench, a roadside sign; a hollow tree is a favorite. The two parties arrive separately. When each is sure he's not being followed, the documents are left at one site, payment in another. Each agent leaves a signal (an empty soda bottle, cigarette pack, and so on) at his respective site, indicating that it is all-clear. If the all-clear signal is not left, the drop takes place at an alternate site, or is scrubbed and rescheduled.

Justice Jargon

A **dead drop** is a secure method of exchanging documents for cash.

On Saturday (Saturday being the KGB's favorite day to conduct spy business), May 18, 1985, Walker drove alone into the suburban Maryland area, unaware that he was the object of one of the FBI's most elaborate arrest procedures ever. His vehicle was shadowed by a wide-ranging escort of 20 unmarked FBI cars and a high-flying FBI chase plane. For hours, Walker routinely followed a tortuous counter-surveillance route mapped out by his KGB handlers. At one point, the FBI followers temporarily lost him, but soon picked up his trail. A further miscue warned off Walker's contact, Aleksy Tkachenko, third secretary at the Soviet embassy and KGB officer. Since he'd committed no crime, Tkachenko was allowed to drive away. Later, he was declared persona non grata and expelled from the United States.

At the exchange site, Walker left a bag of garbage beside a tree and drove away. Recovering the bag, FBI agents discovered that the garbage had been washed clean, to avoid attracting the interest of wild animals. Inside the bag was another bag, the latter containing 129 classified documents. Later that night, agents arrested Walker at a nearby motel. When apprehended, Walker was armed with a handgun, but decided not to try to shoot it out and surrendered.

Investigation revealed the extent of the damage done to national security by Walker. His information allowed the Soviets to read American military codes. Had armed conflict broken out between the U.S. and the U.S.S.R., the Soviets' ability to read those codes would have given them a potentially war-winning advantage.

For his treachery, Walker had ultimately received from the KGB a million dollars (tax-free). A U.S. court sentenced him to life imprisonment. As documented by Thomas B. Allen and Norman Polmar in their book, *Merchants of Treason* (Dell, 1988), when accomplice Jerry Whitworth was sentenced to serve 365 years in prison, he was described by the presiding judge as "a man who represented the evil of banality … a zero at the bone," a description which also accurately described his mentor, John A. Walker. Arthur Walker received a life sentence. John Walker's son Michael was sentenced to 25 years. Daughter Laura Walker Snyder had refused to join the spy ring, so no charges were filed against her.

Ivy Bells

Walking in through the same Soviet embassy front door which had been used by Walker was former National Security Agency employee Ronald W. Pelton. After 14 years as an NSA analyst, Pelton retired and in 1980 offered to sell his knowledge to the Soviets. He was debriefed by Vitaly Yurchenko, KGB security officer at the Washington embassy from 1975 to 1980. Oddly, although the Soviet embassy was under constant surveillance, neither Walker nor Pelton was spotted entering the building.

Pelton's case is unique in that he passed no documents to his handlers, but instead relied on his photographic memory to detail vital information about U.S. intercepts of Russian signal traffic.

KGB officer Yurchenko proved to be Pelton's undoing. During an odd three-month "defection" to the West in 1985, Yurchenko provided clues that led to Pelton's exposure as a Soviet spy.

 Official and Confidential

In August 1985, KGB officer Vitaly Yurchenko began one of the oddest odysseys of modern spy history. He seemingly defected to the United States, during his debriefing exposing American spies Ronald Pelton and Edward Lee Howard. In November 1985, while dining at a restaurant in Washington, D.C., Yurchenko gave his CIA handlers the slip, vanishing, only to resurface at the Soviet embassy. At a press conference, he claimed he had never defected, but had been drugged and disoriented by CIA agents, until finally managing to escape from them. The still-unexplained episode is one of the great Cold War conundrums.

Pelton was interrogated by FBI agents David E. Faulkner and Dudley F. B. Hedgson. Basically, having no hard evidence against him, the ace FBI interrogators skillfully played Pelton into confessing that he'd spied for the Soviets. His own words alone propelled him into a life sentence in prison.

The most damaging information passed by Pelton to the Soviets was the existence of one of the United States' most closely guarded military secrets, an operation codenamed Ivy Bells. Behind the cryptonym lay the fact that U.S. submarines were tapping undetected into an undersea Soviet military communications cable and monitoring the Soviets' top-secret message traffic.

The One Who Got Away

Malice was as important as mercenary considerations in Edward Lee Howard's decision to turn traitor. Howard had been recruited by the CIA with the goal of ultimately becoming a handler running Soviet spies in Moscow. While in training, Howard learned a great deal about ongoing CIA operations in Russia, as well as mastering some of the agency's escape and evasion techniques for eluding capture.

But Howard's misfit personality (drug and alcohol abuser and impulsive sneak thief) led to his dismissal from the agency. While living in Santa Fe, New Mexico, he traveled to Europe, where he made a deal to sell his services to the Soviets. Howard is believed to have exposed Soviet scientist A.G. Tolkachev as an American spy.

Tolkachev was arrested by the KGB and is thought to have been executed. CIA analysts blamed Howard for having "wiped out" the agency's Moscow station spy ring.

Howard's New Mexico location put him in proximity to spy on top-secret research labs at Los Alamos and other such high-tech installations. Like Pelton, Howard was undone by two-way defector Vitaly Yurchenko, whose debriefing provided indirect clues pointing toward Howard.

Justice Jargon

In spy parlance, **dry-cleaning** is the act of shaking off possible tails and pursuers. Counter-surveillance tactics include wearing different coats and changing them, changing modes of transportation, varying routes, and backtracking.

In September 1985, while under FBI surveillance, Howard managed to elude his watchers and disappear. His CIA training came in handy, enabling him to use "*dry-cleaning*" counter-surveillance techniques to elude pursuit and escape to Moscow. He lives there still, and was last reported working as an insurance salesman.

Rogue's Gallery

Other notable alumni of the spy class of 1985 bagged by the FBI include Richard W. Miller, Jonathan Pollard, and Larry Wu-tai Chin.

Miller was an FBI agent, a slovenly foul ball who'd been transferred to the San Francisco field office's counterintelligence unit, where it was thought he couldn't do too much damage. Little did they know. Instead, he was suborned by a sex lure, a female KGB-controlled Russian beauty whose wiles persuaded him to engage in espionage. Miller was fired and then arrested, technically making him a "former" FBI employee at the time of his apprehension. He was sentenced to life imprisonment.

Jonathan J. Pollard, a civilian employee who worked for the Naval Intelligence Support Service, stole classified material and passed it along to Israel. Revelations about Israeli spying on the United States caused a serious, if temporary, breach in relations between the two allies. Pollard was sentenced to life imprisonment. His wife and accomplice was sentenced to five years in prison.

Larry Wu-Tai Chin was a translator and CIA employee who was revealed to have been spying since 1948 for the People's Republic of China. Arrested and awaiting sentencing, in February 1986 Chin committed suicide in his cell.

Some impressive spy catches had been made, but bigger fish remained to be netted.

The Least You Need to Know

- In the late 1970s, the U.S. government made a policy decision to actively prosecute and convict spies.

- The most damage to U.S. national security has been done by walk-ins who volunteer to spy for foreign governments for pay.

- The Foreign Intelligence Surveillance Court (FISC) is where U.S. intelligence agencies make application for electronic surveillance of suspected spies and terrorists.

- Navy communications John Walker and his "family of spies" passed information allowing the Soviets to read coded U.S. naval communications.

- The Year of the Spy, 1985, saw the FBI make a number of high-profile arrests of Soviet-controlled U.S. spies.

Chapter 17

Nightmover: FBI versus the Supermole

In This Chapter

- In the final phase of the Cold War, the Soviets score their greatest spy coup against the United States.

- CIA counterintelligence expert Aldrich Ames is a Soviet double agent

- CIA stonewalling and cover-ups thwart FBI spy hunts

- The USSR falls, but the KGB's successor agency keeps spying on the United States.

- NIGHTMOVER: FBI spy-hunters bag super-traitor Aldrich Ames

The FBI's successes in catching spies and double agents in 1985 was offset by the career of the worst American traitor of the Cold War. He was Aldrich Ames, a career CIA officer who sold his services to the KGB and became the highest-paid spy in history. Betraying the secrets of the CIA's counterintelligence division, which was charged to protect the agency against Soviet subversion and penetration, Ames caused the destruction of the United States's spy networks in Russia. Meanwhile, CIA obstructionism and cover-ups thwarted FBI spy-catchers from bagging the super-traitor for long years—but not forever.

The Mole People

In the spring of 1985, at about the time when the FBI was rolling up John Walker and his family of spies, a new double agent was about to go operational against the United States. Solidly established in the heart of America's top-secret intelligence apparatus, he would become possibly the most dangerous traitor of our time. He betrayed to the Soviets not only top-secret intelligence, but also agents working for the United States, resulting in their execution or imprisonment. His treacherous career spanned the terms of three FBI directors (Webster, Sessions, and Freeh) and outlasted even his original sponsor, the USSR itself. And when the USSR was no more, he continued spying for its successor.

He was career CIA officer Aldrich Ames, whose FBI codename was NIGHTMOVER. By the time the FBI got on his trail—was *allowed* to get on his trail—Ames had already done most of his damage. More than just the most important espionage case of the latter half of the Cold War, the Ames case remains vitally important today in the post–9/11 world as an object lesson in the evils inherent in the lack of interagency cooperation between the CIA and FBI.

Justice Jargon

A **mole** is a penetration agent which the enemy has planted, suborned, or cultivated in an intelligence agency or service. Like its namesake, the mole burrows from within, advancing to the inner workings of the host organization while betraying its secrets. Notable moles include Kim Philby, Aldrich Ames, and Robert Hanssen.

The ultimate nightmare of any intelligence service is to find itself penetrated by a *mole*, a double agent who's reporting on its doings to the enemy. The CIA's British counterpart, MI-6, had been disastrously penetrated by moles, most notably by Kim Philby. Some spy-hunters seriously suspected the onetime head of the MI-5 (the UK's internal security division similar to the FBI service), Sir Roger Hollis, of working for the Soviets.

During the 1950s and 1960s, as a series of high-level British moles was exposed, the CIA and FBI were spared such scandals. Was this because they harbored no such double agents, or merely because the penetrators had gone as yet undetected?

Fear of the latter haunted James J. Angleton, the CIA's Counterintelligence chief. In 1960, believing (apparently on intuition) that the agency had been penetrated by a mole or moles, he began an ultimately disastrous mole hunt that decimated the agency's Soviet division, paralyzing its operations against the foe. The mole hunt was so destructive that some CIA thinkers were led to postulate that, based on the damage the inquiries had done, Angleton himself must be the mole. That goes to show the paranoia that such spy hunts can engender. No such mole was then ever publicly identified; the government paid extensive reparations and apologized to some of those whom Angleton forced from the service.

Cops and Robbers

James Jesus Angleton was a Yale graduate, poet, and WWII OSS agent who became the CIA's oracular head of counterintelligence. A colorful character, an orchid fancier and fly-fisherman, Angleton once famously quoted the poet T.S. Eliot by applying his phrase "a wilderness of mirrors" to the spy world. Revela-tions of Angleton's program opening foreign mail addressed to U.S. citizens led to his firing from the agency in 1974.

Portrait of a Traitor

One of Angleton's staffers was Professor Carleton Ames, a historian whose expertise on Burma led to his early-1950s recruitment by the CIA. Ames, his wife, and his three children, of whom the eldest was son Aldrich ("Rick"), lived for a time in Rangoon. Alcoholism led to the senior Ames's 1954 posting to Angleton's newly formed CIA Counterintelligence staff, in effect sidelining him where it was believed he couldn't do much harm.

In 1962, son Aldrich Ames, 21, was hired by the CIA as a clerk-typist and document analyst against the Soviets. Completing a year of training, he was posted to the agency's Directorate of Operations (DO), its clandestine wing. The CIA gave him a top-secret security clearance, which he held for his 31 years in the agency.

Ames served a tour of duty in Turkey, a period marked by some heavy drinking of his own. He had some wins, but his career was stalling. In 1973, he was assigned to a desk job in the Soviet division, helping support CIA operations against Soviet officials in the United States.

In the mid-1970s, stationed in New York City, Ames was part of the team that successfully handled the defection of Arkady Shevchenko, the USSR's United Nations under-secretary general and highest-ranking Soviet official ever to defect to the United States. The defection was a coup that boosted the careers of those involved with it, including Ames.

In October 1981, the CIA posted Ames to its Mexico City station, a cockpit of Western hemisphere intrigue. Under diplomatic State Department cover, he was chief of the station's Soviet counterintelligence branch and his primary mission was to recruit Soviet and Soviet Bloc agents.

Agency operations were augmented by a local close support team, assisting in surveillance, bugging, wiretapping, break-ins, and so on. Ames's important achievement was the discovery that the support team head, a Mexican national, had never been vetted. When he was, the agency discovered that he had been a double agent who had been working for the KGB for years, which explained why so many operations had gone sour.

Here, while still married, Ames met and courted Columbian Rosario Casas Dupuy, an intellectual from a good family who'd been recruited by the CIA, though not by Ames. He planned to divorce his current wife and marry Rosario. In addition, his record was marred by a number of incidents of public drunkenness.

In 1983, his two-year Mexico City term ended, Ames returned to CIA headquarters at Langley, Virginia, where he became the Soviet branch chief of counterintelligence, overseeing its efforts to detect and neutralize potential Soviet moles who might have penetrated the agency. He was at the heart of the CIA's anti-Soviet intelligence apparatus, with access to identities of CIA sources inside and outside the USSR.

Official and Confidential

In November 1985, testifying before the Senate Intelligence Committee, CIA Counterintelligence chief Gus Hathaway declared, "We have never found a real mole in CIA … There has never been an agent of the Soviets in the center of the CIA itself. We may have failed to find such an agent, but I doubt it." Technically, he was telling the truth. Edward Lee Howard, the spy who escaped to Moscow, had already been fired from the CIA when they learned he was a double agent.

Crossing Over

In March 1984, Ames told his superiors that he wanted to try to recruit Soviets after hours. This was fairly standard operating procedure, especially for deskbound personnel eager for a little operational action. It demonstrated initiative on Ames's part and his superiors readily agreed to the plan. He was required to report all contacts to CIA, which in turn was required to relay all such information to the FBI. The FBI kept close watch on all Soviet diplomats, especially those posted to Washington, D.C.

Because Ames was going to marry Rosario, a foreign national, the CIA's Counterintelligence staff recommended that he be transferred to a less sensitive job. A sensible recommendation, but one which the CIA declined to follow. Big changes were taking place in the life of Aldrich Ames. Divorcing his first wife and paying her alimony was an expensive proposition. Rosario moved in with him, prompting him to buy new furniture, a new car, and more. He had money problems, although nothing more serious than those experienced by millions of other Americans.

Ames knew that he had a valuable commodity to sell to the KGB. No one knows when he first began contemplating treason. Possibly he had it in mind in 1984, when he proposed that he begin meeting with Soviet diplomatic personnel to recruit them; it made a perfect "cover story" to justify any meetings he might have that would be observed and reported. Ames said that he began plotting betrayal in the fall of 1984 and winter of 1985, as his money problems multiplied.

Official and Confidential

The Soviet embassy on 16th Street in Washington, D.C., was housed in a nineteenth century mansion built for George Pullman, inventor of the railroad sleeping cars which bear his name. The entrance was kept under surveillance by the FBI, which failed to detect walk-ins John Walker, Ronald Pelton, and Aldrich Ames.

What is known is that in April 1985, at age 44, after 23 years of honorable employment at the agency, Ames decided he'd rather switch than fight. Switch sides, that is. Like so many other damaging double agents of the period, he was a walk-in, perhaps the ultimate walk-in.

Assuming (or knowing) that the FBI had bugged the embassy, Ames handed a guard an envelope on which he'd written the name of Stanislav A. Androsov, the KGB's chief resident on-site. In the envelope was a letter providing the names of two Soviet officials who'd approached the CIA to volunteer information. Also enclosed was a document with his name highlighted, identifying him as the agency's Soviet Counterintelligence branch chief—the very official who knew the identities of every mole working for the CIA inside Soviet intelligence.

In the note, he requested $50,000 as payment for his services. He left it to the Soviets to follow up on contacting him. Protecting his identity by using a middle man, the Soviets used as a cut-out Sergei Chuvakhin, an embassy first secretary whose KGB status if any is unknown. Meeting with Chuvakhin was justified by Ames's cover that he was trying to recruit the Russian national. At a meeting in the Soviet embassy, Ames was handed a note from Viktor I. Cherkashin, Soviet Counterintelligence chief in Washington. Not long after, while dining together at a restaurant, Chuvakhin passed Ames a bag containing $50,000 in cash.

About this time, spy John Walker was caught and exposed by the FBI. Ames, unconcerned, regarded himself as a "professional" who was "too smart to be caught."

The Big Bundle

Now, Ames made his big move. On June 13, 1985, in his office at CIA headquarters in Langley, he stole between five and seven pounds of secret documents, stuffing them in plastic bags and carrying them out of the building, unopposed, unsearched. While careful about packages and other material being brought *into* the building, the guards did not examine packages personnel carried *out* of the building.

That same day, June 13, while lunching with Chuvakhin at a Georgetown restaurant conveniently close to CIA headquarters, Ames passed him the documents. The largest amount of classified information ever passed to the KGB in a single meeting, it included the names of more than 10 of the most important Soviet sources working for the CIA and FBI, dooming most of them.

In 1985, Ames's counterintelligence duties brought him to work with a joint FBI-CIA squad codenamed *COURTSHIP*, which recruited KGB officers to work for the United States. A prize catch for the unit was the recruitment of two such officers attached to the Soviet's Washington embassy.

Justice Jargon

Although the CIA's charter generally prevents it from conducting operations within the United States, exceptions are made in counterintelligence matters. However, a presidential executive order mandates that the CIA must advise the FBI when it conducts foreign counterintelligence operations in this country. Overcoming a troubled history, in 1980 the CIA and FBI established **COURTSHIP,** a joint operation to try to recruit Soviets stationed in Washington.

In 1982, operating from an office building in Springfield, Virginia, the COURTSHIP unit succeeded in recruiting Lt. Col. Valery F. Martynov, officially a member of the diplomatic cadre at the USSR's Washington embassy. In reality, Martynov was a KGB officer whose mission was to collect scientific and technical information. A rising young officer, Martynov held great potential as a "sleeper agent," one who would continually ascend to ever-higher levels in the hierarchy.

The FBI next recruited KGB Major Sergei M. Motorin, third secretary at the embassy, who was also working for the combined COURTSHIP unit. Both Martynov and

Motorin were recruited by the CIA, using a complex approach mixing blandishments and threats. In both cases, each had done something stupid: One had spent money entrusted to him, the other was in a car accident while in the company of a hooker. They feared exposure and disgrace more than they feared working for the opposition. The recruits were given modest sums of money, but nothing they could get rich on. Such recruitments are complex, ambiguous transactions.

In the course of his work with COURTSHIP, Ames had learned of both Motorin and Martynov, double agents working in the Soviet's Washington embassy. That was too close for comfort. Should either man learn a hint of Ames's secret dealings, they could expose him. The possibility of such discovery was remote, but why take chances? As he later told investigators, "I didn't assume they would ever be involved or become knowledgeable, but accidents happen."

So he deliberately set out to burn both men. Like any canny killer, Ames was wiping out witnesses to his crimes.

In return for his having identified virtually all Soviet agents of the CIA and other American and foreign service, the KGB had set aside a $2 million payment for Ames, which it paid out in sizable installments through Chuvakhin, who passed them along to Ames at their luncheons. By July 1985, Ames had stopped filing reports of his meetings with the Soviets, irritating the FBI, which officially complained several times to the CIA about the lack of information on the Ames/Chuvakhin get-togethers. Nothing was done by the CIA, and Ames failed to file any more reports.

> **Official and Confidential**
>
> The KGB let Aldrich Ames pick his own codename. He chose the cryptonym **Kolokol,** Russian for *bell*. Ames said that the name was a reference to a nineteenth century Russian revolutionary journal of the same name. From the time of Ivan the Terrible, bells have played an important role in Russian history. When "Kolokol" Ames sounded, all the Kremlin—and the CIA— echoed his ringing.

The Dangerous Defector

Having neutralized potential threats at the Soviet embassy, now Ames's greatest fear was that a defector might expose him. That's why he was put into a panic by the August 1985 defection of Vitaly Yurchenko. Like Ames, a walk-in, Yurchenko presented himself at the U.S. embassy in Rome. The highest-ranking KGB officer to come over to the other side, Yurchenko had been in charge of operations against the United States and Canada.

Did Yurchenko know of the existence of the KGB's supermole in the CIA? Ames was noticeably nervous as the time came for Yurchenko's arrival in America. By virtue of his position in the counterintelligence branch, Ames was one of a handful delegated to meet Yurchenko at the airport and participate in his debriefing.

At their meeting, Yurchenko showed no signs that he recognized Ames, allowing the latter to breathe easier. Yurchenko subsequently provided information leading to the identification of KGB double agents Edward Lee Howard and Ronald Pelton. That alone presented a problem for CIA. Burton Gerber, chief of the Soviet division, and Gardner R. "Gus" Hathaway, chief of the counterintelligence staff, hadn't yet told FBI of their suspicions of former employee Howard.

Two years earlier, in 1983, Howard had been observed suspiciously loitering around the Soviets' Washington embassy, and had even confessed to "considering" selling secrets. This the CIA had failed to pass along to the FBI, though required to do so, for only the FBI has the power to arrest spies. They wanted to "handle" (that is, bury) the problem in-house. The FBI first began to learn of Howard during Yurchenko's debriefing. Even then, the CIA kept quiet about the extent of Howard's dealings with the Soviets. Unaware of the seriousness of the threat, the FBI had only light coverage on Howard when he went underground and escaped to Russia.

Before 1985 was done, Yurchenko had defected back to the USSR, if indeed he'd ever defected to the United States at all. As you may remember from Chapter 16, Yurchenko's true motivations are one of the enduring mysteries of the Cold War.

Official and Confidential

In November 1985, when returning to the USSR, Yurchenko was on board the same plane as COURTSHIP double agent Lt. Col. Martynov. Martynov had been ordered to accompany Yurchenko by KGB chief resident Androsov. When Martynov returned home, he was arrested for espionage and eventually executed.

The Yurchenko episode takes on added possible layers of meaning when considered in light of the case of Aldrich Ames. These possibilities include …

◆ Yurchenko was a genuine defector who was unaware of KGB supermole Ames.

◆ Yurchenko was a fake defector sent by the KGB to test Ames's reliability by seeing if Ames reported back on Yurchenko's debriefing to his KGB handlers. (He did.)

◆ Yurchenko was a fake defector who burned Howard and Pelton as a ploy to divert suspicion away from the existence of a mole in CIA.

Black Hole

From Fall 1985 through early 1986, the KGB ran wild in Russia, rolling up about 20 key CIA sources and double agents, all of whom "inexplicably" vanished. They disappeared as if swallowed up by a black hole. It was poor tradecraft, since it risked alerting the CIA that it had been penetrated. The standard course would have been to roll them up slowly, one at a time, possibly even turning them into triple agents, feeding disinformation to the CIA. In either case, their fate would have been the same: execution or at best, imprisonment in the gulag. Only the time span was different.

Ames was worried, and he passed on his fears to his Soviet handlers. They said that the orders for the mass arrests came from higher than the KGB, from the highest ruling circles of the Kremlin.

In any case, nothing happened. The Soviet blackout of sources was explained away at the CIA's Directorate of Operations, rationalized as the result of poor operating procedures by the Russian agents. Or they blamed it on Edward Lee Howard, the Spy Who Got Away. It couldn't be that the upper ranks of the agency had been penetrated by a mole. That was unthinkable.

Besides, after a year or two, the roll-ups stopped. That was because Ames had completed his tour at headquarters in Langley and had been posted to the U.S. embassy in Rome as CIA station Soviet branch chief. While there, Ames opened several Swiss bank accounts to hold his spy gains, and bought his first Jaguar. He also continued spying for the USSR, walking out of the embassy unmolested with bags full of secret documents.

> **Bu Stats**
>
> How much was Ames paid? A 1989 KGB accounting found that nearly $1.9 million was delivered to Ames, with another $800,000 being held in a Moscow account, totaling $2.7 million. With added payments made or guaranteed, the total amount promised or paid was $4.6 million, making Ames the best-paid spy in history.

Spy Hunt

In December 1986, while under fire for illegally funneling profits from Iran arms deals to fund the Contra insurgency in Nicaragua (the Iran-Contra affair), CIA Director William Casey collapsed of a malignant brain tumor, dying six months later. Searching for a candidate with clean hands and no CIA "old boy" ties, President Ronald Reagan nominated FBI Director William H. Webster to become CIA chief.

Installed as new FBI director was William Sessions, the San Antonio, Texas, federal judge who'd presided over the trials of Chagra and Harrelson for assassinating Judge Wood.

In October 1986, learning that COURTSHIP sources Martynov and Motorin both had been arrested and were slated for execution, the FBI formed an investigatory team headed by counterintelligence expert Tim Caruso to analyze how the two spies had been detected. The CIA discreetly formed an understaffed mole hunt unit.

Ames returned to Washington as European branch chief of the Soviet division group, then later as branch chief for Czechoslovakian operations, still passing info for pay to Soviet handlers via personal meetings and dead drops in the Washington, D.C., area.

At the time, CIA employees were polygraphed every five years. Ames passed his April 1991 polygraph test. (When the test results were later reexamined, after the truth about Ames was known, it was decided with 20-20 hindsight that he'd showed "deception" during the polygraphing, and that the examiners had been "too friendly" to him throughout the proceedings.)

That same month, April 1991, saw the opening of a CIA/FBI joint probe begin a search for the mole. FBI agents James P. Milburn (considered the best analyst of KGB operations in the bureau) and James Holt worked with CIA officers in vetting a list of 198 CIA employees with access to the identities, reducing it to 29 priorities. At the top of the priority list stood the name of Aldrich Ames.

Official and Confidential

Located at Buzzard's Point along the Anacostia River, the Washington Metropolitan Field Office (WMFO) is the FBI's first field office and second largest, as well as its premier counterintelligence office, handling surveillance and investigation of foreign spies in the capital. It also carries out criminal probes and conducts most background investigations of high government officials. It's also the home base of the Hostage Rescue Team.

In December 1991, the USSR officially collapsed, replaced by the Russian federation. Ames continued spying, this time for the SVR, the post-Communist successor to the KGB. In 1993, eight years after it began losing its Moscow assets, the CIA formally notified the FBI that Ames was the chief suspect as the mole, and the FBI formally took over the case. In March, the investigation was handed over to the Bureau's Washington Metropolitan Field Office. SAC Robert M. "Bear" Bryant, FBI assistant director in charge of the National Security Division, had overall responsibility for Ames probe. ASAC John F. Lewis Jr., the FBI's number-two counterintelligence official in the Washington Field Office, supervised the 10-month investigation. SA Leslie G. Wiser Jr. led the FBI team that placed Ames and his wife Rosario under surveillance, wiretapping and bugging their home and gathering evidence. Assistant U.S. Attorney Mark J. Hulkower ultimately successfully prosecuted the Ameses for conspiracy to commit espionage and tax fraud.

Operation NIGHTMOVER

When the unit first officially opened the case, FBI agent Milburn said, "This is a guy who must move in the darkness. Let's call it NIGHTMOVER." Ames and the case itself were both codenamed NIGHTMOVER.

Ideally, the FBI wanted to catch Ames in the act, either filling a dead drop with stolen documents or collecting payments from same, and if they could bag some KGB officers at the same time, so much the better. But that was tough to do. Surveillance is tricky. Ames was a trained professional, and the dead drop sites were sufficiently remote to alert the quarry to the presence of any shadowers in the area. Despite surveillance, Ames was operational, visiting dead drops five times and signal sites three times between May 1993 and February 1994.

A trash cover on Ames's garbage yielded a year-old Post-it note, a rough draft of a message from Ames detailing a meeting schedule to his Soviet control. Taking the note to the Foreign Intelligence Surveillance Court (FISC), the FBI was able to obtain a court order to surreptitiously enter and search Ames's house and install bugging devices. Extensive taped conversations caught Ames and wife Rosario discussing his espionage, with Rosario nagging him to keep his tradecraft sharp and not get caught.

Bu Stats

Ames made a yearly salary of $69,843, yet he drove a $40,000 red XJ6 Jaguar (his third Jag) and paid for an Arlington, Virginia, home with $540,000 in cash and another $99,000 on home improvements. From 1985 to 1994, his and his wife's total credit card charges equaled $455,000; his wife owned 150 pairs of shoes.

Someone at the CIA stupidly scheduled Ames to appear at a drug conference in Moscow, but no way was he getting on that plane. The FBI wasn't risking a second Howard-type getaway. On Monday, February 21, 1994, President's Day, acting by prearrangement with the FBI, Ames's immediate supervisor at Langley called, telling him to come to headquarters to receive some special information. Ames jumped in the Jaguar, heading toward Langley. Before he'd gotten more than a few blocks, the street was sealed off before and behind him by Bucars, boxing him in.

As FBI agents closed in, Ames said several times, "There must be some mistake." Told he was under arrest for conspiracy to commit espionage, Ames said "Espionage, me? I hear what you're saying, but you've got to be kidding."

He'd been arrested away from his home, so he couldn't destroy evidence. He was handcuffed and taken away, all in less than a minute. At the same time, agents arrested Rosario at the house. Later, Ames said little, but noted unhappily that if the FBI had arrested him, it probably had a pretty good case.

Endgame?

The damage inflicted by Ames was staggering. Ultimately, he was responsible for the execution deaths of at least ten Russian agents. One such was GRU General Dimitri F. Polyakov, FBI codename TOPHAT, CIA cryptonym GTBEEP, considered one of the West's top cold war spies. After spying for the United States for 18 years, retiring, and returning home to Moscow in 1980, he was betrayed by Ames and executed on March 15, 1988. Because of Ames, three dozen spies were imprisoned and possibly hundreds of operations were compromised, including the neutralization of super-secret National Security Agency (NSA) electronic surveillance and eavesdropping programs.

On April 28, 1994, at a courthouse in Alexandria, Virginia, Aldrich Ames pled guilty to two counts of conspiracy to commit espionage and conspiracy to commit tax fraud, and promised to cooperate fully with the government—which he did in order to win a lighter sentence for Rosario, his wife and the mother of their five-year-old son. The prosecutor noted that the agents Ames had betrayed had died "because Rick Ames wasn't making enough money with the CIA and wanted to live in a half-million-dollar house and drive a Jaguar."

> **Cops and Robbers**
>
> In an interview with TV's *Prime-time Live*, Diane Sawyer asked Rosario Ames how she now felt about her husband. "I despise him," Rosario Ames said. She pled guilty to conspiracy to commit espionage and tax fraud, and was sentenced to serve a term of about five years.

In his statement, Ames said, "Frankly, these spy wars are a sideshow which have had no real impact on our significant security interests over the years." That was his exit line. He was sentenced to life in prison without parole.

NIGHTMOVER was neutralized. But, as you'll see in a later chapter, the nightmare was not yet over, not with the FBI's own supermole, Robert Hanssen, still safely established in place and reporting to his Russian spy masters.

The Least You Need to Know

- CIA career officer Aldrich Ames was a walk-in who sold secrets to the KGB.

- Ames's trusted post in CIA counterintelligence gave him access to the identities of all the agency's Russian agents—whom he betrayed.

- CIA incompetence and cover-ups thwarted FBI spy-catchers from doing their jobs.

- FBI Counterintelligence's Operation NIGHTMOVER caught CIA supermole Ames.

- The USSR's fall did not preclude Russia from continuing spy operations targeted at the United States.

Part 4

New World Order

As the last decade of the twentieth century dawned, the USSR broke apart, drawing to a close the Cold War whose prosecution had occupied the two superpowers since 1945. The Soviet Empire's fall produced not an era of peace, but a dangerous new phase of global instability. Ever more powerful weaponry was available to violent extremist hate groups and individuals, such as the Unabomber and Oklahoma City bomber Tim McVeigh. Espionage operations mounted against the United States by Red China showed that the game of spy/counterspy was far from done. The terror strikes of 9/11 thrust the United States into a new kind of war, one in which the FBI must redefine itself as the nation's premier counterterrorist force, its mission being the prevention of future terrorist assaults.

Chapter 18

Judgment Calls

In This Chapter

- The 1980s emergence of violent neo-Nazi hate groups
- Blueprint for butchery: *The Turner Diaries*
- The Order: a terrorist rampage of bank robberies, bombings, and political murder
- What really happened at Ruby Ridge
- Fiery holocaust at Waco's Ranch Apocalypse

Using a wave of anti–Big Government resentment as their vehicle, American hate groups old and new enjoyed a resurgence in the last decades of the twentieth century. Veterans of the movement, such as the KKK and American Nazi Party, forged new alliances with white supremacists, fundamentalists, and neo-Nazi skinheads. The terrorist organization known as the Order mixed bombing, bank robbery, and political murder until the FBI stopped them. At Idaho's Ruby Ridge, a deadly shootout with separatist Randy Weaver enmeshed the Bureau in controversy, while the siege of David Koresh's Branch Davidian compound in Waco, Texas resulted in horrific tragedy as well.

Internal Insecurity

Much misinformation, disinformation, and outright lies have attached themselves to the Ruby Ridge and Waco incidents in the early 1990s. To properly understand what really happened in both episodes, context is critical. Waco and Ruby Ridge (and beyond them, the Oklahoma City bombing) must be seen as high- (or low-) water marks of the tide of anti-government sentiment that began in the 1980s and earlier.

Seen from a certain perspective, the United States federal government has seemingly endless laws that regulate nearly every facet of a citizen's daily life, as well as formidable powers for enforcing those dictates and punishing the disobedient and defiant. As such, the idea of big government frequently generates a good deal of resentment among the American people. Most citizens respond by expressing their feelings at the ballot box or by exercising their constitutional right to complain.

For others, though, resistance takes a more concrete form. Opposition may include taking such illegal measures as not paying taxes or stockpiling prohibited weapons. In the 1980s, such resistors began to assume a more prominent public profile. A recession in the early part of the decade wreaked havoc on many small farmers and homeowners, causing them to lose their property through foreclosures. A weak national economy multiplied the unrest.

In the fever swamps of U.S. political extremism were some groups whose existence was based on violent opposition to the federal government. First among them chronologically was the Ku Klux Klan, the 150-year-old white supremacist terrorist organization, destabilized and decimated by FBI investigations that put Klan leaders in jail for bombings and other related crimes, but which still retained deep-rooted, hardcore support. Coming up strong was the American neo-Nazi movement with its many offshoots and splinter groups, some of which took their origin in the pre-WWII fascist movement. A third element consisted of militant white racist fundamentalist religious sects, which linked the other two.

A lifelong pillar of Nazism, Christian Identity fundamentalism, and white supremacy was Reverend Richard G. Butler, a veteran hatemonger who gathered about 200 followers to an armed compound in Hayden Lake, Idaho, in 1973 to proclaim the founding of the group Aryan Nations. The compound served as a hub for a growing alliance of neo-Nazis, white supremacists, and the KKK. A leading propagandist for the cause was William Pierce, whose 1978 novel *The Turner Diaries* became for violent anti-government extremists both a bible and blueprint (literally, in the cases of Order founder and mastermind Bob Mathews and Oklahoma City bomber Timothy McVeigh).

Cops and Robbers

William Pierce was a former physics professor and follower of American Nazi Party leader George Lincoln Rockwell, who was assassinated in 1967. Pierce formed the Washington, D.C.–based neo-Nazi National Alliance. Using the pseudonym "Andrew Macdonald," Pierce wrote *The Turner Diaries* (published 1978), a novel depicting the escalatingly murderous exploits of Earl Turner, an assassin for the fanatical white supremacist Organization, whose ruling inner circle is known as the Order.

Law and Order

Some heard the call to move beyond theory to what anarchists had once called "propaganda of the deed"—that is, terrorism. One such was white supremacist Robert Jay "Bob" Mathews. Born 1953, Mathews moved his family to a farm in the town of Metaline in a remote corner of Washington State. Through Pierce's National Alliance, Mathews met and associated with a small cadre of like-minded young neo-Nazis with a number of criminal records and a propensity for violence. A pilgrimage to Richard Butler's Aryan Nations compound at Hayden Lake, Idaho, inspired Mathews in September 1983 to form a radical terrorist group.

Using Pierce's *Turner Diaries* as a blueprint, Mathews's original nine-man group took an oath over the baby daughter of one of its members, vowing to prosecute a racial holy war to free the U.S. from what they regarded as Jewish-controlled federal government tyranny. Ultimately, the group called itself the Order, after the ruling clique in the *Turner Diaries*. It also became known to the initiated as the Bruders Schweigen, German for Silent Brotherhood.

Beginning with armed robbery, Order members held up a Spokane-area adult video store, netting $369 for the revolution. Similar robberies followed in Seattle, as did the band's involvement in printing counterfeit currency. The phony money was at first crude, but later improved in sophistication. A natural progression from forging fake money to forging fake identities followed, providing Order members with driver's licenses, social security numbers, credit cards, and such, all issued to nonexistent men.

Terrorism always being part of the program, the group set off a bomb in a Seattle adult movie theater on April 22, 1984, attacking the pornography symptomatic of the popular culture they abominated. The next day, a Monday, they phoned in a phony bomb threat to the now-sensitized Seattle police. But the threat was only a lure, a piece of misdirection designed to mobilize the police elsewhere while the Order pulled off an armored car heist that netted nearly $500,000.

In late May 1984, Walter West, an Aryan Nations member whose talking out of turn was regarded as a threat to the Order, was murdered by a Brotherhood killer. On June 18, 1984, group members stalked and shot dead controversial Denver radio talk show host Alan Berg. Earl Turner would have been proud of them.

On July 19, 1984, in north California's Ukiah area, the Order knocked over a Brinks truck, escaping with an impressive $3.6 million in loot. But during the heist, leader Bob Mathews had left behind at the scene of the crime a gun, which the FBI traced to an associate of the group.

The dragnet tightened as career criminal Tom Martinez, close to the Order but not a member, told all to Secret Service investigators in order to deal his way out of a charge of passing counterfeit money. The Order broke up, its members going on the run as the FBI closed in.

Official and Confidential

Commenting on the death of devotee Bob Mathews, National Alliance head and *Turner Diaries* author William Pierce remarked opaquely, "It's foolish to think in terms of opposing social or racial trends by violent or illegal means."

On November 25, 1984, Martinez lured Mathews and a second Order member to a meeting in a Portland, Oregon motel. Mathews shot himself out of an FBI trap, wounding an agent and himself being wounded, while his accomplice was taken. Mathews, furious, penned a "declaration of war" against the U.S. government, which was signed by a number of Order members.

Mathews forted up at a hideout at Whidbey Island, northwest of Seattle. On December 7, 1984, a hundred heavily armed FBI agents were on the island, augmented by scores of local law enforcement officers. Ignoring demands to surrender, Mathews held off the besiegers until Saturday night, when flares dropped on the roof of his fortified hideout ignited, burning it down with him inside. Mathews, 31, officially died of smoke inhalation.

In short "order," the remaining members of the Silent Brotherhood were apprehended, tried, convicted, and sentenced to terms in the federal penitentiary.

Incident at Ruby Ridge

Not far from Richard Butler's Aryan Nations compound in Hayden Lake lies Ruby Creek, Idaho, whose Ruby Ridge cabin was home to the Weaver family: Randall "Randy" Weaver, wife Vicki, and their four children. Patriarch Randy Weaver was an adherent of *Christian Identity*, a white supremacist creed whose tenets were vociferously preached by Pastor Butler. An avowed separatist, he shunned the works of the federal government as "Satanic."

Cops and Robbers

Originally propounded in nineteenth century England, where it was known as Anglo-Israelism, the **Christian Identity** movement preaches that the Chosen People, the Israelites of the Old Testament, were not Hebrews but rather Aryan Anglo-Saxons, who migrated to North Europe as the Lost Tribes. God has sent them to be overseers of the world's "lesser races," with the exception of the "Satanic" Jews, who must be destroyed. The creed has wide currency among white supremacist hate groups.

An undercover agent of the Bureau of Alcohol, Tobacco, and Firearms (ATF) persuaded Randy Weaver to supply him with sawed-off shotguns. To make or possess such weapons is a federal offense. Whether Weaver was stung or entrapped depends on your point of view. A credible theory posits that the ATF sought to turn Weaver into an undercover operative, targeted against the nearby Aryan Nations.

Weaver was arrested, posted bond, released, and ordered to appear for trial at a future date. When the date arrived, he failed to appear. He was now a wanted man, a fugitive with federal marshals on his trail. Instead of fleeing, he stayed on his farm, saying that he just wanted to be left alone. If he weren't left alone, well, he had guns to protect himself. But by not fleeing, he put his whole family in harm's way.

On August 21, 1992, four U.S. marshals were on a piece of property adjacent to Weaver's, when along came Weaver, his 14-year-old son Sammy, his adopted son Kevin Harris, and the family dog. The dog barked at the marshals hiding in the bushes. The marshals fled down the mountain. Weaver, Harris and Sammy pursued the marshals and one marshal shot the Weaver dog. Sammy Weaver fired a rifle at the agents, who returned fire. Sammy Weaver was shot dead. In 1995, a Senate investigating committee concluded that he'd been shot in the back while fleeing. Kevin Harris then fired and killed U.S. Marshal William F. Degan. A gun fight broke out that was so intense that the marshals were pinned down by heavy fire. They were not rescued until after nightfall by a state police tactical unit. The federal marshals involved in the initial shootout were later all awarded medals for valor.

A siege developed, resulting in a standoff. The marshals requested help from the FBI, which sent in a Hostage Rescue Team (HRT). An 11-member team surrounded Weaver's cabin. On August 22, at about 6 P.M., an FBI helicopter flew over the site. Weaver, his daughter Sara, 16, and Kevin Harris emerged from the cabin, all carrying rifles.

HRT sniper Lon Horiuchi later said that he thought one of the men was going to shoot at the copter, so he fired at him first. The man, Weaver, was wounded. The trio ran back to the cabin. Horiuchi fired again, missing Weaver, but hitting his wife Vicki, who stood half-hidden behind a partly opened door. Shot in the head, she died almost instantly.

Ten days later, Randy Weaver and the others surrendered. Weaver and Harris were charged with murder; conspiracy to commit murder; manufacture, possession, and distribution of illegal weapons; and failure to appear in court. In July 1993, a jury found Weaver not guilty of murdering U.S. Marshal Degan, ruling that the marshals had fired first. He was convicted of failing to appear in federal court. The original ATF-inspired weapons charge against him was dismissed as entrapment. Eventually, while admitting no guilt or culpability in the matter, the Justice Department paid the Weavers $3.1 million to settle their wrongful death lawsuit against the government.

> **Official and Confidential**
>
> In the aftermath of the Ruby Ridge incident, an Idaho state prosecutor filed charges in the death of Vicki Weaver against FBI sniper Lon Horiuchi. A federal court dismissed the charges.

The U.S. marshals had botched the initial arrest, souring the situation by the time the FBI's HRT got involved. The shooting of Vicki Weaver was a tragic accident. When individuals try to shoot it out with the law, innocent bystanders run the risk of being hurt or killed. Whatever his beliefs, the fact is that Randy Weaver was a damned fool who put his family into harm's way.

In the event, though, the Ruby Ridge incident was a defining moment for the antigovernment movement, who turned it into a national crusade. Opportunistic politicians distorted the FBI's role in the incident, grabbing headlines by making a whipping boy of the Bureau.

For the FBI, though, worse was yet to come. Waco was just around the corner.

Waco: Ranch Apocalypse

The Branch Davidians of Waco, Texas, were a splinter group that had split off from the fundamentalist Christian Seventh Day Adventists. To this group came Texan Vernon Dean Howell, a charismatic evangelical with delusions of grandeur and an obsession with the New Testament's apocalyptic Book of Revelation. Howell, who called himself David Koresh, literally shot his way into leadership of the Branch Davidians, via a gun battle in 1987 at the sect's compound with its then-leader, with whom he'd been feuding. Koresh was acquitted of attempted murder charges and took over the sect.

Cops and Robbers

Vernon Howell, born in 1963, a native of Houston, Texas, was a long-haired, folk-guitar strumming hustler with a facility for discoursing on the Bible in 12-hour sessions. Assuming the leadership of the Branch Davidians in Waco, Texas, Howell renamed himself David Koresh: David, for the king of the Biblical Israelites, and Koresh, the Hebraized form of Cyrus, the Persian king who freed the exiled Israelites in Babylon, allowing them to return to their ancestral home.

Koresh quickly gained complete ascendancy and control of the 120-odd men, women, and children of the sect. His followers needed someone to tell them what to do, a role that Koresh was more than willing to assume. He maintained that he was their divinely inspired leader, a prophet and messiah whose whim was law. In classic cult leader fashion, he used mind control techniques to cement his hold over his followers. Depersonalization, fatigue, and hunger were used to put the members into a vulnerable state, where they could be reprogrammed to give Koresh absolute obedience.

His control techniques included the breaking down of family ties, pitting wives against husbands and children against parents. Koresh relegated to himself the privilege of having sex with the wives, while their husbands were ordered to remain celibate. Female children as young as 12 also became his sexual chattels.

The Ranch Apocalypse

In a chilling prevision of the future, Koresh named the compound Ranch Apocalypse. His paranoia expressed itself in a more concrete form in the early 1990s by his stockpiling of weapons and explosives. He acquired vast quantities of assault weapons, grenades, and crates of ammunition. Presumably they would be used in the End of Days, to protect the sect members against Satanic or godless hordes come to destroy them.

The arms build-up brought Koresh to the attention of the ATF. Monitoring Koresh, they placed an undercover agent in the compound. Koresh's acquisitions of parts for the assemblage of machine guns put him in violation of federal law.

Official and Confidential

Although the siege of the Branch Davidian compound and its fiery aftermath have been popularized under the one-word descriptor "Waco," the compound was actually located ten miles outside of that town, in Mount Carmel.

Wrongway Raid

With the militia movement blazing throughout the Midwest and West, increasing the use of armed resistance against federal officers, law enforcement agents, and tax collectors, the ATF was wise to monitor Koresh's heavily armed doomsday cult. In fact, it would have been derelict in its duty had it failed to keep an eye on him.

But when surveillance turned to action, things went horribly wrong. Moving against Koresh, the ATF seriously miscalculated its strategy and tactics, with lethal consequences. Koresh was known to leave the compound to come into Waco for various reasons. That would have been the optimum time to make an arrest. Instead, looking for some publicity and a favorable media splash, the ATF decided to launch a massive raid against the Branch Davidian compound.

On February 28, 1993, the ATF struck, but not before having invited representatives from 11 different media and news outlets to cover the story. This heavy media presence proved to be self-sabotaging. On a back road, a Branch Davidian encountered a TV cameraman who told him that a raid was imminent. The ATF's undercover man inside the compound alerted them that the element of surprise had been lost.

Despite this, the ATF decided to go through with the raid. A team of 91 ATF agents moved against the compound, only to encounter stiff resistance from well-armed Branch Davidians. In a furious 45-minute firefight, four ATF agents were killed and 15 were wounded, while six Branch Davidians were also killed. The ATF retreated, and the siege was on.

> **Official and Confidential**
>
> What lay behind the ATF's botched raid on the Branch Davidian's compound in Waco, Texas? The agency's legitimate law enforcement concern may have been supplemented by a desire for some good publicity. At around that time, ATF's yearly budget appropriations were coming up, and agency heads wanted to go into that process with a high-profile win under its belt, to offset some of the bad press the agency had received for its role at Ruby Ridge.

ATF having fumbled, the hot potato was handed off to the FBI when President Clinton ordered the Bureau to take over the siege. Again, as at Ruby Ridge, the FBI had been called in after another agency had already made a botch of things. Complicating the big picture was turmoil at FBIHQ, caused by the lame-duck status of Director William Sessions. When William Webster had resigned the post in 1987 to assume directorship of the CIA, President Reagan had appointed Sessions to head the FBI.

Sessions's tenure had been a rocky one, marked by hostile relationships with high-level Bureau and Justice Department officials. Lacking Webster's rigorous sense of probity, Sessions had compromised himself with small but telling abuses of his position. Among these abuses were numerous cross-country junkets and personal trips wrongly labeled as resulting from official Bureau-related duties; tax irregularities stemming from those write-offs; and undue influence wielded by his wife, Alice Sessions, an omnipresent and meddling presence at FBIHQ. Bureau morale suffered from the Director's getting away with infractions for which any other personnel would have been disciplined.

Appointed for a ten-year term, Sessions clung to his post, riding out a fractious four years with the Bush-appointed Justice Department. Seen by the incoming Clinton administration as a holdover from the previous regime, and with the FBI's Office of Professional Responsibility investigating charges against him, Sessions was hanging on to his job by his fingernails.

Inferno

It was in this period of drift and uncertainty at the organization's top levels that the FBI took over the problem in Waco. In charge at the scene was Jeff Jamar, FBI SAC of the San Antonio office. The Hostage Rescue Team (HRT) Commander was working for Jamar. The standoff had turned into a siege. In effect, every man, woman, and child in the compound was now held hostage to the will—and whim—of David Koresh.

Hovering over the confrontation was the malign specter of Jim Jones, the mad preacher whose followers had committed mass suicide in Guyana.

Cops and Robbers

Charismatic preacher Reverend Jim Jones relocated his U.S.-born People's Temple in the crude colony camp of Jonestown in Guyana, on South America's swampy northeast coast. In November 1978, a delegation of concerned relatives and reporters, led by California Congressman Leo Ryan, was massacred by Jones's gunmen. At his command, some 900 People's Temple members drank poisoned Kool-Aid—some voluntarily, others under duress. Jones himself died of a bullet in the temple, most likely self-inflicted.

Parallels between the People's Temple and the Branch Davidians were unsettling. Both Jones and Koresh were charismatic manipulators who wielded near-absolute power over their followers. Both preached an apocalyptic gospel of imminent Doomsday. People's Temple members had practiced mass suicide drills in anticipation of the real thing, while Koresh's followers had also undergone similar drills. A very real possibility existed that Koresh would engulf the compound dwellers in a suicidal conflagration.

At the siege site, days turned into weeks. The Branch Davidians had enough water and food stored away to hold out for a year. Negotiators were frustrated by Koresh's endless mind games and stalling tactics. But the delay served a valuable purpose: In that time, 34 Branch Davidians (24 of them children) came out of the compound to surrender voluntarily.

The FBI unleashed a psychological warfare operation against the Davidians, shining searchlights into the compound at night, blaring discordant music, chants, and even the sound of rabbits being slaughtered through loudspeakers in an effort to pressure the cultists to surrender. This ill-considered tactic, which could only have reinforced Koresh's depiction to his followers of their besiegers as Satanic oppressors who meant the worst for them, apparently came from somewhere high up, back at FBIHQ.

All who were going to come out of the compound had come out. Options were considered. Jeffrey Jamar, the FBI SA in charge at the scene, proposed the use of gas to force the evacuation of the compound. Anesthetic knock-out gas was rejected, on the grounds that it might kill off some of the very old and very young. CS, a kind of tear gas, was selected as the lever to force the surrender of the Branch Davidians. After lengthy conferences with Bureau bigs in Washington, Attorney General Janet Reno authorized the operation.

After 51 days, the clock had finally run out. On April 19, 1993, at about 6 A.M., the Branch Davidians were ordered to come out and surrender. They stayed put. An M-60 tank advanced on the compound, its battering ram knocking down the walls, pumping in CS gas. Throughout the morning, the compound was gassed while tanks battered down much of the main building's exterior. But some of the Branch Davidians were equipped with gas masks, while 30 mile-per-hour winds caused the gas to disperse.

Bu Stats

In the April 19, 1993, final assault on the Branch Davidian's Waco compound, 80 of the sect's members perished, including 24 children. Seven died of self-inflicted gunshot wounds, including Koresh.

At around noon, fire broke out in the southwest corner of the compound. In such an action, fire is always a possibility. Fearing that the Branch Davidians would shoot at firemen, the FBI had earlier ordered fire trucks away from the scene. By 12:20, the compound was blazing out of control. The Branch Davidians didn't come out and were consumed by the flames.

Various investigations, the last conducted by Special Counsel John Danforth, determined that the fire was without question started by the Davidians. HRT members had observed the Davidians starting the fires and trails of accellerents were found inside the compound. The fire had three origination points, all beginning at the same time. Recorded conversations from inside the compound reflect that David Koresh ordered the fires to be lit.

The Branch Davidian compound in Waco, Texas, burns out of control, climaxing the deadly 51-day stand-off between Federal agents and cult members on April 19, 1993.

(Courtesy of Corbis)

Political Fallout

The siege had ended, and now the finger-pointing began. The official line was that the Branch Davidians had themselves set the fire that consumed them. Survivors (there were nine) claimed that the M-60 tank had knocked over containers of kerosene, igniting them. Arson investigators found that a number of fires had been simultaneously set in the main building, with accelerants used to intensify the blaze.

Attorney General Janet Reno said she accepted full responsibility for the action and its consequences. Polls taken in the immediate aftermath of Waco showed that the public by a large majority believed that the Branch Davidians were to blame for their own deaths.

What went wrong? Despite indications to the contrary, the planners clearly thought that ultimately Koresh wouldn't initiate a Jonestown-style mass suicide. They were wrong.

An armed rush would have resulted in the death of scores of FBI HRT members. They would have been trying to rescue people who would have shot them. Many Davidians would have been killed in the shoot out, and they would still have set fire to the building. They believed that the only way they could get to heaven was to die in a fiery gun battle with the government. Death by fire, or gun fire, was their salvation.

Like Ruby Ridge, Waco became a political football. Hostile politicians used it as a club with which to hammer the Clinton administration. Ironically, the controversy allowed beleaguered Director Sessions to hold on to his post for a few months longer. Not until July 19, 1993, was he pushed out of office, becoming the first FBI Director ever to be fired. Replacing him was Louis B. Freeh, former FBI agent and judge.

Waco ultimately became the focus of feverish conspiracy theories fostered by extremists of the political left and right. It couldn't be that it was just a raid gone wrong, it had to be deliberate—the FBI wanted to kill those men, women, and children because of their faith, because they'd armed themselves against the government, and because it would throw a scare into other like-minded individuals.

So believed (or at least said they did) creatures of the extreme right and left. Among them was a Gulf War veteran who made what he described as a "pilgrimage" to the Waco compound during the siege: Timothy McVeigh.

The Least You Need to Know

- Hatemonger William Pierce's novel *The Turner Diaries*, advocating mass slaughter to racially "purify" America, served as a blueprint for like-minded fanatics.

- Inspired by neo-Nazi ideology, the terrorist group The Order unleashed a wave of bombings, bank robberies, and political assassination.

- A botched U.S. Marshals' action against white separatist Randy Weaver led to the FBI's involvement in the Ruby Ridge incident.

- After a 51-day siege, an FBI assault on the Branch Davidian compound in Waco, Texas, culminated in the cultists burning themselves alive.

- A series of small but telling improprieties led to the firing of FBI Director William Sessions.

Chapter 19

American Psychos

In This Chapter

- New technology, including the Internet, empowers malcontents with frightening destructive power

- The Unabomber's 18-year career of anonymous mail package terror bombings

- Violent antigovernment hate groups adopt new tactics to counter FBI sleuths and informants

- OKBOMB: the bombing of a federal building in Oklahoma City kills 168, wounds 500

- Apprehending homegrown, made in the USA terrorist Timothy McVeigh

- The ordeal of Atlanta Summer Olympics bombing suspect Richard Jewell

America's open society is both its strength and its weakness. Each new technological innovation is both promise and threat. For example, the Internet is a wonderful communications, research, and entertainment medium, yet it also allows easy access to potentially dangerous information which can be used against society or the individual. Public dissemination of homemade bombmaking techniques puts ever-greater firepower in the hands of potentially dangerous individuals. Such developments continue to provide great challenges to the FBI. It was not until after September 11, 2001 that FBI agents had the mandate to search the Internet and review websites of terrorists or radical groups. After 9/11 the rules were changed to allow agents to surf the web looking for potential threats to our country.

Prime examples of modern-day threats equipped with devastating firepower are the Unabomber, the antitechnological terrorist whose package bombs targeted people; and Timothy McVeigh, the all-American boy next door turned pathological mass-killer at the 1995 Oklahoma City bombing. The case of Richard Jewell, prime suspect in the 1996 Olympic Park bombing, shows how a false step in the age of 24-hour news cycles can embarrass the Bureau.

Unabom

Changing times produce changing trends in crime. Sometimes an old threat returns in a frightening new guise. The anarchist bombings of 1919 to 1920 helped usher in the transformation of the old Bureau of Investigation into the forerunner of the modern FBI. As the century wound on, technological improvements allowed ever greater powers of destruction to trickle down to the individual. The Internet made a sea of information available on demand, including information on how to make war on society—information that had been previously available, but that required a certain amount of research and digging to unearth. Now anyone with an online computer can download bomb-making specifications and recipes. And now when ideologues, haters, and just plain crazies set their ideas in motion in the real world, the results can be horrendous.

Justice Jargon

The **UNABOM** case was so labeled by FBI investigators because early targets of the bomber included universities ("un") and airlines ("a").

Official and Confidential

FBI investigators offered different theories as to the meaning of the FC initialization on the bomb parts. They were important to the bomber, since they appeared repeatedly, obsessively in each incident. One theory is that they stood for, simply, f*** computers; another, that they meant Freedom Club.

Predating today's ubiquitous on-line computer world, however, is the Unabom case, whose origins begin in an era when bombmaking procedures had to be accessed through books and periodicals. In 1978, at a university in the Chicago area, a package sent through the mail exploded when opened, injuring a security guard. The parcel was a package bomb, conceptually little different from those sent by early twentieth century anarchists to high-profile jurists, legislators, and financial magnates. So began an 18-year reign of destruction unleashed by the anonymous terrorist known as the *Unabomber*, ultimately killing three people and seriously wounding 23. In 1979, a second bomb injured a Northwestern University graduate. In 1980, a fourth bomb injured United Airlines President Percy Wood at his home

None of the victims was personally acquainted with the attacker. They had been selected because to their assailant they represented standard-bearers and enablers of the modern technological world—living symbols of the machine society he so detested.

Odd, oblique, taunting notes accompanied the bombs. The bomber's method of operation featured the use of a handcrafted wooden box containing gunpowder and a construction of hand-tooled metal springs and parts to trigger the explosion. The machine parts, scavenged from junkyards and diabolically reconfigured as arming and triggering mechanisms, were sometimes engraved with the letters FC.

One Man Terror Campaign

The Unabomber was a loner with a grudge against techno-society, expressing it through bombing. In a sense, he was a straggler, the last of a wave of anarchist-protest bombers who'd thrived during the 1960s and 1970s. That era had seen radical terrorists like the Weather Underground bomb draft boards, official buildings, and other symbols of the ruling government. The wave had peaked in the late 1960s, fading with the violent resistance movement that spawned it when the United States disengaged from the Vietnam War in 1974. The Unabomber was something of a product of that era, a late bloomer who began in 1978 when the movement had all but ended, a true believer who continued his one-man nightmare crusade throughout the Reagan era into the online 1990s.

At heart, he was a technophobe, a machine-breaker who targeted for destruction the machine-tenders. His targets were not confined to one geographical region, but stretched nationwide. Continuing to bomb his way through the 1980s, his acts included the 1982 injuring of a University of California, Berkeley, professor of electrical engineering with a package bomb and the 1987 bombing of a computer store in Salt Lake City, Utah. In the latter incident, the Unabomber was seen by an eyewitness, who was unable to furnish much of a description due to the suspect's disguise consisting ofa hooded sweatshirt and dark glasses.

A lone terrorist, operating without a network of associates to betray him, is one of the most difficult of all criminals to catch. Rather than dissuading him, the death of his first victim merely encouraged him to continue. Here was an ideologue who welcomed the blood of his foes in furtherance of his cause. Not since George Metesky, the Mad Bomber, in the 1950s and 1960s had the FBI faced this kind of perpetrator—and he'd remained on the loose for the better part of two decades. The person or persons responsible for the ghastly 1920 Wall Street bombing were never caught. Unabomber would likewise prove to be a tough nut to crack.

Cops and Robbers

George Metesky, known as the Mad Bomber, was a New York City resident who, feeling that he'd been unfairly charged on an electric bill from public utility company Con Edison, conducted an ongoing bombing campaign against the company. Starting in 1954 and continuing until his apprehension in the late 1960s, Metesky set off a number of bombs at sites throughout the city. Unlike Unabomber, Metesky produced a number of injuries but no fatalities—though not for lack of trying.

On June 22, 1993, the Unabomber sent a package bomb to University of California geneticist Professor Charles Epstein. Two days later, a second package bomb was opened by Yale University Professor David Gelertner, author of *Mirror Worlds*, a book theorizing about computer simulations of reality. Both men were severely injured.

In 1993, for the first time ever, the FBI issued an Internet alert seeking tips to Unabomber's identity. It received some 56,000 replies. A widely distributed FBI profile crafted a picture of the Unabomber as a white male in his thirties or forties holding a menial job, a neatly dressed, well-organized individual, able to blend into society.

On December 10, 1994, at his home, New Jersey advertising executive Thomas Mosser, an advisor to such technologically oriented clients as Digital Equipment Corporation and IBM, opened a Unabom mail package and was killed by the blast.

Manifesto for Mayhem

In 1995, the Unabomer contacted *The New York Times* with an ultimatum: If the newspaper would agree to publish his "manifesto," he would stay his destructive hand and refrain from killing. *Times* editors and FBI agents huddled in conference. It was not the policy of the *Times* or the Bureau to yield to terrorist demands. However, with innocent lives in the balance, and a cold investigative trail, officials decided to accede to the demand.

On September 19, 1995, both the *Times* and the *Washington Post* ran, complete and unabridged, Unabomber's 35,000-word manifesto, an antitechnology creed damning computers, the machine age, the Industrial Revolution, and even the concept of community-based agriculture as it has been practiced for the last 4,000 years.

The gamble paid off. In early January 1996, David Kaczynski, a social worker from Schenectady, New York, contacted FBI agents, stating that the manifesto echoed obsessive theories he'd heard espoused over the years by his brother, Theodore.

In 1996, Ted Kaczynski lived in rural isolation in a 12 foot by 14 foot wooden cabin in the woods outside Lincoln, Idaho. On April 3, an FBI SWAT team surreptitiously surrounded the cabin. A Forest Service officer known to Kaczynski approached the cabin, accompanied by two FBI agents. When Kaczynski came out to greet his acquaintance, he was grabbed and arrested.

> **Cops and Robbers**
>
> Dr. Theodore "Ted" Kaczynski, born in 1940, was a mathematical prodigy who graduated from Harvard at age 20, becoming a tenured mathematics professor at the University of California, Berkeley. In 1969, he abruptly quit, resigning his position and dropping out of the system.

Inside the cabin, agents found a nearly completed bomb that was ready for mailing (Unabomer's promise to stop the killing if his manifesto was published was a lie), bomb parts, chemicals, bomb-making tools, and several copies of his manifesto. A typewriter proved to be the one used to write the 56-page manifesto. From the cabin, truckloads of evidence were shipped to the FBI Lab in Quantico, Virginia. In May 1996, the entire cabin was loaded on a flatbed truck and ultimately taken to a secure storage facility in Sacramento, California, site of Kaczynski's 1998 murder trial.

In a letter to the *Times*, Kaczynski had written, "We are an anarchist group calling ourselves FC," but no evidence was ever developed to indicate the existence of such a group or any accomplices in the Unabomber attacks. Although subject to the death penalty should he be found guilty of first degree murder and other capital charges, Kaczynski was allowed to accept a plea bargain to plead guilty on all counts in exchange for a life sentence in January 1998.

At his May 4, 1998, sentencing hearing at a Sacramento court, Kaczynski issued a brief statement saying that the government had misrepresented the facts in the Unabom case, that he hoped the public would reserve judgment until hearing all the facts of the case, and that he intended at some future date to respond to the government's assertions. He was given four life sentences without the possibility of parole. Brother David Kaczynski received a $1 million dollar reward, which he said he was going to share with the Unabomber's victims and their families.

OKBOMB

A native of upstate New York, Timothy V. McVeigh enlisted in the U.S. Army and served as a sergeant in the Gulf War, where he received a Bronze Star for valor. McVeigh, who until then had evinced only enthusiasm for an Army career, achieved a coveted goal of being allowed to take Special Forces training to become a Green Beret. However, unable to meet the rigorous physical standards required, he was dropped from the program.

Although the Green Berets are an elite fighting force whose standards can only be met by a select few, McVeigh was ashamed of his failure. It was as if a switch had been flipped in his mind. If he couldn't become a Green Beret, why then, the Army was no damned good, and neither was the whole rotten government of which it was a part. Such was his thinking, which ripened into fanatical hatred of the U.S. government. Honorably discharged into civilian life, McVeigh cultivated a taste for ultra-right, antigovernment , militia-style politics.

He also developed a deep and abiding enthusiasm—bordering on reverence—for *The Turner Diaries*, the novel written by neo-Nazi William Pierce advocating assassinations, bombings, and mass murder to overthrow the federal government and institute a racial extermination of non-Aryans.

For a time, McVeigh worked the gun show circuit in the Midwest and West, supporting himself by selling copies of *The Turner Diaries*. He also had a fondness for quoting Jefferson's maxim about the Tree of Liberty requiring frequent waterings of "the blood of patriots."

As noted in Chapter 17, McVeigh made a "pilgrimage" to David Koresh's Branch Davidian compound in Waco, Texas, during its besiegement by federal agents. That siege's fiery climax of mass death for the cultists enraged McVeigh, who saw it an infamy crying out for vengeance.

Justice Jargon

Among neo-Nazis and the white supremacist movement, Rahowa (sometimes RaHoWa) is shorthand for **racial holy war,** their fervently sought Holy Grail, a genocidal war of extermination to "purify" the U.S. (if not the world) of Jews, blacks, and all non-Aryans.

Among neo-Nazis, white supremacists, and violent antigovernment militias, the Great Beast is the FBI, whose greatest weapon is the informant. To guard against this threat, the movement espoused the doctrine of "leaderless resistance." Essentially, this meant operating in small cells of from three to five members with no overt ties to established organizations. If any members of the cell are taken, they can only betray their immediate fellows, insulating the parent organizations from prosecution. Many such leaderless cells, following the objectives of the larger ideology to which they're all in thrall, will ultimately produce the much-sought goal of a *"racial holy war."*

ATF agents who'd served at the Waco siege were posted to the office at the Alfred P. Murrah Federal Building in Oklahoma City, Oklahoma. On April 19, 1995, shortly before 9 A.M., hell was unleashed on that site, as a powerful blast pulverized the building, killing 168 citizens, including 19 children, and injuring 500 people.

It was the greatest peacetime terrorist strike ever inflicted on the U.S., one only to be surpassed by the terror strikes of September 11, 2001. Mindful of the 1993 bombing of the World Trade Center, citizens and law enforcement alike initially believed the Oklahoma City bombing to be the work of Middle Eastern or Islamist terrorists.

Yet FBI investigators found the date of the blast highly significant: April 19, the second anniversary to the day of the fiery conflagration at the Waco compound. It was also one day before the birthday of Adolf Hitler, a milestone among the neo-Nazi movement.

Justice Jargon

ANFO is an acronym for ammonium nitrate soaked in fuel oil—basically, fertilizer soaked in diesel fuel. Due to the commercial availability of both components and its high explosive yield, the mixture is a favorite of homemade bomb makers unable to access state-supplied conventional explosives.

Criminalists and forensic technicians determined that the building had been struck by a truck bomb, specifically a truck filled with 4,000 pounds of the potent homemade explosive *ANFO*, which is fertilizer soaked in diesel fuel.

Experts determined that a rear axle found some distance from the blast site came from the truck used to house the bomb. The axle furnished a vehicle identification number (VIN), which was used to identify the truck. An FBI trace on the number revealed that the vehicle had been a 20-foot yellow Ryder rental truck that had been rented from Elliott's Body Shop in Junction City, Kansas.

Owner Eldon Elliott identified the renter as one Robert Kling, a man with a crew cut, beady eyes, and a long, thin, pale face. The shop's mechanic said that Kling had been accompanied by a second man with dark hair, thick eyebrows, and a wide, thick-featured face. Elliott also remembered having seen the second man.

FBI sleuths tagged the two Unsubs (unknown subjects) as Unsub One and Unsub Two. Sketches of both men were widely distributed in the region. Several witnesses at the scene identified Unsub One as the man they'd seen in the area of the yellow Ryder truck shortly before the blast.

A Junction City motel owner recognized Unsub One as the person who'd rented a room from April 14 to April 18, registering as Tim McVeigh of Decker, Michigan. The Michigan address cited by McVeigh was discovered to be that of brothers James and Terry Nichols.

Official and Confidential

The Austrian made Glock pistol is a favorite of terrorists, criminals, and other clandestine types because of its accuracy and reliability. Available in 9mm, .45 caliber, and .40 caliber, there are also a few .357 and 10mm models. Contrary to popular belief, they contain metal parts and will not go through an x-ray or metal detector.

The searchers didn't have to look far for McVeigh. He was already in custody, having been arrested by an Oklahoma state trooper who'd stopped his vehicle about an hour-and-a-half after the bomb blast, at a site some 75 miles distant from the crime scene. Stopped for driving without license plates, a classic piece of dumb luck that no one could have predicted, McVeigh was also found to be in possession of a .45-caliber Glock semiautomatic pistol, which he did not use to try to shoot his way to escape. Most likely, he had no idea that the FBI would identify him so quickly, and decided not to risk a gun fight with a state patrol officer, when the chances were that he would just walk out of jail a free man.

Held in the county jail, McVeigh was an hour away from a bail hearing when the FBI contacted the local sheriff, advising him to hold the suspect until FBI agents could come and pick him up, which soon followed.

The FBI investigation generated 28,000 interviews and the collection of some three and a half tons of evidence. McVeigh's accomplice was discovered to have been his Army buddy Terry Nichols, who was also arrested and charged with the crime. Brother James Nichols was subsequently cleared of any involvement. Terry Nichols did not fit the sketch of Unsub Two, whom the FBI ultimately classed as an innocent passerby who'd been in the shop the same time as McVeigh but had no connection to him. Unsub Two has never been found or identified.

When originally apprehended by the Oklahoma state trooper, McVeigh had in his possession *The Turner Diaries*, which features the bombing of a federal building as an overture to race war. Government prosecutors maintained that McVeigh had committed the bombing as "payback" for Waco and in hopes of igniting violent antigovernment uprisings. While in custody, McVeigh proved to be surprisingly reticent and close-mouthed, except to deny being part of any larger conspiracy. Authorities developed information that indicated that McVeigh had had contacts with *Turner Diaries* author William Pierce's neo-Nazi National Alliance; with the Aryan Nations compound in Hayden Lake, Idaho; and with Elohim City, a militant Christian Identity compound of several dozen white supremacist families. The links were provocative but opaque and elusive, and they failed to produce any solid evidence of a conspiracy.

Official and Confidential

Located near Oklahoma City, Elohim City is a stronghold for Identity movement (see Chapter 18) fanatics, and has been associated with the violent antigovernment group The Covenant, Sword, and Arm of the Lord (CSA). On April 19, 1985 (note that date), a CSA plot had been broken up by federal agents, a plot involving a rocket attack on the Alfred P. Murrah Building. The author of that plot, Richard Snell, was executed for other capital crimes on April 19, 1995, the same day as the Oklahoma City bombing. The existence of other, perhaps peripheral OKBOMB conspirators besides McVeigh and Terry Nichols remains a vexing question.

McVeigh was tried, convicted, and sentenced to death for the bombing. At the 11th hour, a snag developed that threatened to delay or possibly even derail McVeigh's execution date, a date long-anticipated by most of the U.S. population.

To discourage the development of conspiracy theories, the Justice Department (without the input of FBI Director Freeh) had entered into a unique agreement to furnish McVeigh's defense with all documents relating to the investigation. This agreement covered not only documents that might bear on the defendant's guilt or innocence, which they were legally obligated to provide, but all documents in any way related to the case, period. This obligation imposed a Herculean, perhaps even impossible task on the FBI, since virtually all its field offices had generated some paperwork involved with the investigation.

In 2001, as Execution Day neared for McVeigh, the FBI notified McVeigh's attorneys that it had failed to turn over to them some 3,000 pages of documents relating to the case. The Justice Department was forced to request a stay of McVeigh's execution until they could examine the material, which eventually totaled 4,034 documents.

Finally, a judge ruled that the documents had not been vital to the defense and that their unavailability had not prevented the defendant from receiving a fair trial.

The execution went forward, with McVeigh dying by lethal injection and taking his secrets with him. The Oklahoma City bombing, which he'd hoped would ignite a nationwide uprising, instead marked the decline of the violent antigovernment militia movement, as the horrendous human consequences of its militant rhetoric were made clear in real flesh and blood terms.

Jolting Jewell

The ugly side of being the prime suspect in an FBI investigation of a high-profile crime was demonstrated in the case of Richard Jewell, a case that boomeranged against the Bureau to create a public relations disaster.

Held in and around Atlanta, Georgia, the 1996 Summer Olympic games were a focus of worldwide media interest and attention. On July 27, at a little before 1 A.M. at Centennial Square, a plaza at the heart of the grounds, a suspicious object was noted by security guard Richard Jewell. The object was an abandoned green backpack. While the area was being evacuated, the knapsack-bomb exploded, killing two people and wounding 111. Had the bomb not been detected and the warning given, casualties would undoubtedly have been much higher. The outrage was also a global humiliation for the host country, the United States, a humiliation maximized by the intensive 24-hour Internet and cable TV news cycle. Heavy pressure for a quick solution came down from high up in Washington, D.C.

Initially hailed as a hero, Jewell enjoyed his 15 minutes of fame, describing to TV news crews and reporters how he'd spotted the disguised infernal device. But his mini-celebrity soon become notoriety. Within three days after the bombing, the *Atlanta Journal-Constitution*, a leading, nationally well-respected newspaper, printed a story from an unnamed law enforcement source stating that Jewell was the FBI's lead suspect in the Olympic bombing case. The article noted the phenomenon of persons who set fires or plant bombs in order to play the hero by "discovering" the danger.

A pair of FBI investigators "invited" Jewell to attend what they described as a video-taping of a Bureau instructional film about first-responders at emergencies. They misrepresented themselves, preying on his vanity and ego—acceptable tactics that have been ruled legal by the courts but which might not be found so acceptable in the court of public opinion, especially in a case targeting the wrong man.

Official and Confidential

Time and again, the courts have ruled that the use of deception by law enforcement agents against a crime suspect is a legally permissible tactic, as long as the suspect has been given and understands his or her Miranda rights. This tactic allows investigators to falsely tell the suspect that he's been witnessed doing the crime, that an accomplice has put the finger on him, that a key piece of evidence such as a weapon has been recovered, and other ruses that might prompt the suspect to confess.

The interview was held downtown at the Atlanta field office. Fearful that it might compromise a future prosecution, Director Louis Freeh (known to oversee important ongoing investigations) phoned the field office, ordering that Jewell be given his Miranda warning. This was objected to by the on-site SAC and a U.S. attorney who was also present. Their fear was that once Jewell had been Mirandized, he'd cease cooperating. Freeh made it an order.

At the interrogation, Jewell was read his rights, but was told that this was only a formality, a bit of red tape necessary to continue with the training video they'd told him would make him a "superstar." Not buying, Jewell requested a lawyer, and the interview ended. He was not arrested, but was allowed to go freely.

For the next 80 days, Jewell got the treatment that comes with being the prime suspect in a major FBI investigation and being publicly named as that prime suspect. The *Journal-Constitution* followed with more articles from "informed sources" attesting to Jewell's probable guilt in the bombing. In the print and TV news media, profiles appeared, indicating that Jewell's psychological background was consistent with the park bomber. His name was traduced, dragged through the mud. His home, where he lived with his mother, was exhaustively searched by the FBI, which confiscated his guns and even 22 of his mother's Walt Disney videotapes.

And then, lo and behold, after three months of being left out to hang, Jewell was publicly cleared by the FBI of the crime. Subsequent developments in the case led to the naming of a new prime suspect, Eric Robert Rudolph, a militant anti-abortion zealot also wanted in the bombings of two abortion clinics and an Atlanta nightspot. An accomplished shooter, outdoorsman, and genuinely dangerous man, Rudolph fled to the woods, evading pursuit. He remains at large to this day.

The FBI SA who misled Jewell about his rights was suspended for five days without pay, while the SAC received a letter of censure.

Ultimately, the Justice Department settled with Richard Jewell, paying him a hefty damage settlement. Jewell's lawyers accused the FBI of having fingered Jewell as the prime suspect to the *Journal-Constitution*, a charge denied by the FBI, which noted that a member of the numerous law enforcement agencies also involved in the case could also have leaked the information. Protecting the confidentiality of its sources, the newspaper has refused to identify the leaker. As of this writing, Richard Jewell's attorneys intend to prosecute a multi-million dollar civil suit against the newspaper for damages incurred by their client.

The Least You Need to Know

- From 1978 to 1996, Unabomber Ted Kaczynski's campaign of mail package bombings killed three people and seriously wounded 23.

- Countering the threat of FBI informants and penetration, starting in the 1980s violent antigovernment hate groups adopted the tactic of using small, three to five person cell groups.

- The April 19, 1995, truck bombing of the Murrah Federal Building in Oklahoma City killed 168 and wounded 500, making it the most devastating peacetime terror strike until September 11, 2001.

- Timothy McVeigh, with accomplice Terry Nichols, committed the Oklahoma City bombing to "avenge" the Waco Branch Davidians and in hopes of triggering violent antigovernment uprisings.

- Mishandling the interrogation of 1996 Olympic Park bombing suspect Richard Jewell (later cleared), created a public relations fiasco for the FBI.

Chapter 20

Wen Ho Lee: Phantom Menace

In This Chapter

- ◆ The USSR's fall heightens Sino-American spy tensions and intrigue
- ◆ Did China steal America's top-secret W-88 thermonuclear warhead?
- ◆ The FBI uncovers shocking security lapses at U.S. atomic weapons labs
- ◆ Scientist Wen Ho Lee: Master spy or fall guy?
- ◆ Solution Unsatisfactory: Resolution of the Lee spy trial

During the U.S./USSR Cold War superpower rivalry, the CIA encouraged extensive contacts between U.S. atomic scientists and their Red Chinese counterparts. The Soviet Union's fall highlighted the potential threat to U.S. strategic interests held by the People's Republic of China (PRC). In 1992, a PRC atomic weapons breakthrough seemed to indicate that the Chinese had engaged in massive espionage and theft of U.S. atomic weapons secrets. 1995 saw the start of the FBI's five-year investigation into PRC espionage at top-secret U.S. nuclear weapons making facilities. Charged with massive theft of atom secrets, scientist Wen Ho Lee's controversial high-profile trial resulted in a cloudy outcome and public relations headaches for the Bureau.

The Big Steal

In 1995, Department of Energy (DOE) counterintelligence chief Notra Trulock notified the FBI that the secret of making the W-88, the United States' most advanced nuclear warhead, had been stolen by spies for the PRC. Intelligence indicated that in 1992, PRC atomic weapons scientists had built and successfully tested a working model along the lines of the *W-88*, a significant technological breakthrough. Allowing for the ability to fit a number of independently targeted nuclear warheads on a single intercontinental ballistic missile (ICBM), the technology could put scores of millions of Americans living on the Pacific coast under potential nuclear threat. It might even alter the global balance of power.

Heading both DOE's intelligence and counterintelligence branches, Trulock believed that the W-88 had been stolen as a result of espionage at one of the nation's top-secret nuclear weapons designing facilities. Many federal agencies are equipped to investigate potential cases of espionage, but only the FBI has the power to arrest those suspects. Trulock had now officially reported his suspicions to the FBI.

Justice Jargon

The **W-88** nuclear warhead is a vital component of America's atomic weaponry, the latest in a series of warheads designed for submarine-launched ballistic missiles. The W stands for *weapon*, while 88 is the series number. The warhead is a miniaturized H-bomb whose size allows for the arming of several independently targeted warheads on a single missile.

What followed was a five-year investigation carried out against a stormy backdrop of controversy and national uproar over alleged Chinese spy theft of vital U.S. atomic secrets—the "crown jewels," as a federal prosecutor would later describe them. The search would expose a culture of appalling institutionalized security violations at the nation's top-secret atomic weapons labs. Ultimately, its focus would narrow to one man, scientist Wen Ho Lee, and the question of whether he was the most dangerous traitor since the Rosenbergs or a scapegoat for the DOE's systemic security failures.

East-West Atomic Enigma

Behind it all lay a curious episode of post–Cold War intrigue. Earlier in 1995, a walk-in had presented himself to Taiwanese authorities, claiming to be a defector from mainland China and carrying a bundle of top-secret PRC atomic weapons documents.

The documents revealed that PRC scientists were aware of certain key design features of the U.S.'s W-88 warhead. The CIA polygraphed the defector. When asked whether he was acting for a foreign intelligence agency, his answers indicated deception. The possibility was considered that he was actually acting on behalf of the PRC, alerting U.S. military planners to the fact that China had W-88 type warheads, to deter U.S. intervention on the side of Taiwan should hostilities occur between it and China.

Whatever the messenger's motive, the documents demonstrated the existence of PRC atomic espionage against the United States and the nation's awareness of certain aspects of the W-88. That much was certain.

Official and Confidential

The United States's key atomic weapons design facilities are three national laboratories: Los Alamos, Sandia, and Livermore. Los Alamos National Laboratory (LANL) is located in Los Alamos, New Mexico; Sandia is located in Albuquerque, New Mexico; Livermore is in California. All three labs are operated by the University of California and overseen by the Department of Energy. Los Alamos and Livermore handle nuclear weapons design, whereas Sandia engineers the nonnuclear bomb and weapons technology.

Believing that Trulock lacked the evidence to back up his assertions, the FBI declined to open an investigation. Trulock went back to work, in the summer of 1995 convening a working group of about 20 expert nuclear weaponeers and CIA analysts to probe whether the PRC had stolen the secret of W-88. DOE counterintelligence investigator Dan Bruno opened an Administrative Inquiry (AI) into the subject.

Bruno's investigation was hampered from the start because he was operating under false premises. Perhaps reflecting his boss Trulock's belief that the W-88 secret's loss was due to excessive contact between U.S. atomic weapons lab scientists and their PRC counterparts, Bruno focused on the three national weapons labs: Los Alamos, Livermore, and Sandia. Yet the W-88 information had been widely disseminated at the Pentagon and among a number of civilian defense contractors, any one of which might have been responsible for the loss. Of the labs, Livermore failed to keep adequate records of its scientists' foreign trips and contacts, so it, too, was arbitrarily excluded from the investigation. Bruno's spy hunt became focused exclusively on Los Alamos National Laboratory (LANL).

Tiger Trap

At LANL, the DOE investigation became increasingly focused on one man, Taiwanese American nuclear scientist Wen Ho Lee. Lee was a figure not unknown to the FBI or the CIA, both of which in the past had had ongoing relationships with him. Lee first came to the notice of the FBI under suspicious circumstances in December 1982, during a spy hunt operation codenamed Tiger Trap. FBI Foreign Counterintelligence (FCI) agents were investigating scientist Gwo-Bao Min, suspected in the passing of neutron bomb secrets to the PRC. A wiretap on Min's phone picked up an apparently unsolicited call from Lee to Min, who were strangers to each other. Lee expressed anger on Min's troubles from being a suspected spy and offered to help find out who had "squealed" on the scientist. Min quickly cut off the call.

FBI agents tracked down Lee, then working at Los Alamos. Lee and Min were both originally from Taiwan, and Lee said that he'd assumed that Min was suspected of spying for Taiwan. What he hadn't known was that Min was suspected of spying for China. While being readied for a polygraph test, Lee volunteered the information that, starting in 1980, he'd been forwarding unclassified documents on reactor safety to Taiwan. The agents then recruited Lee into fronting for a *false flag* effort against Min. One day Lee walked up to Min, confronting him, trying to lure him into agreeing to spy for China.

Min wasn't buying and brushed off Lee. His partcipation in the episode concluded, Lee's initial attempted obstruction of the FBI counterintelligence operation investigating Min should have ensured the revocation of his security clearance, effectively prohibiting his access to classified data and materials.

Instead, LANL security officers were not notified of his activities, ensuring his continued employment at X Division, the lab's atomic weapons making branch—an astonishing security lapse, and not the last in the strange case of Wen Ho Lee. Specializing in hydrodynamics, mathematically modeling the behavior of fluids in nuclear reactors, he was a hardworking if unspectacular performer.

> **Cops and Robbers**
>
> Born in 1939 on the island of Taiwan, in 1964 Wen Ho Lee came to the United States, where he received his master's in mechanical engineering. In 1978 he went to work at Los Alamos, two years later becoming a member of the computational section of the Theoretical Design Division, also known as X Division, a top-secret atomic weapons–making branch.

> **Justice Jargon**
>
> A **false flag** operation is one in which an agent pretends to be working for a foreign country or intelligence agency to determine where the targeted subject's true allegiance lies.

Lee's wife Sylvia, also a LANL employee, was deeply involved as a volunteer in the hospitality arrangements for delegations of visiting Chinese scientists, serving as translator and hostess. This activity caused her to be recruited by an FBI agent in 1984 for regular debriefings of information she'd overheard in the course of her hostessing chores. Later, a CIA agent also made use of Sylvia Lee in the same capacity. Wen Ho Lee, too, was ultimately recruited for the effort by the CIA and FBI.

Official and Confidential

During the late Cold War period, the CIA backed a program encouraging U.S. nuclear researchers to participate in scientific exchange missions with the PRC. The scientists attended conferences, delivered research papers, met their opposite numbers, and toured PRC nuclear labs and facilities. Back in the United States, they would be debriefed by the CIA. During the visits, their PRC counterparts were equally if not more aggressive in seeking information from them.

Lee made more than a dozen visits to China, attending scientific conferences and seminars. During routine briefings held when he returned from these trips, Wen Ho Lee said that he'd not been contacted by Chinese scientists seeking to persuade him to pass along confidential scientific data. This piqued security officials, since all the other personnel who'd attended the conferences along with Lee had all reported some sort of approach designed to wean data from them. Why had Wen Ho Lee alone escaped their importunities? Perhaps he'd had them but failed to report them, a security violation.

In 1994, a high-ranking delegation of PRC scientists was visiting Los Alamos. Although he was not part of the hosting group, Wen Ho Lee sought out the PRC delegation and was warmly embraced by Hu Side, the head of the IAPCM, China's counterpart to Los Alamos.

Security investigators were frankly baffled by the incident they called The Hug. Surely, if Lee had passed information to the Chinese, they would have tried to hide their acquaintance with him, not advertise it publicly in front of their LANL hosts.

Prime Suspect

Early on in investigator Dan Bruno's Administrative Inquiry, both Wen Ho and Sylvia Lee came to the forefront of the list of potential suspects. On October 31, 1995—Halloween—DOE counterintelligence director Notra Trulock presented another briefing to the FBI, one in which Wen Ho Lee was presented as a prime suspect in spying for the PRC.

But Trulock's briefing to the FBI had not been conducted entirely in good faith. What Trulock failed to explain to Bureau spy-hunters was that the working group of LANL expert scientists and CIA analysts had concluded that the secrets of the W-88 hadn't been stolen from the facility by a mole burrowing from within. In fact, they weren't even sure that the PRC had stolen the secret of the W-88. Trulock held their conclusions from the FBI.

In May 1996, the results of Dan Bruno's AI were passed to the FBI. The short list of potential atom secrets theft suspects had narrowed to one name: Wen Ho Lee.

Handling local investigative chores at the lab was the FBI's Albuquerque, New Mexico office, whose top priorities included narcotics trafficking, border-crossing fugitives, and crimes committed on Indian reservations. In recent years, the FBI and LANL had had an uneasy relationship. Security conditions at Los Alamos were so lax and loose that in 1994, the FBI had pulled out all personnel stationed at the labs.

The FBI investigation was hampered from the start by withholds and misleading information. Withholds in the case of DOE's Trulock burying the working group's conclusion that the W-88 hadn't been stolen from the lab, and misleading information as when agents were wrongly led to believe that they lacked legal authority to examine Lee's computer files at LANL. In fact, according to security regulations, they did have that right, but for several years the computer went unexamined.

Justice Jargon

The Justice Department's **Office of Intelligence Policy and Review (OIPR)** is responsible for making applications to the FISC for warrants for electronic surveillance and more of targeted suspects.

In February 1997, probers wanted to go to the Washington, D.C., Foreign Intelligence Surveillance Court (FISC), to get a warrant to wiretap and bug Lee, but the supervening agency, the Justice Department's *Office of Intelligence Policy and Review (OIPR)* didn't think there was enough evidence and refused to apply for a warrant. The result was that investigators were blinded in terms of their electronic surveillance capacities.

In spring of 1998, Wen Ho Lee spent three weeks in Taiwan. In August, FBI desperation shone through when they launched a clumsy and abortive false flag ploy against Lee. In 1983, Lee himself had played the central role in a false flag operation against suspected neutron bomb spy suspect Gwo-Bao Min.

Now Lee was on the receiving end of a similar gambit. Adding to the ill-considered, slapdash nature of the affair was the fact that the agent ostensibly trying to recruit

Lee to spy for the PRC spoke Cantonese, when it was generally well known that Chinese intelligence officers speak Mandarin. In any event, Lee brushed off the approach, although contrary to regulations, he failed to notify security officers about the contact.

In fall of 1998, Trulock delivered his briefing to the House of Representatives' *Cox Committee*, originally formed to investigate Chinese influence-buying in the last election, but which had broadened its scope to probe classified technology transfers from the United States to the PRC.

Justice Jargon

Chaired by California Representative Chris Cox (Republican), the **Cox Committee** was formed to investigate illegal Chinese campaign contributions during the 1996 Presidential race. Its scope expanded to probe illegal technology transfers by U.S. companies whose satellites were launched into space atop Chinese rockets. Following leads supplied them largely by Notra Trulock, the Committee's final report reflected his arguable conclusion that the PRC had committed massive espionage and theft of U.S. atomic secrets.

Grand Theft Atomic

In December 1998, on his return from a trip to Hong Kong, Lee was polygraphed at the behest of LANL by technicians employed by private security firm Wackenhut. Prior to the test, Lee volunteered the information that during a 1988 visit to a conference at Beijing, he'd received a surprise visit at night in his hotel room from two PRC scientists. One was Hu Side, later head of China's nuclear weapons program, the one who during his 1994 LANL visit had embraced Lee so warmly. Lee told investigators that the duo had asked him for information about classified nuclear warhead data, which he'd refused to give them. Contrary to regulations, he'd failed to report the meeting until now.

Wackenhut's operators concluded that Lee had passed the test. His admission about the 1988 Beijing meeting led to the suspension of his security clearance pending further investigation, resulting in his being transferred over to the unclassified side of the lab. The lack of clearance meant that he was barred from entering his former office. This proved to be of some paramount importance to Lee, for in the next few months he made numerous failed attempts (and several successful ones) to enter his office.

In February 1999, FBI experts said that their examination of the Wackenhut polygraph records showed that Lee had not passed the test. The FBI now administered its own polygraphing of Wen Ho Lee, a test he failed.

On March 5, 1999, FBI agents asked Lee for permission to search his office, which he granted. Searchers found manuals for working the mathematical bomb codes, manuals that Lee shouldn't have had. Worse, an investigator found Lee's notes on "How to Move Files."

The next day, March 6, *The New York Times* broke a front-page story about possible espionage at Los Alamos. On orders from a panicked FBIHQ and against the recommendation of the female FBI FCI agent who'd been working the case, on March 7 she reluctantly conducted an confrontational interview with Wen Ho Lee, demanding to know what exactly he'd done, threatening him with the loss of his security clearance and job, and reminding him of the fate of the Rosenbergs, convicted atomic spies who'd gone to the electric chair protesting their innocence. Lee steadfastly maintained his innocence.

On March 23, an investigator discovered in Lee's lab a printout of a computer files directory that listed as unclassified files that he knew were classified weapons files.

Computer security at LANL was virtually nonexistent. The computer section was divided into two halves, one classified and the other unclassified. But no safeguards existed to keep users from going into the classified section, labeling the files as unclassified, and downloading them to the unclassified side, for later retrieval.

Here's what Wen Ho Lee had done: Starting in April 1988 and continuing for eleven years, he'd ultimately downloaded 430,000 pages of classified files. Downloading them from the unclassified section to a computer in a trailer outside the facility's restricted area, he'd then transferred the data to a number (between 15 and 25) of blank quarter-inch tapes.

It was the most massive collection of mathematical atomic weapons codes ever amassed by a single individual. Getting those tapes back or at least accounting for them would ultimately become the government's top priority, even more than sending Wen Ho Lee to jail. But for now, a wrongway probe had somehow come right, with agents discovering what looked like the biggest atomic secrets espionage case since Klaus Fuchs and the Rosenbergs.

In December 1999, Wen Ho Lee was arrested. Federal prosecutors filed a 59-count indictment against Lee for violations of the Cold War–era Atomic Energy Act, charges which upon conviction could lead to a sentence of life imprisonment.

On Trial

At a bail hearing, federal prosecutors argued that national security demands mandated that Lee remain in custody. The government presented a series of witnesses to argue that Wen Ho Lee had stolen the "crown jewels" of mathematically coded U.S. atomic secrets, and that the transfer of the tapes to a foreign country (that is, China) might irrevocably alter the United States' global strategic posture. The tapes being so important, the government argued, it was necessary that Wen Ho Lee be kept in isolation, so that he would be unable to cue a confederate to the location of the tapes.

The judge agreed. Wen Ho Lee was remanded to the custody of the Santa Fe county jail, where he was kept in a single cell in an isolation ward designed to secure the inmates from the general jail population. So that he might not reveal the locale of the tapes through intermediaries to a confederate, he was kept in solitary confinement. For the same reason, he was not allowed to receive visits from family or friends. Each day, he was allowed a one-hour exercise period, alone (save for a guard) in the courtyard.

 Official and Confidential

While Lee was in jail, events happened that would radically affect the prosecution and outcome of the government's case. The lead prosecutor, a hard-driving and aggressive case winner, was revealed to have engaged in several questionable sexual affairs with employees of the U.S. Attorney's Office, leading to his relegation to a secondary role and ultimately his withdrawal from the prosecution team. Then the judge in the case, who'd consistently ruled in favor of the prosecution, was forced to recuse himself when accused of having made improper sexual advances to a female member of the defense team. His replacement was considerably more skeptical about the merits of the government's case.

Outside the courtroom, charges that Lee had been racially profiled and targeted because of his ethnicity found resonance in parts of the Chinese-American community, which rallied to his support.

The atmosphere had changed materially when Wen Ho Lee had a follow-up bail hearing. The defense called an FBI agent to the stand, pointing out that he'd testified under oath in the previous hearing that Lee had requested the use of a colleague's computers on the pretext of using it to file a job resumé, only to use it to download data. This activity showed intent to deceive on Lee's part, a subterfuge that worked against him. The defense now cited a transcript of an interview with that same colleague, in which he stated that Lee had indeed said that he planned to use the computer to download some data. What's more, the FBI agent had to have known that fact, since he'd been the one who'd interviewed the colleague.

In other words, the FBI agent had misrepresented the facts under oath. Confronted with that misrepresentation by the defense, he now claimed he'd forgotten the facts at the time, making an honest mistake. The defense intimated that he'd lied, making much of the fact that during the time of his initial testimony, the transcript of the colleague's interview had been unavailable to the defense.

Defense experts followed, all stating that in their opinion, the mathematical codes copied by Lee did not have the strategic importance ascribed to them by the government, that they were not the crown jewels, and that their mere possession would not give another country the ability to build the W-88, which was protected by other top-secret features not mentioned in the 1995 PRC defector document drop.

With Wen Ho Lee on the verge of being released on bail, it was time for both sides to make a deal. The government wanted the tapes more than they wanted Lee. Lee now said that he'd made more tapes than he'd previously admitted to, that there might have been as many as 25. He said that he'd thrown them in a Dumpster behind the lab. The FBI sent a team of agents in bio-hazard spacesuits to comb through the

Official and Confidential

Commenting on career and personal reverses he'd suffered in the aftermath of the case of Wen Ho Lee, former DOE counterintelligence chief Notra Trulock, who'd gotten the whole W-88 flap started, observed, "If I'm such a mastermind, how come I'm unemployed and broke?"

city dump, probing the area where that period's Los Alamos garbage would have been located. An assiduous search finally located some unclassified tapes, but not the ones being looked for. The tapes have never been found, and the only "proof" that they've been disposed of is the dubious word of Wen Ho Lee.

In the plea bargaining, the government dropped all but one of the 59 counts it had filed against Lee, leaving one felony count of downloading classified information, to which Lee pled guilty. At a hearing in early September 2000, the judge sentenced Lee to time served, which amounted to 277 days.

Final Analysis

While the spectacle of a 60-year old man being kept in solitary confinement for 9 months is unpleasant, the fact is that most of his troubles were brought on by Wen Ho Lee himself. Throughout his career, from his 1979 hiring by LANL (and possibly before that), Lee lived a double life of subterfuge and deception. The question of his spying for other countries remained unresolved, but what is known for certain is that he was a liar, a manipulator, and a thief.

The extent of his copying of nuclear weapons codes proves him guilty of the theft of the single greatest horde of atomic secrets of all times. The final dispensation and destination of those missing tapes is unknown, but standard operating procedure in the intelligence field requires that all the information contained therein must be considered compromised and steps taken to remedy that vulnerability.

The most likely explanation for Lee's behavior was that he was engaged in industrial espionage, the "industry" in question top-secret atomic weapons making. Possibly he planned to take those tapes with him to his next job, in whatever country that might be, using the storehouse of technical data they contained to enhance his bargaining position as he sold his services to the next bidder—but who knows?

The Least You Need to Know

- The fall of the Soviet Union highlighted U.S. rivalries and international intrigue with the People's Republic of China.

- In the early- to mid-1990s, evidence indicated that the PRC had acquired top-secret data relating to the W-88, the United States' advanced miniaturized thermonuclear warhead.

- Misleading information and withholds by Department of Energy top brass hampered the FBI's atomic spy hunt from the start.

- A two-decade pattern of suspicious behavior by scientist Wen Ho Lee culminated in the revelation that he'd downloaded the most massive hoard of atomic secrets ever.

- Prosecutorial missteps resulted in Lee's plea-bargaining his way to freedom and a black eye for the Bureau.

Chapter 21

The Enemy Within: Robert Hanssen

In This Chapter

- ◆ CIA turncoat Aldrich Ames's FBI counterpart was Bureau analyst Robert P. Hanssen

- ◆ Beginning by spying for Soviet military intelligence GRU, Hanssen soon switched to the KGB

- ◆ From 1985 to 1991, Hanssen was the KGB's top source for U.S. top secrets

- ◆ Hanssen's computer skills and access to other spy agency data gave his treachery unprecedented depth and breadth

- ◆ The KGB defector who identified Ames also set Hanssen's downfall in motion

Supermole Aldrich Ames was the deadliest traitor in the CIA, but not in the entire U.S. intelligence community. Ames alone was not responsible for the multiple betrayals that had wounded U.S. spy operations during the period he was active. Unpleasant and ugly though it was to contemplate, evidence indicated that at least one other such supermole was also planted in high intelligence circles, passing top-secret material to the Soviets.

There was such a traitor: FBI analyst Robert P. Hanssen. During his lengthy career as a double agent, he passed thousands of pages of classified documents to the KGB, becoming their greatest source ever of U.S. secrets. Outlasting the Cold War, Hanssen continued spying for the Russians until the day of his arrest by FBI agents.

FBI Supermole

A trusted, high-ranking U.S. intelligence officer turns traitor, conducting a years-long campaign of betrayal, systematically selling the nation's most prized secrets to the enemy. Because of him, the identities of double agents were revealed, billion-dollar intelligence operations were ruined, and vital national security and global strategic interests were compromised.

This describes the activities of Aldrich Ames, the supermole in the CIA's Soviet counterintelligence bureau, whose 1994 arrest for spying and subsequent sentence of life imprisonment should have ended the U.S. intelligence community's double agent nightmare.

Justice Jargon

Security classifications of government data are based on how much damage their being compromised will do to national security interests. **SECRET** data would cause serious damage; **TOP SECRET** would cause exceptionally grave damage.

It did not, because Ames was not one but two of a kind. During the years Ames was operating as a Soviet spy, another trusted U.S. intelligence operative was also busily selling out the nation's secrets. Unknown to each other, he and Ames were in a sense doubles, twins in treason. This second supermole was FBI agent Robert Philip Hanssen, a rare traitor from the Bureau's ranks who became the KGB's greatest U.S. source of top-secret intelligence data.

Background to Treason

Born in 1944, Robert Philip Hanssen was an only child whose father was a Chicago policemen who'd worked on the department's Red Squad, rousting communists and other subversives. A dysfunctional relationship existed between father and son. When Robert was about six years old, his father whirled him around in circles until the boy threw up; another time, he held the boy upside-down by his ankle until the child urinated on himself. For twisted psychological reasons of his own, the senior Hanssen continually sought to tear down his son's confidence, and was constantly belittling him. One of the most bizarre episodes occurred when young Hanssen took his driver's license test. Although he'd passed, his father bribed the examiner to fail him, a subterfuge of which the teen was painfully aware.

Robert "Bob" Hanssen was a good student—bright, but lacking social skills. He evinced an early and consuming interest in spies, code breakers, and such. At college, he took courses in Russian. Rebelling against his father's desire that he go into medicine, Hanssen received an MBA and became a certified public accountant.

Obscure yet powerful impulses drew him to choose a career in law enforcement, his father's profession. Hired by the Chicago Police Department, Hanssen joined an internal affairs unit whose mission was to catch crooked cops. In 1968 he married Bonnie Wauck, whose brother was an FBI agent. A Lutheran, Hanssen converted to Catholicism, his wife's religion. Early in the marriage, Bonnie learned that her husband had a girlfriend, triggering a painful confrontation between the two. He promised to be good and she forgave him. They set about raising a big family, ultimately having six children.

In 1976, America's Bicentennial year, Hanssen joined the FBI. A computer whiz with an accountant's concern for detail, he helped compile a database listing all Soviet agents, their backgrounds, and home addresses while posted in the United States.

It wasn't long before Hanssen decided that the FBI was an organization of incompetent timeservers, none of whom were as smart as he was. In 1978, he was posted to New York City, an expensive place to live that exacted financial hardship on a family man with an FBI agent's salary. A year later, he decided to give treason a try. Contacting agents of the GRU, the Soviet military intelligence apparatus, he sold them secrets for $20,000, including identifying General Dmitri Polyakov as a double agent working for the west. Codenamed TOPHAT by his FBI handlers, Polyakov had been a vital U.S. intelligence asset for more than two decades. Hanssen's fingering of Polyakov was the first blow of a one-two punch, the second and fatal blow falling several years later, when CIA turncoat Aldrich Ames similarly identified Polyakov as a double agent. Aldrich's identification was the confirmation needed by the KGB to set in motion Polyakov's arrest and execution for spying.

Bu Stats

During 25 years with the FBI, Robert P. Hanssen was never given a polygraph test.

This identification was the beginning of what could be called the twinning of Ames and Hanssen. Either turncoat would have been an extraordinary intelligence asset for the KGB, but the two of them together formed a uniquely potent combination.

Working independently, each unaware of the other's existence, Ames and Hanssen served as an invaluable control mechanism by which the KGB could cross-check the data of both.

In 1980, arriving unexpectedly at their Westchester home, Bonnie Hanssen surprised her husband (while he was examining some documents, which he then clumsily tried to conceal. Thinking that he had a note to or from a girlfriend, she demanded to see it and Hanssen contritely gave it up. The missive wasn't a love letter, but rather a note contacting the GRU to negotiate further betrayals.

Hanssen said that it wasn't so much a case of treason as of venality and that the "secrets" he'd sold the Soviets were unimportant material. To placate Bonnie, he agreed to stop his spying, confess his sins to the Church, and use the Reds' pay-off money for charitable works. He did confess his espionage to a priest. Like dealings with a doctor of lawyer, what takes place in the confessional is a privileged communication, which means its confidentiality is protected by the laws of both church and state. No priest would violate the seal of the confessional to report Hanssen's treason to the authorities.

Template for Treachery

Hanssen stopped spying for the GRU and continued working for the FBI. In 1981, he was transferred to Washington to pull administrative duties at FBIHQ. For the next few years, his spying career was on hiatus, only to come roaring back in 1985. That year saw the birth of Hanssen's sixth child, and his transfer to New York City, where he was assigned to supervise a counterintelligence squad monitoring KGB activities.

The Year of the Spy, 1985, saw Hanssen hatching out a plan to contact not the GRU but the more prestigious and potent KGB. Knowing that the FBI didn't open mail addressed to KGB agents at their home residences, Hanssen used the mail as his vehicle. While temporarily in Washington, D.C., to take care of some administrative work at the Bureau, he mailed an envelope to the home of a KGB officer operating as a lesser functionary at the Soviets' Washington embassy. Had the FBI conducted a mail cover on the addressee, they would have seen a Maryland postmark on the letter, rather than one from New York City which might trail back to Hanssen.

Inside the letter was a second envelope, sealed and inscribed with a message warning the recipient to pass it unopened to Viktor Cherkashin, the KGB's number-two officer in Washington.

> **Cops and Robbers**
>
> An old-school Soviet spy and spy handler, Viktor I. Cherkashin was the handler for both U.S. intelligence agency supermoles Aldrich Ames and Robert P. Hanssen. Cherkashin held their identities very closely, cutting out the middle levels and sharing it only with the top bosses of the KGB. Cherkashin's role in the greatest intelligence double coup of the Cold War earned him many honors and medals, including the Order of Lenin.

At the embassy, Cherkashin unsealed the inner envelope, which held a letter from an unknown correspondent offering to spy for the Soviets for money. It was signed simply "B" (for Bob?). As a way of establishing his credentials in this first letter, B identified three KGB officers who'd turned double agent and were spying for the United States: Motorin, Martynov, and Yuzhin. Hanssen's identification of the double agents confirmed CIA turncoat Aldrich Ames's earlier naming of them, leading to the execution of the first two and a lengthy imprisonment in the gulag prison labor camps for the third. Also included in the letter were other nuggets of valuable classified data.

The writer's terms were specific: His identity would remain unknown, even to his KGB handlers and he would never meet them face-to-face. Contact would be maintained through a system of signal sites and dead drops. It was a unique proposition, one which went contrary to all rules of KGB tradecraft. But a wise operative knows when to break the rules, and Cherkashin agreed to the terms.

Hanssen's next step was to leave a package of stolen classified documents at a dead drop site under a bridge in a Washington area park. In it was a letter telling the KGB how to transfer the pay-off money (another dead drop). Hanssen used the alias Ramon, once the alias of a successful Chicago Police Department undercover agent. The Soviets paid him a sum of $50,000.

Official and Confidential

Robert P. Hanssen's aliases for Soviet spy dealings included the letter B, and the names G. Robertson, Ramon Garcia, and Jim Baker. Ramon was the name of a successful Chicago Police Department undercover agent. Not known for having a sense of humor, Hanssen might have been having fun with the alias "Jim Baker"—James "Jim" Baker being President George H.W. Bush's Secretary of State, campaign manager, and troubleshooter.

The KGB's G-Man

In 1986, while further establishing his spy operation, Hanssen initiated phone conversations with KGB officer A.K. Fefelov, a rare episode of direct contact which he would later have cause to regret.

In 1987, Hanssen was posted to FBIHQ's Intelligence Division as a member of the Soviet Analytical Unit. It was an unfortunate accident of history that Hanssen's ascent coincided with a period when the FBI was making a concerted effort to share intelligence with other agencies, giving him access to their classified data. It's been said of him that where other spies have sold out individuals, he sold out entire intelligence systems. His macro-treason was empowered by his technical-computer expertise and his access to the classified files of such agencies as the CIA, National Security Agency, and the Defense Intelligence Agency.

So pleased were the Soviets with the quality of his work, that in addition to direct dead drop cash payments, they also set up a bank account for Hanssen, into which some $800,000 was ultimately paid.

One of Hanssen's major coups was the betrayal of a tunnel that had been built under a new Russian embassy building sited in the Mount Alto region of Washington, D.C. Designed by the National Security Agency and monitored by the FBI, the tunnel was dug using specially built silent drilling equipment to avoid discovery. The listening post used sophisticated laser equipment to electronically surveil the embassy. Hanssen alerted the Soviets to its existence, rendering useless an operation which had cost over $1 billion to construct.

Hanssen gave the KGB the U.S. Continuity of Government Plan, a top-secret blueprint for keeping the U.S. government intact in case of atomic attack. By revealing the chain of command and logistical data to the Soviets, it increased their chances of waging a first-strike nuclear attack against the United States. It was especially hazardous given the belief held in some upper ranks of the Kremlin that their country could survive and even triumph in a nuclear war. By revealing this data, Hanssen increased the threat of world atomic holocaust.

He delivered to the other side the FBI's Double Agent Program, a guide detailing what FBI counterintelligence agents looked for in sizing up and recruiting potential Soviet double agents to spy for America. This coup prompted not only cash payments but also a letter of thanks from KGB boss Vladimir Kryuchkov.

Beginning in 1988, Hanssen augmented his document drops with the inclusion of computer disks. Reaching out to get a fellow traitor off the hook, in 1989 Hanssen intervened to protect U.S. diplomat Felix Bloch, target of an FBI counterintelligence probe.

> **Cops and Robbers**
>
> The French intelligence service detected State Department official Felix Bloch, the number-two man at the U.S. embassy in Vienna, passing a valise to a KGB officer while they were dining together at a restaurant. Bloch later claimed to have been unaware of the other's KGB affiliation, saying he thought the other was a stamp collector and the valise had contained a stamp collection. Fired from the State Department for making false statements, Bloch was thrown into penury. Working as a supermarket checkout bagger, Bloch was arrested for stealing several bags of groceries from his employer.

French intelligence officers tipped off the FBI about diplomat Bloch's meeting with a KGB agent codenamed "Pierre." FBI FCI probers began closing in on Bloch. Learning of the investigation, Hanssen alerted the KGB, which tipped off Bloch. The investigation was derailed, preventing Bloch's arrest for spying, but he was dismissed from his post, destroying any value he might have had for the Soviets.

Private Life of a Traitor

Hanssen's profile showed a mass of quirks and contradictions. A dour individual with limited social skills who favored dark suits, he was nicknamed "Dr. Death" and "the Mortician" by FBI co-workers. He and his family belonged to prestigious, exclusive St. Catherine of Siena Church in Virginia, a church attended by many FBI top brass, including Director Louis Freeh and his family. Some of Hanssen's children attended the same exclusive private school as Freeh's. Hanssen and his wife were members of Opus Dei, a highly conservative Catholic organization with potent Vatican connections.

Yet beneath his dour surface lay bizarre psycho-sexual predilections. Using his own name, Hanssen posted on the Internet "erotic" stories about his wife, Bonnie, concerning her unknowingly exposing her nudity and thereby sexually exciting strange men. The stories were untrue, sexual fantasies about which his wife knew nothing. Hanssen was an exhibitionist who rigged a closed-circuit video camera to allow a lifelong male friend of his to watch Hanssen having sex with his wife—again, without Bonnie's knowledge. Even among the most private intimacies of domestic life, Hanssen was addicted to the thrill of betrayal.

A strip club habitué, Hanssen liked to tell the dancers that his real interest was in saving their souls. In 1990, he cultivated the acquaintance of exotic dancer Priscilla Sue Galey, a veteran stripper performing at a Washington club. The relationship ripened, with Hanssen giving her gifts of money and jewelry. He took her on a trip to Hong

Kong, paying her bills, yet traveling separately and maintaining separate hotel rooms. She later wondered if he'd been grooming her for a role in his operation, perhaps as a courier.

He gave her a gift of a used Mercedes and a credit card, instructing her to use the card only for auto-related expenses. In 1991, when a bill showed that she'd used the card to buy cigarettes and presents for family members, he took back the card and summarily ended the relationship, cutting off all contact with her. Subsequently, she became a crack cocaine addict and prostitute, in 1993 spending a year in jail for selling drugs.

What worried Hanssen was ever-increasing turmoil in the Soviet system, symptoms of the imminent collapse of the USSR. In December 1991, he broke off spying for the Russians. One of the things that convinced him to close down operations was the official visit to FBIHQ by a KGB delegation. Soon after, the USSR fell and the KGB officially ceased to exist.

Justice Jargon

Predating the 1917 revolution as the Okhrana, the Czarist secret police, the Russian secret police system flourished throughout the history of the USSR under various names, such as the OGPU, MVD, NKVD, and ultimately, KGB. The KGB was a key element, perhaps the most vital one, not only of the Soviet Empire but of the entire Russian societal infrastructure. Officially disbanded in the early 1990s, the organization was resurrected first as the SVR, and is currently constituted as the FSB.

Spy, Interrupted

Hanssen's hiatus from spying lasted from 1991 to 1999, when the accession of former KGB officer Vladimir Putin to the premiership of Russia reassured Hanssen that the risk of discovery had lessened enough to warrant his getting back in the game. Plus, with his 25-year retirement date from the FBI upcoming in April 2001, he could use the extra money, not to mention the ego-boosting psychological "lift" he derived from what he imagined was the awe and respect in which his Russian spy handlers held him.

Resuming contact and operations, his letters took on an ever-more needy, manic quality, at the same time that his new Russian handlers' tone became crisper, more businesslike, tasking him with specific assignments.

Further stirring up the pot was the Gusev affair. Russian intelligence scored a coup by planting a sophisticated bugging device concealed in the ornamental molding of a chair in a conference room down the hall from the office of Secretary of State Madeleine Albright. To avoid discovery, instead of constantly transmitting, the bug was intermittently activated by a remote control wielded by agent S.B. Gusev, officially attached to the Russian diplomatic corps. The set-up required Gusev to park his car on a street near the State Department building. He gave himself away by constantly feeding fresh quarters into the parking meters—a dead giveaway, since diplomatic personnel in Washington, D.C. are notoriously heedless of such things as parking tickets and fines.

Official and Confidential

In a March 2000 letter to his Russian spy contacts, Hanssen wrote: "One might propose that I am either insanely brave or quite insane. I'd answer neither. I'd say, insanely loyal."

The exposure of CIA supermole Aldrich Ames failed to explain all of the intelligence losses that had occurred during his heyday. Analysts realized that there had to be another highly placed mole in upper U.S. intelligence ranks. The predominant theory (at least around the FBI) was that the other mole was also a member of CIA.

In another case of doubling with his CIA counterpart, Robert Hanssen was undone by the same Russian defector who'd burned Ames. Codenamed Avenger, the high-ranking KGB defector who'd first tipped spy-hunters to Ames later put the CIA in touch with a Russian double agent inside the FSB. The FSB officer sold CIA the mole file, which included tapes of a 1986 telephone call between KGB agent Fefelov and the mole. Two FBI agents listening to the tape declared the mole's voice to be that of Robert Hanssen.

Also included in the file was a plastic garbage bag in which an early document dump had been delivered to a KGB dead drop. An examination of the bag yielded a fingerprint belonging to Hanssen.

Because of the difficulty in proving espionage cases in court, the FBI wanted to catch Hanssen in the act of passing information or making a pick-up at a dead drop site. At FBIHQ, he was transferred to a different department, one where he could do little damage and was watched constantly. He was shadowed, his car searched. Sensing the dragnet closing around him, Hanssen decided to make one last drop.

On February 18, 2001, at Virginia's Foxstone Park, Hanssen placed a package of documents at a dead drop site under a bridge. Returning to his car, he was surrounded by FBI agents and arrested. Agents also found a second drop site, where the Russians had placed a package containing $50,000. Characteristically, as he was being collared, Hanssen said, "What took you so long?"

Congressional laws passed in the wake of the Ames case allowed for the death penalty in peacetime cases of espionage, where the betrayals had resulted in the deaths of agents. Hanssen was liable on that score, and Attorney General John Ashcroft wanted to seek the death penalty, but was dissuaded by the argument that U.S. spy hunters needed to keep Hanssen alive in order to verify information about other such traitors that might surface in the future.

Bu Stats

During his traitorous career, Robert Hanssen identified nine double agents. Making 24 dead drop package deliveries, he sold the KGB a total of 6,000 pages of classified documents and 27 computer disks.

Pleading guilty in July 2001, Hanssen was given a life sentence with no possibility of parole. Cleared of any involvement in the case, his wife Bonnie was allowed to claim 55 percent of Hanssen's pension ($40,000 a year)—his survivor's pension, what she would have been allotted had he died in the line of duty. Believing that divorce is a sin, she remains married to him.

Given the intricate layers of deception in the world of spy/counterspy, the disturbing possibility exists that the Russians themselves might have burned Hanssen, whose period of utility was drawing to a close, in order to divert suspicion from the existence of another mole or moles operating in high U.S. intelligence circles.

The Least You Need to Know

- Supermole Robert Hanssen was the greatest traitor in FBI history.

- Officially disbanded in 1991, the KGB survived the fall of the USSR, renamed the SVR and currently the FSB.

- As the Soviet Union was replaced by the Russian Federation, Russian spying on the United States continued unabated.

- In 25 years at the Bureau, Hanssen was never polygraphed—a major security lapse.

- Hanssen is now serving a life prison term, but the possibility exists that other such supermoles remain hidden in the U.S. intelligence community.

Chapter 22

9/11 and Beyond

In This Chapter

- TRADEBOM: The 1993 World Trade Center bombing
- Osama bin Laden and al Qaeda's murderous rise
- The terror strikes of 9/11
- Could 9/11 have been prevented?
- Aftermath: The FBI's mission redefined

The 1993 World Trade Center bombing by Islamist radical terrorists was a forerunner of worse things to come. Paramount among the post–Cold War enemies of the United States was Osama bin Laden, founder of al Qaeda, a mobile, elusive, and deadly terrorist organization dedicated to waging "holy war" against America. On September 11, 2001—a date memorialized as simply 9/11—al Qaeda plotters unleashed the most deadly attack ever to strike on American soil. In its aftermath, the FBI's fundamental mission has been redefined, making its top priority not law enforcement but rather the prevention of terrorist acts.

TRADEBOM

Coming events sometimes cast their shadows before they occur. The ugly post–Cold War shape of things to come may be said to have first manifested itself on February 26, 1993, when a bomb went off at New York City's World Trade Center complex. Exploding in an underground parking garage, the bomb killed six people, injured hundreds, and menaced some 50,000 people inside the site's famed twin towers.

Codenamed TRADEBOM, the attack was investigated by 300 FBI agents. Early on, an ATF agent located the remains of a Ford Econoline van that had been used to deliver the bomb. Its vehicle identification number tagged it as a yellow van belonging to a Ryder rental truck agency in Jersey City, New Jersey. Records showed it had been rented by one Mohammed A. Salameh, 25, a Jordanian national. Shortly after the blast, Salameh had appeared at the rental agency, claiming that the vehicle had been stolen and demanding the return of his $400 security deposit.

Official and Confidential

The date of the February 26, 1993 bombing of the World Trade Center coincided with the second anniversary of the expulsion of Iraqi forces from Kuwait City during the Gulf War. Coincidence?

Cops and Robbers

Mohamed bin Laden, patriarch of the bin Laden clan, was a Yemeni emigrant to Saudi Arabia whose connections to the ruling House of Saud dynasty helped him become a multi-millionaire construction magnate. Islamic law allows a man to be legally married to four wives at the same time. His fourth wife, a Syrian, bore him a son, Osama, one of the patriarch's 53 offspring.

Salameh's arrest led to the discovery of a radical terrorist cell operating under the aegis of Egyptian fundamentalist cleric Sheikh Omar Abdel Rahman, a (literally) blind fanatic hatemonger based in a Jersey City mosque. The group's stated motive for the WTC bombing was to "punish" the United States for its support of Israel. Sheikh Omar, bomb plot mastermind Ramzi Yousef, and a half-dozen or so fellow conspirators were ultimately convicted and imprisoned for their crimes.

Basest of the Base

Osama bin Laden first came to prominence during the late Cold War struggle to force the Soviets out of Afghanistan. In 1979, he formed the Islamist terrorist organization al Qaeda, literally "the base," as in the base of a pillar. His rise was fueled by his access to his share (about $30 million) of the bin Laden family fortune. In addition to his own personal fortune, bin Laden was also able to draw on contributions from wealthy Islamists, including members of the Saudi royal family.

With the end of the Soviet occupation of Afghanistan, Osama next turned his ire toward the United States, professing to take particular offense at U.S. troops setting foot in Saudi Arabia, home of the Muslim holy sites of Mecca and Medina, during the Gulf War.

Terror Trail

Al Qaeda operates on the cell method, by which the membership is divided into small groups or cells, ensuring that if one member is captured, he can only identify the members of his cell, thereby insulating the rest of the organization.

A mobile organization with several thousand members scattered worldwide, al Qaeda uses the technology and infrastructure of Western secular societies to attack those societies with the aim of destroying them. Scorning all things non-Islamic, it uses such devices as cell phones, e-mail, and stolen identities to further its purpose. Cunningly, it also uses the West's civil liberties and constitutionally guaranteed rights to shield against capture and prosecution, rights which are nonexistent in the despotic theocracies which spawned the terrorists.

In 1996, in Dhahran, Saudi Arabia, a band of terrorists "inspired" by the teachings of Osama bin Laden used a truck bomb to destroy the Khobar Towers barracks, killing 19 U.S. servicemen. FBI Director Louis Freeh directly oversaw the investigation and found that Saudi officials were obstructing the probe. The FBI also developed evidence that indicated that the terrorists had received assistance from elements of the Iranian government. On June 22, 2001, Freeh's last day as FBI director, indictments were handed down, charging 13 Saudis and a Lebanese with the crime. Whether they will ever actually stand trial remains in question.

On August 7, 1998, al Qaeda operatives succeeded in simultaneously detonating truck bombs at U.S. embassies in the African cities of Dar es Salaam, Tanzania; and Nairobi, Kenya. The bombings killed a total of 224 people and wounded 5,000.

In mid-December 1999, FBI agents arrested al Qaeda member Ahmed Ressam, taking him at a Canadian border crossing when he attempted to bring a carload of explosives into the United States as part of a plan to bomb Los Angeles International Airport.

A key milestone on the road to 9/11 was the October 2000 bombing of the naval destroyer USS *Cole* while it was moored in the waters off Yemen, a small coastal state on the Arabian peninsula (and perhaps not coincidentally, the original home of the bin Laden clan.) The terrorists filled a small motorboat with explosives and rammed it into the *Cole*, detonating the bomb. The blast killed 17 sailors and blew a big hole in the side of the ship, narrowly avoiding sinking it.

A team of FBI investigators headed by John P. O'Neill arrived in Yemen to investigate. Before long, the probers unearthed links between the suicide ship-bombers and high-level officials in the Yemeni government.

> **Cops and Robbers**
>
> FBI agent John P. O'Neill, head of the New York City field office's counterintelligence and counterterrorism, was dedicated to the pursuit and capture of Osama bin Laden. O'Neill headed the investigation into the October 2000 suicide boat-bombing of the USS *Cole*. Retiring from the Bureau, he took a job as security director for Manhattan's World Trade Center complex. In a tragic irony, several weeks after taking the post, he was killed in the terror attacks of 9/11.

The mood in Yemen turned ugly toward the agents. In an appalling act of toadying to the host government, U.S. State Department officials forgot which country they came from and sided with the Yemeni government, ensuring that the FBI agents were prohibited from carrying firearms with which to protect themselves in the steadily worsening hostile environment—thereby sinking the investigation.

This craven acquiescence surely must have contributed to the al Qaeda leadership's belief that the United States was too corrupt and cowardly to defend its interests or retaliate when struck, paving the way for 9/11.

The U.S. government's answer to all of these attacks was essentially to do nothing. President Clinton ordered the bombing by cruise missiles of a Sudanese chemical factory and an Afghani terrorist training camp, two ineffectual public relations gestures. The attack on the *Cole* and the two embassies garnered a criminal investigation by the FBI, but no military response for what was an act of war. This lack of response no doubt caused bin Laden to believe the United States was weak and had no resolve.

Apocalypse Now

On September 11, 2001—like December 7, 1941, a date that will live in infamy— 19 al Qaeda members hijacked four separate airplanes, turning them into devastating flying bombs. The hijackers were divided into three 5-man teams and one 4-man team. Boarding aircraft like any other passengers, they struck when the planes were aloft, using knives with blades shorter than 4 inches and box cutters that they had legally carried aboard to take control of the planes. Unlike previous hijackings, these would feature no prolonged hostage dramas, no assailants issuing pompous manifestos and nonnegotiable demands. Hostage-taking wasn't what these hijackings were about. Occupying the planes' cockpits, al Qaeda pilots took over the controls.

At 8:45 A.M., Eastern Standard Time, American Airlines Flight 11 slammed into the World Trade Center's north tower. At 9:05, United Airlines Flight 175 hit the complex's south tower. The planes' blazing jet fuel created an inferno so intense that it melted the buildings' vertical support beams, causing them to pancake, collapsing floor by floor. Both towers fell, with tremendous loss of life.

American Airlines Flight 77, flying out of Washington's Dulles Airport, crashed into the Pentagon at 9:40. Aboard hijacked United Airlines Flight 93 out of Newark, cell phone calls alerted passengers of the previous crashes. Storming the cockpit commandeered by the terrorists, the passengers heroically fought them to the death, the plane crashing in a field in Stony Township, Pennsylvania. (Captured al Qaeda members have since identified Washington's Capitol building as the intended target of Flight 93.)

> **Bu Stats**
>
> Eleven crew and 81 passengers were lost on American Airlines Flight 11; 9 crew and 56 passengers were lost on United Airlines Flight 175; 6 crew and 58 passengers were lost on American Airlines Flight 77; and 7 crew and 38 passengers were lost on United Airlines Flight 93. Almost 3,000 people were killed in the World Trade Center attacks; in the attack on the Pentagon, 189 people were killed.

This was war, a terrorist Pearl Harbor, the most devastating single strike ever launched against the continental United States. Truly the "Crime of the Century," the assault triggered the most massive investigation in FBI history. Early on, Bureau counterterrorism experts believed that the attacks were the work of bin Laden. A key clue to the source lay in Afghanistan where, one day earlier on September 10, al Qaeda members had assassinated Northern Alliance leader Massoud. It was a case of al Qaeda and its Taliban hosts securing their home turf by eliminating a key leader of the opposition in advance of the overseas assaults.

Passenger seat numbers, airport video monitoring tapes, and similar leads quickly established the identities of the 19 hijackers, 15 of whom came from Saudi Arabia.

FBI sleuths learned that the 9/11 plot originated with an al Qaeda cell in Hamburg, Germany, its members trained in camps in Afghanistan, hosted by the extreme Islamic fundamentalist Taliban government. Closely allied with bin Laden, Taliban chief Mullah Omar provided a secure environment for al Qaeda.

The seed for 9/11 was first planted, perhaps, in 1994, when Algerian terrorists who'd hijacked an Air France plane threatened to crash a plane into Paris' Eiffel Tower.

In 1995, Manila police broke up a plot to simultaneously explode bombs aboard 12 U.S. planes flying trans-Pacific flights, leading to the apprehension of Ramzi Yousef, architect of the 1993 World Trade Center bombing. He'd also plotted to crash a plane into CIA headquarters in Langley, Virginia.

Another signpost was the 1999 hijacking of an Air India jet, where al Qaeda members cut a passenger's throat and let him bleed to death, terrorizing the crew and passengers. The jet was flown to Kandahar, Afghanistan. In the aftermath, the FBI opened a liaison office in New Delhi, India, cooperating with Indian counterterrorist efforts.

The 9/11 strike was masterminded by Egyptian Mohammed Atta, whose terror team was originally intended to comprise 20 members. But key coplotter Ramzi bin al-Shibh's request for a U.S. visa was denied four times, allegedly leading to his substitution by Zacarias Moussaoui, the so-called "20th hijacker" (whose August 2001 arrest is believed to have prevented his participation on 9/11).

The terror team penetrated U.S. society, living among unsuspecting neighbors. A handful of members attended flight schools, claiming they wanted to qualify for pilot's licenses and learning how to fly the big jumbo jets. A question exists as to how many of the hijackers realized that they were on a suicide mission. One theory is that only the pilots knew the truth, and that the others, the "muscle" required to handle the physical tasks of taking over the aircraft, were unaware of their imminent fates. Buttressing this version are the words of bin Laden himself, seen crowing on a post-9/11 al Qaeda video that most of the hijackers didn't know they were on death flights.

Official and Confidential

In the immediate aftermath of 9/11, President George W. Bush declared, "We will make no distinction between the terrorists who committed these acts and those who harbor them."

Bu Stats

The cost of financing al Qaeda's 9/11 terror strikes totaled somewhere around $500,000. Economic damage inflicted by the strikes on New York City alone are estimated to have caused an $80 billion loss.

In the aftermath of 9/11, the FBI launched the most massive investigation in its history. Areas of concentration focused on unearthing the hijackers' pasts and back trails, identifying and apprehending those who had handled their logistics (car rentals, procuring false or stolen identities, and so on), and disrupting the flow of funds into al Qaeda, especially those channeled through the medium of seemingly innocuous "charities." A priority was improved coordination and cooperation with other international law enforcement agencies.

Post-Mortem

Could 9/11 have been prevented?

The short answer: Probably not.

It's a truism to note that the world has changed since 9/11. Those changes are as different as peace and war, life and death. Having long been isolated domestically from the results of foreign turmoil, the vast majority of the American public, including top policymakers, were unable to conceive of the heightened level of threat menacing the U.S. in recent years. Those few who were aware were unable to persuade their fellow citizens of its gravity. Between 1993 and 1999, the FBI thwarted some 40 attempted terrorist plots, including an al Qaeda plan to bomb New York City landmarks including the Holland and Lincoln tunnels.

The 1993 WTC bombing and the 1995 Oklahoma City bombing both took place on U.S. soil yet failed to effect any real or significant changes in national security procedures. The 1998 African embassy bombings and the 2000 attack on the *Cole*, occurring in distant lands, had even less influence on U.S. policy and public opinion.

Extremely restrictive guidelines imposed on the FBI by the Justice Department following the Church Committee hearings in the 1970s remain almost totally unchanged. These guidelines limit the FBI's ability to monitor and apprehend terrorist groups before they can commit their crimes. Neither Congress nor the White House seems willing to make the changes that FBI line agents believe are necessary.

Justice Jargon

The FBI investigation of 9/11 is codenamed PENT-TBOM, combining Pentagon with an extra letter T, for the Trade Center. The anthrax investigation is codenamed AMERITHRAX.

Adding to the woes of a stricken nation was a series of sinister anthrax attacks. Anthrax, a deadly disease communicable to both livestock and humans, is spread via microscopic spores. It is a key component in biological warfare. On October 2, 2001, in Atlantis, Florida, a photo editor died from exposure to the virulent germ-borne disease. He'd been employed at the American Media building, publisher of the *National Enquirer* tabloid newspaper. Investigation determined that the site had fallen prey to an unknown anthrax attacker. The building was sealed up and abandoned, and remains so to this day.

A short time later, an assistant to NBC-TV news anchorman Tom Brokaw was stricken with anthrax after opening a letter addressed to her boss, a letter which released a cloud of white powder containing the spores. Similar Trojan Horse–style anthrax letters were sent to Senate Majority leader Tom Daschle, Vermont Senator Pat Leahy, and others.

The anthrax attacks killed 5 people, seriously sickened 18, and caused the temporary closing of three Senate office buildings and several mail sorting facilities contaminated by the spores.

Handling the AMERITHRAX investigation was the FBI's Washington Metropolitan Field Office (WMFO). Were the attacks the product of foreign state-sponsored biowarfare, of a homegrown U.S. militia or neo-Nazi group, or of a Unabom-style lone nut? DNA testing identified the anthrax as belonging to the Ames strain, originating from a strain kept at an agricultural college lab in Ames, Iowa. The strain had been disseminated to many U.S. research facilities, making its point of origin difficult to track.

Investigators theorize that a Unabom-style researcher is responsible for the attacks. Attorney General John Ashcroft has publicly identified Dr. Steven Hatfill as, not a suspect, but rather a "person of interest" in the case. Hatfill has held a number of press conferences complaining of FBI and Justice Department harassment. He has been charged with no crime, while the AMERITHRAX investigation holds the possibility of becoming the Bureau's Richard Jewell II.

Warning Signs

FBI Director Robert S. Mueller III took office barely one week before 9/11. In the first weeks following the assaults, he issued several public statements stating that no information existed that could have prevented the terror strikes of 9/11. By late May 2002, he had altered that position, publicly saying that 9/11 might have been detectable.

Information had surfaced indicating several pre–9/11 lapses by the FBI. In March 2001, a Phoenix, Arizona, flight instructor reported to the Federal Aviation Administration (FAA) his suspicions that a student was using a fake pilot's license. The license was discovered to be genuine, but the student later became one of the 9/11 hijackers.

A July 2001 memo from Phoenix, Arizona, FBI SA Kenneth Williams to FBIHQ, noting the suspicious behavior of flight students of Middle Eastern origin, warned that bin Laden's al Qaeda agents might be enrolling in U.S. flight schools as a prelude to terrorist attacks. Mueller, who was unaware of the memo's existence until several days after 9/11, conceded that the information should have been shared with the CIA.

More damning was the May 21, 2002, 15-page letter of whistle-blower Cynthia Rowley, general counsel for the FBI office in Minneapolis, Minnesota. In it, she charged that FBIHQ supervisors and lawyers had aggressively blocked the field office's efforts to investigate Zacarias Moussaoui, and warned Mueller of the risks inherent in continuing to publicly maintain that the FBI had had no prior warning of 9/11.

Cops and Robbers

Zacarias Moussaoui, 33, a French national of Moroccan descent, attracted suspicion at the Minnesota flight school he was attending by paying $6,000 in cash for lessons, and by his lack of interest in learning about aircraft takeoffs or landings. An admitted al Qaeda member and bin Laden loyalist, Moussaoui is the only person thus far charged with participating in 9/11, a charge which he denies. It is alleged that he was to have been the 20th hijacker, the missing fifth man on the team which hijacked Flight 93.

In August 2001, a Minnesota flight school manager notified the FBI of his suspicions regarding student Moussaoui, who was quickly jailed on immigration charges. The Phoenix memo and two Minneapolis memos regarding Moussaoui both went to the same FBIHQ office, but the information they contained was never correlated.

In that same month of August 2001, the Minneapolis office requested that FBIHQ lawyers go to the Justice Department's Foreign Intelligence Surveillance Court (FISC) to seek a warrant to examine the hard drive of Moussaoui's computer. (Examined after 9/11, the computer yielded information on airplanes, crop-dusting—a potential bio- or chemical warfare delivery system—, and a telephone number in Germany for a suspected member of al Qaeda, what has been described as a virtual "blueprint" for 9/11.)

The effort was blocked by FBIHQ supervisors and lawyers, who stated that there was not enough evidence to apply for a warrant. They also downplayed the significance of information on Moussaoui supplied by French intelligence that might have led to the issuing of said warrant. A Senate Judiciary Committee later found that there was "ample evidence to confirm these suspicions" and press for the warrant. Singled out for criticism were supervisors in the Radical Fundamentalist Unit.

Director Mueller has referred the supervisors' activities to the Justice Department's Inspector General for investigation. He publicly declared his gratitude to Ms. Rowley for alerting him to the situation and stated that no career handicap would afflict the whistle-blower. For decades, the FBI has acted under the Attorney General's Guidelines for Domestic and International Terrorism. They are very restrictive and to violate one of the guidelines can cause serious damage to an agent's career. Over time, agents have learned that while they could get into trouble by giving approval to such cases, they could never get in trouble for saying "no." Under the administration of

Janet Reno, the Department of Justice's interpretation of the guidelines became even more restrictive, and the agents reflected the attitude of the Justice Department, which had the ultimate authority.

Also, a serious disconnect was bubbling under in the summer of 2001 between the FBI and the FISC. Compounding an environment of bad feelings and negative publicity generated by the Wen Ho Lee debacle, the FISC review board accused FBI lawyers with supplying misleading information in some 75 other Clinton administration–era applications for warrants.

It must also be noted that in the pre-9/11 climate, an FBI investigation of students of Middle Eastern origin attending U.S. flight schools would undoubtedly have triggered charges by the forces of political correctness that the Bureau was engaging in so-called discrimination and racial profiling.

The events of 9/11 also exposed a serious technology gap in the FBI's computer infrastructure. The Bureau's obsolete desktop computers were unable to communicate between different in-house divisions, not to mention communicating with other agencies. The desktop models lacked scanning or multimedia capabilities, even the ability to send and receive e-mail. During the height of the 9/11 investigation, FBIHQ and field offices had to exchange reports and photos of suspects by putting them on CD-ROMs and delivering them by couriers. Even today, an FBI agent cannot send a photo via e-mail. The FBI databases, of which there are at least 40, are not networked and there is not a search engine that is effective for any of them.

Official and Confidential

When it comes to pre-9/11 intelligence lapses, the FBI does not stand alone. The record shows that on August 6, 2001, CIA officers briefed President George W. Bush of the threat embodied in bin Laden's resolve to attack the U.S.

Remaking the Bureau

By late May 2002, revelations of FBI lapses had Director Mueller fighting hard for his political life. Although the flubs had taken place during the tenure of previous Director Louis Freeh, Freeh was gone and Mueller was on the political firing line. He retained the strong support of Attorney General John Ashcroft, who'd been instrumental in Mueller's appointment to the post.

On Wednesday, May 29, 2002, Mueller regained the initiative, holding a wide-ranging press conference to announce a radical redefinition of the FBI's fundamental mission, a "redesigned and refocused FBI," one putting "prevention [of terrorist acts] above all else."

Mueller's ready acknowledgement of red flags missed by the FBI, and his ambitious restructuring plans for the organization, were generally felt to have solidified Congressional and public support for his leadership. The timely reorganization plan also helped secure FBI autonomy and head off any plans to establish a separate Domestic Intelligence Division as part of the administration's planned Homeland Security apparatus.

After 80 years as the nation's preeminent law enforcement agency, the FBI would now be reinventing itself as the nation's premier counterterrorist force. Its Number One priority would no longer be the solution of criminal cases, but rather the prevention of terrorist acts before they happened. Steps taken to further the goal of increasing the FBI's capability of analyzing information regarding terrorist threats and preventing new attacks included:

- The reassignment of several hundred anti-drug agents, 59 white collar crime agents, and 59 violent crime agents to counterterrorism.

- The creation of an Office of Intelligence to coordinate information collection and analysis.

- The hiring of 400 new analysts for posting at FBIHQ and field offices.

- The hiring of hundreds of new linguists and information technology experts.

It must be noted that there are many who question the wisdom of some of Director Mueller's actions. They maintain that terrorism is, quite simply, a crime, and the only way to prevent an act of terrorism in this country is to arrest the terrorists and charge them with a criminal offence. The Director has also indicated that he will reduce the FBI's work in the field of bank robbery, yet many terrorist groups finance their activities through bank robberies.

Cops and Robbers

In September 2002, a joint U.S./Pakistan operation captured one of the most wanted men on the planet: alleged 9/11 co-plotter and organizer Ramzi bin al-Shibh. Yemeni national bin al-Shibh , 30, was Mohammed Atta's roommate in Hamburg, Germany, where the suicide plane plot was hatched. Believed to have been the intended 20th hijacker, bin al-Shibh's inability to get a visa to enter the U.S. is likely to have led to the designation of Zacarias Moussaoui as his replacement. A key link between the hijackers and al Qaeda, bin al-Shibh allegedly played a major support role in the 9/11 plot, channeling funds from Europe to team members in the United States. His capture ranks as a major counterterrorism success, but whether or not Pakistani dictator Musharraf will allow bin al-Shibh's extradition to the United States remains to be seen.

As a further sign of interagency cooperation, daily joint briefings of the President are currently being conducted by CIA Director George Tenet and FBI Director Mueller.

At the same time, Attorney General Ashcroft announced the lifting of Justice Department guidelines which had been put into place in the Watergate era in response to COINTELPRO abuses. Among them were self-imposed restraints prohibiting agents and analysts from surfing the Internet for clues and leads. Investigators were now allowed to search public databases, websites, and online chat rooms for leads to terrorist operations.

At the dawn of a new millennium, the inexorable tides of history confront the United States of America with perilous new challenges, challenges which threaten our national survival itself.

Challenges that will be met—and mastered —by the FBI.

The Least You Need to Know

- In the post–Cold War era, terrorist organizations pose a grave threat to the United States.

- Wealthy Saudi Osama bin Laden founded the worldwide Islamist terror network al Qaeda, "The Base."

- On September 11, 2001, 19 al Qaeda hijackers suicidally crashed jet airliners into the World Trade Center and the Pentagon, the deadliest attack ever to strike on U.S. soil.

- Post–9/11, the FBI's primary mission has been redefined from law enforcement to the prevention of terrorist acts.

Appendix A

Joining the FBI

The FBI is now hiring, and, in the aftermath of the terror strikes of September 11, 2001, the Bureau has received a record number of applications.

FBI special agents must have a four-year college degree, be a United States citizen, be available for assignment anywhere at any time, be between 23 and 36 years of age, and be in excellent physical condition. It is also a general requirement that candidates have three years of professional work experience. Special entry programs exist for those having four-year degrees in computer science or accounting. They also exist for attorneys, CPAs and linguists.

All candidates must pass a thorough background investigation as well as a polygraph and drug urinalysis test.

At this time, the FBI is seeking persons proficient in the following skills: computer science, engineering, foreign counterintelligence, military intelligence, and physical sciences. Foreign-language skills are being sought in Arabic, Farsi, Pashtu, Urdu, Chinese, Japanese, Korean, Russian, Spanish, and Vietnamese.

The FBI is an equal opportunity employer. For further information, visit the FBI Jobs website at www.fbijobs.com and apply online.

Those male and female applicants who are accepted for training will report to the FBI Academy in Quantico, Virginia, to begin taking an intensive 16-week course designed to transform them into FBI agents.

About 1 in 20 applications is accepted. Like recruits entering the armed forces, the trainees take an oath swearing to protect and defend the Constitution of the United States.

The FBI Academy is located on the site of Quantico Marine Base. In layout and design it is much like a college campus, complete with classroom buildings and dormitories for trainees. The academy is part of the Bureau's Training Division. During the 16-week training period, the trainees are schooled in the law, in principles and methods of scientific criminal investigation, interviewing techniques, crime scene analysis, computer skills, counterintelligence, methods of surveillance, and other skills vital to developing well-rounded, professional law enforcers.

The physical side of crimebusting is not neglected, as trainees are required to achieve a rigorous standard of physical fitness. Martial arts and self-defense techniques are important for confidence building and street credibility. Trainees must qualify on the firing range with pistol, shotgun, and carbine. Upon successfully completing the course, the graduate is ready to begin his or her first day on the job as a newly minted FBI agent. Then the real education begins.

Interestingly, the FBI's Behavioral Science Services Unit, famed for its profiling of serial killers and other violent predators, is also part of the Training Division.

Appendix B

Glossary

agent provocateur One who creates a crime to incite, entrap, and punish the criminal or discredit the cause for which he (the agent) pretends to be working.

al Qaeda Radical Islamist terrorist organization founded in 1979 by Osama bin Laden; responsible for 1998 U.S. embassy bombings in Kenya and Tanzania, attack on USS *Cole* in Yemen, and the 9/11 terror strikes against the World Trade Center and the Pentagon.

Alien and Sedition Act World War I–era legislation which authorizes the deportation of noncitizens who advocate the violent overthrow of the U.S. government.

AMERITHRAX FBI codename for the investigation of the Fall 2001 anonymous anthrax mailings which killed five people, sickened eighteen, and closed three Senate office buildings.

anarchism Literally, "no government;" believers hold government is oppression and must be destroyed.

ANFO Acronym for Ammonium Nitrate soaked in fuel oil; basically, fertilizer soaked in diesel fuel, which is a highly explosive mixture favored by homemade bomb makers unable to access state-supplied conventional explosives. The 1995 Oklahoma City bombing was accomplished by a truck bomb filled with ANFO.

Apalachin Upstate New York site of a 1957 gathering of the nation's top crime bosses whose exposure conclusively proved the existence of the Mafia.

black-bag job A surreptitious break-in at a targeted area or residence, though not necessarily a burglary—nothing need be taken, as when documents are photographed.

Bolshevik Majority wing (*bolsheviki*) of Russian Social Democratic Party, which under Lenin's leadership stressed extremist revolutionary Marxism; in 1919 renamed the Communist Party.

bug A hidden microphone or other broadcasting device which is covertly planted in the targeted area or residence.

Bureau of Investigation (BI) Founded in 1908, the BI was an investigatory branch of the Justice Department and a forerunner to the FBI.

Cambridge Ring A network of students at Britain's Cambridge University who were recruited by Soviet agents during the 1930s to serve as deep penetration double agents. Members included traitors Philby, McClean, Burgess, and Blunt.

cell Method of organizing a clandestine organization by which the membership is divided into small groups or cells, ensuring that if one member is captured, he can only identify the members of the cell, insulating the rest of the organization from discovery.

central intelligence A service that coordinates all government intelligence efforts and analyzes all intelligence information, orchestrating covert intelligence operations of various military and federal branches.

Central Intelligence Agency (CIA) Founded in 1947, the CIA is a civilian service that is part of the executive branch, answering to the President and operating through the National Security Council. The CIA's mission is intelligence collecting, analysis, and the integration of domestic, foreign, and military policies.

COINTELPRO (Counterintelligence Program) An FBI operation that used wartime counterintelligence techniques against peacetime domestic foes. Not an investigation, it was a proactive operation designed to disrupt, harass, and ultimately neutralize the targeted operation from within.

Communism According to Vladimir Lenin and the Russian Bolsheviks, all social, cultural, economic activities are regulated by a single authoritarian party representing the workers. The doctrine holds that class warfare is the central dynamic of history, with a goal of promoting a world communist revolution.

concurrent jurisdiction   The power of local, state, and federal courts to hear the same case. High-profile crimes sharing such concurrent jurisdiction are often tackled by multi-agency task forces, teaming local or state police with the FBI.

countersurveillance   Tactics for eluding surveillants, which includes wearing different coats and changing them, changing modes of transportation, varying routes, and backtracking.

coup d'état   Literally, French for a blow or strike against the state. A coup d'état is a sudden decisive use of force to subvert or overthrow an existing government.

COURTSHIP   A joint CIA/FBI operation established in 1980 to try to recruit Soviets stationed in Washington.

cryptography   Literally "secret writing," it is the art and science of code making and code breaking. Experts in the field are cryptanalysts. To put text into its coded form is to encrypt it; to decode it is to decrypt it.

custodial detention list   An index of persons to be rounded up and held in preventative detention in times of national emergency. Later renamed the Security Index (SI).

dead drop   In espionage, a secure method of exchanging documents or cash. The dead drop site is located in a covert area off the beaten path. One agent leaves a package at the site; the other picks it up. The two agents never meet, maximizing security from detection.

dry-cleaning   In spy parlance, the act of shaking off possible tails and pursuers.

false flag   An operation in which an agent pretends to be working for a foreign country or intelligence agency in order to determine where the targeted subject's true allegiance lies.

fascism   A program for setting up a centralized autocratic regime with an ultra-nationalist agenda, exercising regimentation of industry, commerce, and finance; and imposing rigid censorship and the forcible suppression of opposition.

FBIHQ   FBI headquarters in Washington, D.C.

fellow travelers   Sympathizers to the communist cause who are not card-carrying Party members.

field offices   FBI field offices are located in major cities throughout the United States and in San Juan, Puerto Rico. There are 56 field offices in all.

fifth column   Secret pro-enemy forces who are committing espionage, sabotage, and subversion behind defense lines.

five families The five Mafia crime families which dominate New York City. They are the Bonanno family, the Columbo family, the Gambino family, the Genovese family, and the Lucchese family.

Foreign Intelligence Surveillance Act (FISA) Congressional act which established the Foreign Intelligence Surveillance Court (FISC). All U.S. intelligence agencies seeking authorization for electronic surveillance must apply to the FISC court. In 1981, the act was expanded to include break-ins.

Foreign Intelligence Surveillance Court (FISC) The most top-secret court in the land, the FISC meets in the Department of Justice building, in chambers secure from electronic surveillance. In cases involving national security, it issues warrants authorizing intelligence agencies to bug, wiretap, or break-in to targeted areas or residences.

G-men Abbreviated form of Government Men, the phrase is popularly believed to have been coined by gangster Machine Gun Kelly, but more likely was coined by writers friendly to the Bureau. The term has come to mean FBI agents.

general intelligence The gathering of background information on a particular subject, as opposed to information gathered during the course of an investigation to develop a criminal case for prosecution.

German-American Bund Pro-Nazi organization formed in 1933 as the Association of Friends of the New Germany, the Bund was a creature of Germany's Nazi Party. Its goal was the subversion, destabilization, and collapse of the U.S.'s constitutional democracy, replacing it with a homegrown Nazi overlordship subordinate to the Third Reich's Führer, Adolf Hitler. In 1938, when membership peaked, the Bund had 100,000 members.

graymail A variant on the word "blackmail," it is the threat of exposing government secrets in order to avoid prosecution for espionage.

GRU An acronym for Glavnoye Razvedyvatelnoye Upravlenie (Chief Intelligence Directorate of the General Staff), the GRU was the Soviet military intelligence service. Its principal target was industrial and scientific technical intelligence.

Huston Plan Devised by Nixon White House staffer Tom Charles Huston, the Huston Plan mapped out a wide-ranging plan for unprecedented coordination of all agencies carrying out domestic intelligence operations. Active opposition by J. Edgar Hoover prevented it from ever becoming operational.

illegals In Russian spy jargon, spies without diplomatic immunity. They operate according to the residentura system, as residents hiding in deep cover in the host country, where they run an apparat, a secret network.

JODIL Codename for the operation to get gangster and bank robber John Dillinger.

KGB Acronym of Komitet Gosudarstvennoy Bezopasnostie (Committee for State Security). Primarily responsible for USSR internal security, the KGB was the last incarnation of the secret police apparatus which had been known as MGB, NKVD, OGPU, GPU, and at birth, the Cheka.

Lindbergh Law Passed by Congress in response to the Lindbergh baby kidnapping, the law made kidnapping a federal death penalty crime. A second amendment clause stated that if the victim in a kidnapping case had not been safely returned within seven days, it would be *presumed* that the victim had been transported interstate, an elastic clause that gave the BI jurisdiction to get involved.

leak The anonymous dissemination of information by the government to friendly press contacts, who protect the anonymity of the tipster by ascribing the item as having come from an unidentified "inside source," "high-level official," and so on. The term *leak* may come from the fact that the information is distributed piecemeal, in drips and drabs.

legat Short for legal attaché, the legat is an FBI agent or office stationed in other countries to work with local law enforcement authorities on criminal matters within FBI jurisdiction. The Legat program focuses on deterring crime that threatens America such as drug trafficking, international terrorism, and economic espionage.

Mafia Of Sicilian origin, the Mafia provides the central organizing component of the national crime syndicate in the United States. Generally, members refer to it as "Our Thing," or more formally, "This thing of ours"—in Italian, "La Cosa Nostra," often abbreviated in FBI reports as LCN.

mail cover Surveillance operation which monitors the mail received by the subject of an investigation, documenting the envelopes' return addresses. The envelopes themselves are left unopened, their letters unread.

Mann Act Also known as the White Slave Traffic Act, a Congressional law passed in 1910 to curb massive organized prostitution rackets. Named for its sponsor, Illinois Republican Representative James Mann, the act made it a federal crime to transport a female across state lines for "immoral purposes." Congress gave the BI the responsibility of enforcing the law.

Marxism The political philosophy of Marx and Engels that makes the class struggle the fundamental force in history.

MI-5 British Intelligence component responsible for domestic security, similar to the FBI.

MI-6 British Intelligence component charged with foreign security and intelligence, similar to the CIA.

mole A penetration agent which the enemy has planted, suborned, or cultivated in an intelligence agency or service. Like its namesake, the mole burrows from within, advancing to the inner workings of the host organization while betraying its secrets. Notable moles include Kim Philby, Aldrich Ames, and Robert Hanssen.

NIGHTMOVER Codename for both CIA turncoat Aldrich Ames and the FBI operation to get him.

Office of Intelligence Policy and Review (OIPR) Justice Department office responsible for making applications to the Foreign Intelligence Surveillance Court (FISC) for warrants for electronic surveillance and more of targeted suspects.

Office of Strategic Services (OSS) World War II–era civilian intelligence agency under the control of the military's Joint Chiefs of Staff. OSS's mission was espionage, counterespionage, sabotage, propaganda, psychological warfare, and covert action. Dissolved at war's end, it was the forerunner of the CIA.

Official/Confidential files Files collected by J. Edgar Hoover containing items believed to be too important or sensitive to be kept in the Bureau's general files. Documents included key procedural and jurisdictional authorizations, and potentially explosive data about highly placed politicians (including presidents) and private citizens, such as their drinking habits, sexual proclivities, arrest records, politically suspect beliefs and associations, and the like. They were kept in Hoover's office, as were his Personal files, which held material relating to Hoover himself. The latter could include anything from copies of licenses for his dogs, to ultra-sensitive material.

OKBOM Codename for the FBI investigation into the 1995 bombing of the Alfred P. Murrah Federal Building which killed 168 people.

organized crime Criminal activity that runs on a systematic, businesslike basis. Generally, the driving engine of most organized crime is vice operations such as gambling, prostitution, and narcotics, while labor racketeering and extortion are also highly profitable.

Pentagon Papers A 7,000-page, 47-volume study originally entitled "United States-Vietnamese Relations, 1945–1967." Prepared in the last days of the Johnson administration in 1968, the classified Defense Department study documented the history of U.S. involvement in the Vietnam War.

PENTTBOM Codename for the FBI investigation of the terror strikes of 9/11, combining Pentagon with an extra letter T, for the Trade Center.

Public Enemy Term for a high-profile gangster or racketeer, originally coined by the Chicago Crime Commission and picked up shortly after by some of the New York City tabloid newspapers. The phrase was in common use by the time it was used as the title for the movie *Public Enemy*, made in 1931.

Rahowa (sometimes RaHoWa) Among neo-Nazis, skinheads, and the white supremacist movement, a shorthand term for Racial Holy War, a much-desired (by them) genocidal war of extermination to "purify" the U.S. (if not the world) of Jews and blacks, in fact all non-Aryans.

Red Squads Local police investigative units specializing in collecting information and intelligence on prominent communists, socialists, and other extreme leftists within their jurisdiction. Most major cities had Red Squads, with those of Chicago, Los Angeles, and New York City being among the most formidable. The units were also long-lived, some of them remaining in operation well into the 1970s.

resident agencies Smaller than field offices, satellite offices maintained in smaller cities and towns. There are about 400 resident agencies in the United States.

RICO Act Part of Congress's Organized Crime Control Act of 1970; known as the Racketeer-Influenced and Corrupt Organizations (RICO) Act; federalizes the prosecution of two or more people committing two or more crimes in a racketeering pattern. Its stiff sentencing guidelines and asset forfeiture provisions have made it a bulwark of the Justice Department's war on organized crime.

security classifications The categorization of government data based on how much damage their being compromised will do to national security interests. SECRET data would cause serious damage; TOP SECRET would cause exceptionally grave damage.

sedition The incitement of discontent or resistance against legally constituted authorities or the government. The Constitution's free speech provision protects citizens against being prosecuted for sedition.

signal site Communication system used in conjunction with a dead drop system. An agent leaves a signal (strip of tape, colored thumbtack, and so on) at a designated site, such as a stop sign, telephone pole, or suchlike. The signal indicates if the prearranged dead drop site is all-clear. If the all-clear signal is not left, the drop takes place at an alternate site, or is scrubbed and rescheduled.

Smith Act Originally passed in 1940, the Smith Act made it illegal to advocate the overthrow of the U.S. government by force or violence. From about 1948 to the mid-1950s, Smith Act violations were effectively used to prosecute and convict the leadership of the U.S. Communist Party.

socialism Social and political organization based on collective or government ownership and management of the means of production and distribution of goods.

SOG Seat of government, a Hoover-era term for the Bureau's headquarters in Washington, D.C., headed by the director and assistant director.

special A case important enough to merit a number of agents assigned to it alone. Each special headed by an agent on-scene, with the ability to call up as many agents and resources needed to follow up leads.

special agent (SA) An active investigator who may be regarded as the FBI's equivalent of police department detectives. SAs wear no uniforms but instead wear plainclothes on the job.

special agent in charge (SAC) Agent in charge of an FBI field office.

Special Intelligence Service (SIS) World War II–era FBI branch operating in Central and South America. FBI SIS agents thwarted Axis espionage and sabotage efforts. Post-war, SIS was disbanded, its operations taken over by the newly established CIA.

spook A spy or similar clandestine operator in the argot of the intelligence community.

sting An FBI deception operation carried out on an unsuspecting suspect.

task force Investigative team whose members are recruited from a variety of law enforcement agencies working toward a single goal. A federal organized crime task force might typically consist of representatives from the FBI, DEA, Justice Department lawyers, INS, IRS, and local and state agencies.

TRADEBOM Codename for the FBI investigation into the February 26, 1993, bombing of the World Trade Center.

trash cover Surveillance operation which monitors a suspect's trash and garbage output for clues.

tribunal A military trial proceeding, though not a court martial, which allows for looser rules of evidence and greater secrecy, excluding the public and the press.

UNABOM Codename for the FBI investigation into the case of package bomber Ted Kaczynski, an antitechnology nut who operated from 1978 to the mid-1990s. The case was so labeled because early targets of the bomber included universities and airlines.

unsub Unknown subject.

Venona World War II–era ultra top-secret program which decrypted voluminous Soviet cable traffic between the USSR's Washington embassy and Moscow, providing FBI counterintelligence agents with numerous leads exposing Red double agents and spy networks.

W-88 The latest in a series of warheads designed for submarine-launched ballistic missiles. The W stands for "weapon," while 88 is the series number. The warhead is a miniaturized H-bomb whose size allows for the arming of several independently targeted warheads on a single missile.

walk-in A volunteer spy, one who often literally walks-in to the embassy or consulate of the country to which he intends to offer and/or sell his services.

watch listing The acquisition of telegrams and cables sent by or intended for the person being watched.

weapons of mass destruction Conventional or unconventional delivery systems for the use of lethal nuclear, biological, or chemical (NBC) material. A missile or bomb is a conventional delivery system, anthrax-tainted letters are unconventional.

wiretapping When a third party listens to a private telephonic communication. In the dawn of such techniques, the phone conversations would be intercepted by physically "tapping" into the line, usually by splicing into it with a wire whose other end would be connected to a pair of headphones, worn by an agent secreted nearby in a closet or basement. The agent would take notes of the conversation. As the technology improved, the tap wire was connected to recording devices. Ultimately, evolving sophistication did away with the need for an actual spliced wiretap, with the monitoring being done via electronics.

Appendix C

Booking the Bureau: Further Reading

For almost a century, the FBI has been a key factor in the dynamics of U.S. and world history. Its chronicles would fill several libraries. Those interested in delving deeper into the subject are advised to add some or all of the books listed below to their own personal libraries.

The History of the FBI

Gentry, Curt. *J. Edgar Hoover: The Man and the Secrets.* Norton, 1991.

Kessler, Ronald. *The Bureau.* St. Martin's Press, 2002.

———. *The FBI.* Pocket Star Books, 1993.

Powers, Richard Gid. *Secrecy and Power: The Life of J. Edgar Hoover.* Free Press, 1987.

Sullivan, William with Brown, Bill. *The Bureau: My 30 Years in Hoover's FBI.* Pinnacle, 1982.

Summers, Anthony. *Official and Confidential: Secret Life of J. Edgar Hoover.* Putnam, 1993.

Theoharis, Athan Editor. *From the Secret Files of J. Edgar Hoover.* Ivan R. Dee, 1991.

Turner, William W. *Hoover's FBI.* Thunder's Mouth Press, 1993.

General History Topics

Benson, Michael. *Encyclopedia of the JFK Assassination.* Facts on File, 2002.

Bushart,Howard L.; Craig, John R.; and Barnes, Myra. *Soldiers of God.* Pinnacle, 1998.

Flynn, Kevin and Gerhard, Gale. *The Silent Brotherhood: Inside America's Racist Underground.* Free Press, 1989.

Higham, Charles. *American Swastika.* Doubleday, 1985.

———. *Trading With the Enemy: The Nazi-American Money Plot 1933-1949.*

Hougan, James. *Secret Agenda.* Ballantine Books, 1984.

Kessler, Ronald. *Sins of the Father: Joseph P. Kennedy and the Dynasty He Founded.* Warner Books, 1996.

Lukas, J. Anthony. *Nightmare: the Underside of the Nixon Years.* Bantam, 1976.

Mairowitz, David Z. *The Radical Soap Opera.* Avon, 1974.

Navasky, Victor S. *Naming Names.* Viking, 1980.

Radzinsky, Edward. *Stalin.* Doubleday, 1996.

Reeves, Thomas C. *The Life and Times of Joe McCarthy.* Stein and Day, 1982.

———. *A Question of Character: A Life of JFK.* Free Press, 1991.

Rodriquez, Felix and Weisman, John. *Shadow Warrior.* Pocket Books, 1989.

Sann, Paul. *The Lawless Decade.* Fawcett, 1971.

Singular, Stephen. *Talked to Death: The Murder of Alan Berg and the Rise of Neo-Nazis*. Berkley, 1987.

Summers, Anthony. *Arrogance of Power: Secret World of Richard Nixon*. Viking, 2000.

Toland, John. *Rising Sun: The Decline and Fall of the Japanese Empire*. Bantam, 1970.

White, Theodore H. *Making of the President 1960*. Pocket Books, 1961.

True Crime and Punishment

Ahlgren, Gregory and Monier, Stephen. *Crime of the Century: the Lindbergh Kidnapping Hoax*. Impala Books, 1993.

Davis, John H. *Mafia Kingfish: Carlos Marcello*. Signet, 1989.

Demaris, Ovid. *The Boardwalk Jungle*. Bantam, 1986.

Gage, Nicholas Editor. *Mafia, USA*. Dell, 1972.

Hellmer, William with Mattix, Rick. *Public Enemies: America's Criminal Past 1919-1940*. Facts on File, 1998.

Mustain, Gene and Capeci, Jerry. *Mob Star: the Story of John Gotti*. Alpha Books, 2002.

Nash, Jay Robert. *Bloodletters and Badmen*. Warner Books, 1973.

——— . *Crime Chronology 1900-1983*. Facts on File, 1984.

Neff, James. *Mobbed Up: Life of Jackie Presser*. Dell, 1989.

O'Brien, Joseph F. and Kurrus, Andres. *Boss of Bosses: The FBI & Paul Castellano*. Simon and Schuster, 1991.

Rappleye, Charles & Becker, Ed. *All-American Mafiosi: The Johnny Rosselli Story*. Barricade Books, 1991

Scheim, David F. *Contract on America: the Mafia Murder of JFK*. Zebra Books, 1988.

Sterling, Claire. *The Octopus*. Touchstone Books, 1988

Wellman, Paul I. *A Dynasty of Western Outlaws*. Pyramid Books, 1964.

All About Spies

Allen, Thomas B. and Polmar, Norman. *Merchants of Treason*. Dell, 1988.

Costello, John. *The Mask of Treachery*. Warner Books, 1988.

Hoover, J. Edgar. *Masters of Deceit*. Cardinal, 1958.

Lamphere, Robert J. and Schactner, Tom. *The FBI-KGB War*. Berkley, 1986.

Nizer, Louis. *The Implosion Conspiracy*. Fawcett, 1973.

Ranelagh, John. *The Agency: Rise and Decline of the CIA*. Simon and Schuster, 1986.

Stober, Dan and Hoffman, Ian. *A Convenient Spy: Wen Ho Lee*. Simon & Schuster, 2001.

Vise, David A. *The Bureau and the Mole: The Unmasking of Robert P. Hanssen*. Atlantic Monthly Press, 2002.

Wise, David. *Mole Hunt*. Avon, 1992.

——— *NIGHTMOVER*. HarperCollins, 1995.

Woodward, Bob. *Veil: Secret Wars of the CIA 1981-1987*. Pocket, 1988.

Magazine and Journal Articles

Broad, William J.; Johnston, David; and Zernike, Kate. *Anthrax Inquiry Draws Protest From Scientist's Lawyer*. New York Times, August 8 2002.

Hersh, Seymour H. *Mixed Messages: Why the Government Didn't Know What It Knew*. New Yorker, June 3 2002.

Johnston, David and Van Natta Jr., Don. *FBI Stumbles in Terror War*. New York Times, June 3 2002.

Lewis, Neil A. *FBI Chief Admits 9/11 Might Have Been Detectable*. New York Times, May 30 2002.

Shenon, Philip. *Senate Report on pre-9/11 Tells of Bungling at FBI*. New York Times, August 28 2002.

Van Natta Jr., Don. *Government Will Ease Limits on Domestic Spying by FBI*. New York Times, May 30 2002.

Index

Cummings, Homer S., 52
Custodial Detention lists, 79

D

Danforth, John, 234
Dasch, George, 86
Daschle, Tom, 278
Daugherty, Harry M., 34
DCI (director of central intelligence), 203
dead drops, 205
Dean, John, 157, 163, 172, 175-176
decryption, 109
Degan, William F., 229
DeLoach, Cartha "Deke," 145, 157
Department of Justice, establishment of, 21
Dewey, Thomas E., 105, 119
Diamond, Jack "Legs," 48
Dillinger, John, 20, 53, 56, 58
    birth of, 56
    death of, 58
    jail breaks, 56
director of central intelligence (DCI), 203
Director of the FBI, nomination of, 3
Directors (FBI), 10
    See also Hoover, J. Edgar
    Bielaski, A. Bruce, 24
    Burns, William J. "Billy," 34
    Finch, Stanley W., 22
    Flynn, William J., 26
    Gray, L. Patrick, 167
    Kelley, Clarence M., 167
    Mueller III, Robert S., 278
    Sessions, William, 218
    Webster, William H, 179, 184
Disney, Walt, 105
Divisions (FBI), 10-12
Donovan, William J., 42, 45, 51, 91-92, 105, 112
    Central Intelligence Agency, proposal of, 96
    COI (coordinator of information), appointment to, 93-95
    firing of, 97

OSS (Office of Strategic Services), appointment to, 95
Dorfman, Allen, 193
Doyle, William, 63
dry-cleaning (spying), 207
Drys (Prohibition), 35
du Pont, Irénée, 65-66
du Pont, Lammot, 65
du Pont, Pierre, 65
Dulles, Allen, 127, 133, 144, 162
Dupuy, Rosario Casas, 212
Dzerzhinsky, Feliks, 68

E

Eagle, James "Jimmy," 183
Ehrlichman, John, 158, 172, 175-176
Eighteenth Amendment
    ratification of, 35
Eisenhower, Dwight, 111, 125, 130, 132, 144
electronic intelligence
    (elint), 16
Eliot, T. S., 211
Elitcher, Max, 110
Elliott, Eldon, 243
Ellsberg, Daniel, 159-163, 175-176
Elson, Edward L. R., 163
encryption, 109
Epstein, Charles, 240
Espionage Act (1917), 24
European immigration
    early twentieth century, 21
    late nineteenth century, 21

F

facism, 62
facist movement
    American Liberty League, 63-64
    Black Legion, 66
        creation of, 65
    Bund, the, 66-68
    Clark's Crusaders, 65
    du Pont brothers, 65

N

W-X-Y-Z